COMPOSING FEMINISM(S)

How Feminists Have Shaped Composition Theories and Practices

Research and Teaching in Rhetoric and Composition
Michael M. Williamson and Peggy O'Neill, series editors

COMPOSING FEMINISM(S)

How Feminists Have Shaped Composition Theories and Practices

Kay Siebler

Buena Vista University

HAMPTON PRESS, INC.
CRESSKILL, NJ 07626

Printed in the United States of America

Library of Congress Cataloging-in-Publication Data

Siebler, Kay.
Composing feminism(s) : how feminists have shaped composition
   theories and practices / Kay Siebler.
      p. cm. -- (Research and teaching in rhetoric and composition)
Includes bibliographical references and index.
ISBN 1-57273-711-5 -- ISBN 1-57273-712-3 (pbk.)
1. English language--Rhetoric--Study and teaching. 2. Report writing--
   Study and teaching (Higher). 3. Feminism and education. I. Title.

PE1404.S54 2007
808'.042082--dc22

                          2007031382

Hampton Press, Inc.
23 Broadway
Cresskill, NJ 07626

Dedicated to Edward Siebler, Dennis Alcorn and all the other White Hats who have gone on. I know you are somewhere out there soaring above on wings strong and true. Wild Geese. Also to Effie, Ellie, Eula, and Estel. The sacrifice was worth it.

Contents

Acknowledgments

My life has been shaped by the feminist teachers I have encountered. This project would not have been possible without the unconditional support of Kate Ronald, Cindy Lewiecki-Wilson, Katie Johnson and Carolyn Haynes. I thank these four scholars and teachers for giving me insightful feedback and encouragement along the way, as well as being fantastic models of feminist teachers. A special thanks to Kate for her friendship that sustains itself over miles and time zones. This project also would not have been possible without the open hearts and minds of Lynn Worsham, Harriet Malinowitz, and Jackie Jones Royster. Without these three women the heart of this project would not have been half as interesting. These three feminist educators and scholars opened their lives to me and allowed their work to be scrutinized and written about here. They are upstanding examples of feminist teaching and feminist mentoring. I learned truck loads from each of them and there are no words to express the brilliance and generosity of their spirits. To you, dear reader, I suggest skipping right to chapter 3 and read from there. That is where my heart sings, recording the lives and work of three of favorite my academic role models. I also want to thank all the feminist teachers who showed me the way from grade school on: Mrs. Eklund, Mrs. Olson, Pat Lotspiech, Ms. McCoy, Sue Stehly, Barbara DiBernard, Joy Ritchie, Fran Kaye, Dick Streckfuss, Mike Strickland, Wude Starks, Luming Mao, Rodrigo Lazo, Elizabeth Nesbitt, Conrad Wrezenski, Peter Steinfeld, Kathy Kapitan, Doc Whitlatch, Anna Formicella-Elsden, and Carla Offenberger. I am a better teacher following these models of good, feminist teaching. My pedagogy reflects what I have learned from them. Special thanks to Ginny Jane and Nanny who "hurrahed" me every step of the way, always positive and encouraging. And to Bunhead, who never hesitates to say how proud she is.

Introduction

Personal Journal: July 10, 2001

I went to V.J.'s today, first visit since I got back to Nebraska. She told me that Barbara had asked after me, so I need to call her. As I was walking home, laden with the trappings of good friendship (home-baked cookies, a huge clutch of flowers from her garden, and the warm buzz of good conversation still in my head) I again remembered how central Barbara is to this project. It was 1985. I was a fifth-year senior (journalism major) at UN-L when I signed up for her Women's Literature course that rocked my world. The poignancy of that moment in my life is that profound, and perhaps that simple. I can't even remember why I signed up for the course in the first place. Had someone recommended it? Or perhaps someone specifically recommended Barbara as an instructor? Did I just need three more credit hours to round out my schedule (I had always been a sucker for English courses: the candy of my school work)? Perhaps it was all just the gentle poke of fate.

After 18 years of formal education, that class was the first time I remember reading women's writing. That in and of itself sent me to the stratosphere. It was the first year that Norton had published their Norton Anthology of Literature by Women, so that was the course text. The pages, onion thin and almost transparent, reminded me of bible pages, an apropos analogy. I read that book cover to cover: 2,400 pages, writing in the margins and filling up corners of white space with thoughts and ideas. Barbara didn't assign the entire text, but once I started reading, I couldn't stop. It was like a compulsion. So, the text was life-changing. It was the one book I carried with me to Morocco as a Peace Corps volunteer. But it wasn't just about the book. It was also the way Barbara conducted the course. For the first time in a college classroom we were sitting in a circle. I remember feeling giddy that I could actually look around and see other people in the class, and really listen to what they had to say. Instead of students talking to the teacher, answering pointed questions to impress, they were talking to each other. _We were talking to each other_. I was also a bit intimidated. More than once I thought, "These people are so smart." The other astonishing difference was the amount of feedback Barbara gave on my work. We had journals due every week and as a journaling freak I filled up pages and pages of thoughts and reflections. My love of personal self-reflection and the surprise of reading women's words exploded in my class journal. Profound pleasure also came, though, in reading Barbara's response to my work, hearing her thoughts, and feeling her push me to think of things in different directions. I must have been relatively quiet in class, stunned, perhaps, which is hard for me to believe (now I always have to check and double-check my talk time in a classroom), because once she wrote something along the lines of, "You write such interesting things in your journals. I wish you would share them in class discussions. Others can learn from your insights." That floored me. Again, I had never considered that others would find my ideas interesting, let alone learn from them. And even more odd was my belief that I _shouldn't_ share my bright ideas with others because they were mine and I should save them to impress the teacher, a conditioned response to the traditional classroom where performance was only related to getting the teacher's attention, not interacting with other members of the class. That class literally moved my world in various directions. I became a different student, understanding the purpose of the classroom to be interaction and exchange. This way of teaching, although I didn't identify it then as feminist pedagogy, fascinated me and became the model for the type of teaching I would try to do as a Peace Corps volunteer. And the politics of curriculum development would never, ever be transparent to me again. When the class ended I cried. But I also felt anger. Why hadn't I read women's voices until my last year at the university? Why had I been an unempowered, passive student for so long? Why didn't other teachers really listen and hear what their students had to say?

Today walking home from V.J.'s, sweating in the hot, mid-day humidity, I felt that anger and righteous indignation all over again. This project, almost twenty years later, began in that Introduction to Women's Literature classroom. It began with Barbara. What would I be doing, who would I be today if I hadn't landed in that course? And how in the world did Barbara manage to do what _she_ did, transgressing the norms in such profound ways? How many other lives did that feminist teacher change as dramatically as my own?

Do you remember the first moment you found yourself in a feminist classroom? I do, and it changed the way I thought of teaching and how I chose to enact my own pedagogy. But it wasn't until 20 years later that I knew there was a name for what I had experienced in that undergraduate women's literature course. And even, as a graduate student in composition and rhetoric, when I began learning about feminist pedagogy, I became frustrated with the lack of attention it received. Yes, in this field we talk a great deal about feminist issues and feminist approaches to teaching composition and rhetoric, but we seem to eschew serious discussions on feminist pedagogy. "It is too difficult to define," some say. "It is just a gender-focused pedagogy," I have heard. "It forces students to adopt feminist ideologies," critics charge. "It's O.K. for Women's Studies classes, but not appropriate for other disciplines." Or, the most common response I got when I explained to people about *this* project, "That's not feminist pedagogy, that's just good teaching!"

None of these statements are true. They are all petty myths surrounding this complex, living pedagogy that has shaped composition theory and practice for the past 30 years. Yes, it *is* "good" teaching, but it also *feminist*.

A substantial body of work exists describing feminist pedagogy, creating a rich tapestry of methods and practices as a definition. Most articles on the subject are still published by Women's Studies journals. It is unclear to me whether this phenomenon reflects a bias by scholarly journals that aren't specifically Women's Studies against the idea that feminist pedagogy can be separated from Women's Studies or whether it indicates that the scholars themselves perpetuate the stereotype of coupling feminist pedagogy with Women's Studies by only submitting such articles to those types of journals.

From the articles and books that have been published on the subject over the past three decades there is missing a synthesis of the scholarship on feminist teaching, which would provide a clearer definition of how scholars and teachers define feminist pedagogy. This type of information, a more comprehensive, historical definition of feminist pedagogy, is in part what this project is about. To synthesize a short definition of feminist pedagogy from my research, feminist pedagogy is a keen awareness of classroom dynamics, continually striving to confront issues of power and authority as they play out between students and teachers; it is an attempt to move students to critical consciousness, especially in regards to racism, classism, sexism, homophobia and other ideological forces that create hierarchies; it is a commitment to creating connections between the external world and the classroom, creating a learning environment that is high energy, using the kinetics of a classroom as a critique of traditional models of education. A feminist learning community harkens back to the definition of feminism as "creative energy for change and critique," empowering students to become active learners (Morley and Walsh 1).

So, first we need to tease out a historical definition of feminist pedagogy. But there is an inherent connection between feminist pedagogy and composition. Current trends of writing instruction have changed as a result of feminist influence. This argument is one very important to this work as I believe that feminist practices are an integral part of contemporary composition theories and practices, but that this feminist history is not acknowledged in the field by most scholars. Instead of seeing feminism/feminist as a category within composition studies, my research suggests that feminism in fact has helped define contemporary composition theories and practices. In other words, feminism is not a "special" category in composition, but infused in mainstream composition theory and practice, although not recognized as such.

Chapter one is devoted to the specific and unique history of feminist pedagogy. In the first chapter I articulate the influences of feminist ideas and theories on composition teaching practices. I discuss feminism and feminist teaching practices as they first made their way into the academy, in the form of Women's Studies courses, and how those cultural shifts changed the theories and practices of composition. What I document, however, represents only one view of *a* history, not *the* history.

Because I am examining the formal education system, when and where women and feminists entered, and the change that resulted, the resources available to examine perspectives other than the white, male, privileged class perspective are limited.[1] Scholars such as Susan Jarratt are researching historical black colleges and universities and the voices of women at those sites of learning, but nothing that I have read has investigated the role of women specifically as teachers in such institutions. In the past few years there have been articles and books focusing on women in administrative positions at historically black colleges and universities. There has also been research on Native American boarding schools, institutions of education that the federal government established to force native children to assimilate to the dominant culture and which resulted in the coerced betrayal and abandonment their own cultural heritage. These schools were often run by religious orders, many times by women in the vocation of nuns. However, investigation of the role of women teachers in these systems is outside the scope of my project. To narrow my research on women in education, I will be looking at the public university system and the ways feminists changed that system specifically in regard to methods of teaching.

After contextualizing feminist pedagogy in a historical moment, in chapter two I compile a definition of feminist pedagogy that is an amalgamation of definitions culled from scholarly books and articles across the disciplines, published over the past three decades. In chapter two I show how feminist theories and practices have become so infused with composition theories and practices that we are remiss in not recognizing how inherently "feminist" composition is.

The historical definition of *feminist pedagogy* in chapter two is collaborative because it comes from many scholars who have added different themes to the definition, or who have further developed a theme outlined by a previous scholar. How can I offer a history of and a definition of feminist pedagogy without creating a view that implies there is only *one* type of feminist pedagogy or that feminist teaching includes certain attributes, but not others? This is the crux of a complicated conundrum. My answer to this prickly question is probably not satisfactory, but what I am attempting to do is reclaim a history that has been erased or lost, to give face and name to feminist practices and show how infused they are in the field of composition, and in doing so, I hope to give credit where credit is due: to feminists scholars in this field and other fields who have changed the way we approach teaching at the college level.

The last three chapters document how three well-known feminist educators in the field of composition are enacting their feminist pedagogy. Each of these chapters takes on a different tone and character as a result of my field research with each of the three women, Lynn Worsham, Harriet Malinowitz, and Jacquie Jones Royster.

A final chapter offers a reflection of this project in the spirit of being overt with my audience about my feelings towards and reflections on the project.

Interspersed with my research on the history of feminist pedagogy and the field studies of three feminist composition scholars and teachers who are practicing feminist pedagogy are excerpts from my teaching and research journals. These journal entries are selected from the journals I kept throughout this project. These excerpts are intensely personal and my hope is that they allow the reader to understand my struggles and triumphs and why I invested in this work. In the journals I hope to lay open myself for critique. I want the reader to not only get another context of who the author is, but hear the scholar and teacher at her work and how I struggle with and enact *my* feminist principles in the classroom and in my scholarship. These journal entries are also intended to interrupt or disrupt the text, to offer another tear in the history and the scholarship of feminist pedagogy, to complicate and create tension. In the field of composition and rhetoric we talk about context a great deal. The journal entries are my way of offering context to the reader of where I am and what I am doing and thinking as a feminist scholar and teacher. These self reflections are challenges to the reader to open up their own inner world for critique, a primary tenet of feminist teaching.[2]

WHEN AND WHERE I ENTER

Every writer and researcher comes to a project with blinders on. Feminist researchers work to scratch the scales away from our eyes to see more clearly or at least to be honest about what is clouding our vision. In coming to this project, the biases I most struggle with are those of my whiteness and my activist roots. Because I came to feminism as a grassroots activist, devoting many years of my life to working with and against organizations, agencies, government, and other institutions to create material change in women's lives, I feel most akin to academics who clearly relate theory to practice. In the same way that I need to find connections between theory and practice, I am interested in seeing how differently theories can be enacted based on context.

Another key prejudice is my white perspective. It is through that lens that I see the world. Throughout the project I needed to check that perspective. I vigorously try to push myself to recognize these prejudices in the project and interrogate them when I see them. The clincher in that statement, however, is *when I see them*. They are everywhere, and yet they are often hidden from me. These biases will inherently play out not only in how I attempt to write this history of feminist pedagogy, but in the way I collect data and interpret the data I find during research.

Not only do I identify as feminist, causing me to privilege feminist approaches in my teaching and research, but I also identify as a white, able-bodied, bisexual woman. All these identities shape my perspective. My whiteness prevents me from truly understanding what a feminist of color, or a woman of color who does not identify as a feminist, experiences in the academy or the classroom. Because often I am read by students and others as heterosexual, I can hide my bisexual identity when it benefits me and use it as a way to confront homophobia. The decision whether to name my sexual orientation is mine to make, unlike other people who are read as homosexual, regardless of their sexual orientation, and have to confront homophobia regardless of whether or not they choose to.

All these locations and identities influence my approach to this research. My interests will be drawn, and biases will play out, in relation to these identities. I will try to confront the privileging of these perspectives when I see them in my research. I am sure there will be areas where these identities influence my perception when I am not aware, indeed they influence every word that I write and every thought that I have, so the most I can hope to accomplish is being as overt and aware with myself and my audience as I can be, hoping my audience will use feminist critique to point out ways in which my research is biased when I neglect to do so.

Chapter One

Trying to Figure It Out

When Rapunzel Escapes the Tower and Runs Amuck

Documenting history is a tricky thing. For a feminist historian, the accusatory questions loom threateningly before the pen is put to paper: Whose voice is being left out? Whose perspective is being privileged? What perspectives are lost to us forever? Even as I begin to document the history of feminist pedagogy, a short history as history goes, I feel almost paralyzed by these questions. Questions of where to start and who to include immediately call into question the choices I make. By virtue of these choices, I give voice to some and silence others. I exclude and include, and the choices seem largely arbitrary based on who I have read, who has influenced my work and teaching, and who has been cited and written about before. The ideological machine creaks and moans as I run my hands over it, picking through the pieces it has spit out in its churnings, trying to document and analyze *one* history of teaching that is part of the machine and yet somehow a deviation of the typical product generated. Although these theories and voices are part of the machine, they have also disrupted it, jammed it, as Worsham (1992) has written, and thereby altered it in significant ways. Feminist theory and pedagogy, as well as the status, location, and power of feminists in the academy, have changed the practice of teaching composition. In fact, feminism(s) and feminists have largely defined the current practices of composition pedagogy. Somehow along the way, these practices and theories were disconnected from their feminist roots. In other words, there is a disconnect between the contributions feminism(s) and feminists have made to composition and how we define *current composition theory*. There is a strong voice of feminism in the field of composition, but the contribution of feminism and feminist theory moves far beyond that which is labeled as feminist.

THE POWER TO NAME

Even to begin my project I must rely on the documented, which means published, records of feminist teaching. The first mention of feminist pedagogy *that I could find*[3] appears in 1982. Two articles that year gave name to feminist pedagogy: a chapter written by Culley (1982) in MLA's publication *Teaching Women's Literature from a Regional Perspective* and an article on curriculum development written by J. Miller (1982) and published in *Journal of Curriculum Development*. Culley's article names feminist pedagogy as an innovative approach to the pedagogy of literature where diaries and personal histories constitute the texts and work of the course. Culley also identifies the need to connect course work to the lives of students as part of feminist pedagogy. She writes that the structure of the course moved beyond a challenge to canonical texts: "The nature of the course *changed the authority structure of the classroom*, the modes of research and strategies for *sharing knowledge*, even the *relationship between the classroom and the local community*" (P. 88 italics added). These themes of students as knowing subjects, creating connections to the community, and subverting the authority of the teacher and even the academy mark the first themes of feminist pedagogy. Central to this discussion is the work of recovery of women's voices and experience, reinforcing the centrality of *women's* identities and experiences to feminist pedagogy even as we now acknowledge that the identity of woman is socially constructed. The same year that Culley published her article, Miller's (1982) article, "The Sound of Silence Breaking: Feminist Pedagogy and Curriculum Theory" defined feminist pedagogy as an innovative way to approach curriculum design integrating voices and texts by Traditionally Marginalized People (TMP),[4] subverting teacher authority, and opening up curriculum development to student choices. If we understand these articles as signifying the beginning of feminist pedagogical theory, it would be easy to overzealously view the documentation of such a short history as a relatively simple task (1982–present). But who was practicing or naming these or other pedagogical strategies as feminist before this date without the benefit of publication? Who first named certain classroom practices as feminist, and how long did it take before the taxonomy was legitimized in a publication? How did we, as a culture, as an institution (academia), arrive at the moment of publication, of naming (as late as 1982)?

The Stilted Distortion of (his)Story

History is a culture's narrative of itself (Hennessy, 1993), the stories we tell each other about who we are, as a group. Therefore, within one story, depending on *who* is telling that story, a specific perspective becomes dominant. Even when we hear the three bears' voices ("Someone's been eating my porridge!"), we are rooting for Goldilocks. It is her story, after all—her hunger and fatigue that finds respite and satiation at the home into which she breaks, enters, sups, and sleeps. The Bears are only hanging around on the fringes to provide the conflict that Goldilocks triumphantly overcomes. With any history, any narrative, there is conflict; it is at the root of what makes a good story. But to avoid the tunnel vision and blinders of typical history-writing, feminists, among others, have demanded a rigor of historicization or the contextualization of the story, overtly articulating whose perspective is privileged, whose perspective is left out, and the implications of those choices. The conflict that creates a good history needs to be contextualized by asking questions such as, Whose voice is missing? Whose location is privileged? Why and how are these gaps and hierarchies changing the story? (de Lauretis, 1980).

Equally crucial to the story is how the data are collected, the information from which the story springs. The identity and location of the people who collect and interpret the data, and their agenda even before they begin pouring over it, change the story in significant ways. In the telling of histories, there is no neutrality because we are all victims of ideology, and these ideological forces become regimes that rule our thoughts and perspectives. Some scholars believe there are ways to question "The White Guy In My Head," and therefore move in directions that are counter to what the White Guy says. Feminism and a feminist approach to history-making offer a method by which to begin the critical questioning of the story. Questioning whose reality the story represents may be evidence of how this questioning can happen. Feminism offers a way to push the dominant ideological boundaries and demand new perspectives. The question then becomes, does feminism become a part of ideology or, if not, does it construct an equally oppressive ideology of its own? This causes me to return to the historicization questions: Who is being left out? Why?

In recording the history of feminist pedagogy, I must first look at the subculture, or secondary ideology, that is feminism, understanding that even when doing so I am choosing a specific feminist ideology informed by my own position as a feminist (queer, White, privileged class, educated, teacher, writer, activist). The subcultures of feminism interact with and react to the dominant culture with the objective of forcing change in the dominant culture.[5] In historicizing feminist pedagogy, I need to look at what forces in the dominant culture, and in various other subcultures, created the space for contemporary feminism. What created *this* history, the one I am choosing to write about or even construct? The most obvious force in any history of feminism is the mere presence of women, and, specifically in this history, the presence and power of women in the academy both as students and teachers. When females enter male-defined and male-dominated institutions, we anticipate that change will occur to the institution's culture. The patriarchal foundation will shift to include a different perspective or embody a different approach. Although this statement comes dangerously close to essentializing not only the category of *women* or *female*, but also how individual women will alter a structure that is male-dominated, my belief is that, regardless of how any given female/woman enters or works within any given institution, the patriarchy feels that presence and change occurs. Did the U.S. Supreme Court change when Sandra Day O'Connor first donned the robe? Will the foundations of the Catholic Church tremble when the first female priest offers up the Eucharist? A person who lived the experience of being a TMP will bring that perspective to the institution and thereby insert a new perspective or agenda, although the perspective being brought will be as varied as that person's individual experiences and identity. Nearly two decades ago, Fuss (1989) argued—on behalf of Luce Iragaray—that an essential identity of female does not necessarily mean a homogonous, single experience or voice. Regardless of how the physical reality of how woman or feminist enters the male-dominated academy, there are some females who were/are more adamant and diligent about wanting to work toward change than others.

Historically, pedagogy shifts according to social and political movements external to the academy and how these movements define knowledge creation and education. Feminism first entered the academy as concern about the education of females, a result of the women's rights movement during the 1960s and 1970s, where activist feminists were working to gain equal access to patriarchal systems of power, higher education being one of these. My argument focuses on how 20th-century feminism changed methods of teaching, leadership, and scholarship, these changes manifesting themselves at the site of feminist pedagogical practices—specifically, how these theories and practices shaped contemporary composition. The field of composition is an example of the historical erasure of how feminism shaped teaching practices. Therefore, there is a need to show how most contemporary composition scholarship, teacher training, and teaching practices reflect this feminist influence.

Project Journal: October 22, 2000

I finished a draft of the first chapter today: the history of feminist pedagogy in 65 pages or less. The draft feels good, but damn history is hard to write. At every turn I kept thinking, "I am leaving out X! What am I suppose to do about that?" In the end, I felt like I couldn't do much about leaving things out. If I were writing a book just on the history of feminist pedagogy, perhaps I would be able to do more in-depth history making. The most discomforting part is that I feel this is a very white history. It is obviously privileged class (because I am talking about academia, a context systematically denied anyone outside of privilege). For the most part things such as sexuality and able-bodiedness, spirituality, and all those "other" identities that are traditionally marginalized are erased, teachers don't identify in their scholarship these identities, at least historically. So, those discussions, or the lack of those discussions, feels less problematic. But the issue of race and ethnicity does feel problematic. I'm so very white. The texts I am reading are so very white. Beyond a smattering of texts (like those written by hooks, Villanueva and Freire) the focus of what I am reading seems to be gender with occasional nods to ethnicity, sexuality and other stuff. So, I look at the draft of Chapter 1 and I feel as if I have fallen exactly into that trap myself. Can I gnaw off my leg to escape? Is there an escape?

I forwarded the draft to the writers' group. It felt great to do that, but the stance of my perspective will probably be a conundrum to them as well (all white women!). Before I forwarded them the draft I took out all the personal narrative in my latest revision. It didn't feel right there, and it felt like a bad decision to take it out (no personal interrogation or self-disclosure??). The most difficult part of this project right now is coming to terms with the fact that I can't escape my biases, but even as I begin to point to them I become lost in sea of black holes that show me just how spotty this history is.

THE POWER OF PEDAGOGY

Pedagogy represents an interesting point for research in the academy because it is one place where TMP have access to power through teaching and learning. Through teaching, and their agency to construct their own classrooms as they desired, women and other TMP gathered power for change. When the administration allows teachers to control their class and curriculum, the pragmatic work of teaching shifts power away from the administration to the teachers. Policy change or administrative change is more difficult to accomplish than implementing changes in one's own pedagogy. This type of systemic administrative and cultural change requires great numbers of people advocating change as a collective. Administrative and structural shifts involve creating coalitions of people working together to initiate change from a common goal. But with teaching strategies, TMP teachers have the power to create change through how they construct their classrooms, building an environment where teachers and students feel more empowered. Feminist teachers also create slow change throughout the acad-emy as their students become ambassadors to other courses and disciplines, asking teachers to adopt the types of empowering teaching strategies they experienced in feminist classrooms. Of course, when administrators man-date standard syllabi or curricula, the power of individual teachers diminish-es. In these cases, some power remains with the teacher within the site of the classroom and in the way that the teacher chooses to execute the syllabi or curricula. How teachers choose to implement these standard curricula can either support or subvert the larger ideologies of education.

In chronicling the evolution of feminist pedagogy, there are several ide-ological forces at play. The most obvious represents the dominant culture's relegation of women and other TMP to outsider status—outsiders to the power structures that produce ideology. One example of how these power structures play out in education is the lower status of teachers (largely female) in relation to administrators (largely male). Ideology is also reflect-ed in classroom rituals. In most traditional or public educational institu-tions, from the age of 5, students are asked to sit in rows, color in the lines, raise their hands, line up to go to the lunch room according to gender, and stand with hand over heart to say the Pledge of Allegiance (Martin, 1999). Ideology of the dominant culture is present in these rituals, routines, and practices of schools, but largely transparent to students and educators (Aronowitz & Giroux, 1993). These standards or norms create an ideology that reflects the dominant culture in both macro-and micro-systems: Gender distinctions and obedience to hierarchy reflect the macro ideology of the culture; raising hands, sitting in rows, looking to the teacher for the "right" answers to questions, and taking notes from what is written on the board by the teacher reinforce the micro-ideology of most traditional class-rooms and reinforce an obedience to power. Because of these sorts of prac-tices, Gramsci (1988) believes that critical thinking cannot be learned in schools.[6] These practices and school rituals inherently reflect state ideology. Feminist teachers, however, commit their classrooms to disrupting these types of systems and practices of domination. Educational theorist and teacher bell hooks offers a definition of *feminism* that fits particularly well with feminist pedagogy: "eradicating the ideology of domination that per-meates western culture on various levels, sex, race, class to name a few, and reorganizing United States society" (Kramarae & Treichler, 1985, p. 59). Perhaps Gramsci would have more hope for educating students to critical consciousness if he considered hooks' definition and feminist pedagogy.

That is not to say that disruption is easy. When a feminist teacher comes to the institutional ideology of education, bringing her feminist principles to bear on that ideology, she threatens the system.[7] Teachers who attempt to subvert the ideology of education are often met with resistance not only by the administration, but by their own students, who feel displaced or uncomfortable with disruptions to the normal classroom practices they have been conditioned to accept. Feminist teachers struggle to help students move toward critical consciousness within the ideology of education. Can institutions with patriarchal ideologies be reformed by subcultures? By virtue of their pedagogical strategies, feminist teachers say "yes." A more complex question is, Are feminist teachers exchanging one ideology for another, with neither being particularly more or less empowering for individual students since each student will need and demand different things from a classroom community? I address this question specifically in the section entitled "Skeptics" at the end of chapter 2.

Another concern when considering whether feminist pedagogy can change education ideology is whether academics can see beyond their own collusion with the system. Academics, regardless of their political beliefs, may be the "most indoctrinated part of the population" because they have obediently and submissively passed through many gates to get where they are (Chomsky, 1991). In some cases, feminist academics may support, rather than subvert, the ideologies of education. When a feminist supports the status quo, one only hopes that she does so knowing that she is making the choice consciously and has specific reasons for abiding by institutional norms. Feminist pedagogy demands transgression of traditional educational systems and rituals, always with an eye to empowering students and moving them toward critical consciousness. Some feminists may be tempted to appear to support traditional ideologies of education, but take a stand to resist or subvert these practices within their own classrooms.[8] Feminist pedagogy provides a way in which teachers can transgress or ignore institutional practices that are not feminist, replacing them with practices that are feminist within the microcosm of individual classrooms.

Because of the power located in the site of teaching, feminist pedagogy is an important part of the history of women in the academy and, more recently, feminist change in the academy. I want to make the distinction between feminists in the academy and feminist teachers. Feminists who work in the academy are not necessarily feminist teachers. Feminist teachers (either male or female) are teachers who are committed to feminist pedagogy as a specific way of enacting their feminist beliefs in their lives. Feminist academics do not necessarily identify as feminist teachers or enact feminist pedagogy.

FROM WHENCE SPRANG FEMINIST PEDAGOGY

Most of the things I have read about [feminist pedagogy] have gotten on my nerves. They make all these points for being feminist that aren't necessarily. And of course all the touchy-feely stuff. I don't really under-

stand why they have to define certain things they do as feminist. (Harriet
Malinowitz, personal interview)[9]

When I tell people that I am doing my research in the area of feminist pedagogy, I am often met with quizzical looks. Many ask me what feminist pedagogy is. When I offer a distilled definition of what I have come to believe
is feminist pedagogy, many people ask, "Why is that *feminist*?" I answer this
question with more questions: Why do we ask "Why is that considered
feminist pedagogy?" when we never ask, about other pedagogies, "Why is
that considered liberatory pedagogy" or "Why is that considered *critical*
pedagogy?" Why do we feel the need to question the definition of what
feminist pedagogy is when we do not feel the need to call into question
other definitions?

Feminist pedagogy sprang from liberatory and critical schools of pedagogy used by feminists in the early Women's Studies courses in the United
States. Since the late 1980s, in publications such as *The Feminist Teacher* and
anthologies such as *Meeting the Challenge*, feminist teachers have been writing about how to apply feminist pedagogical principles in courses other than
Women's Studies. However, most of these scholarly works focus on one
theme or principle of feminist pedagogy as it is implemented in a classroom
with articles devoted to collaboration; attention to race, class, gender; and
issues of teacher authority. Through my research on feminist pedagogy, I
have compiled a more comprehensive definition, organizing that definition
into themes. Here I offer 16 themes that comprise a contemporary, more
comprehensive definition of feminist pedagogy.[10] These themes have been
extrapolated from books and articles on the subject of feminist pedagogy
published over the past 30 years.[11] This definition of feminist pedagogy
presents a more comprehensive and historical view of how feminist teachers
approach their work. To see how contemporary composition scholars,
teachers, and leaders enact their feminist pedagogy, I used classroom observation, conversations, analysis of scholarship and speeches, and observation
of meetings as part of my ethnographic studies of three prominent feminist
educators and leaders in the field of composition. The results of these ethnographies are discussed in chapters 3 to 5.

Personal Journal; July 26, 2000

After lunch I went over to the Psych department to sit it on a graduate seminar entitled "Feminist Pedagogy." I had talked to the
instructor and she said it would be great to have me sit in. It's a
small class (five students besides myself), graduate students from
the psych department (3) and the English department (2). The
instructor is great, but the course is very basic. The reading is light

and most of it feels outdated, or seems to reflect the "Women's Ways of Knowing" approach to feminist pedagogy, which feels more like a consciousness raising group than a classroom. Many of the articles on the reading list I have taught in my Intro to Women's Studies course in the "History of the Second Wave" section. The interesting thing is that the prof made the disclaimer that she often is accused of assigning too much reading. Wow. That probably speaks to the difference between the classes I am used to, English department classes where there is a book or so assigned for each class period, and other disciplines where the focus isn't so text-based. [. . .] We began class with a "check in." That was a blast from the past! I haven't done "check ins" since the CR-like coven I was a member of about twelve years ago, and I am very skeptical about how well this approach will "work" in a graduate class. Is this feminist pedagogy? It appears it is according to this teacher, but I think there needs to be more rigorous questioning both by the group and self to embody the critical self reflection that to me earmarks feminist pedagogy. The teacher is very soft-spoken in that new-age therapist sort of way and she said she wanted this to be a "safe space," another tag phrase that puts me on edge because I hear the subtext to that as being, "Everything is validated; no confrontation; no conflict." One young woman spent a lot of time talking about how much she hated her students, how they didn't respect her, how racist they are. That is the problem with "check-ins": it can quickly disintegrate into emotive processing with little or no analysis. It's going to be really fascinating, though, to watch how this teacher practices her feminist pedagogy in this class where the subject is feminist pedagogy. I am deeply grateful that she is allowing me to day-trip into the course.

Through conducting my research and hearing people's response to my project, I have come to believe that one of the most common misconceptions about feminist pedagogy is that feminist pedagogy is a good fit for Women's Studies classes, but cannot or should not be applied to other disciplines. This belief implies that feminist politics ground the content of a course or that a student must adopt a feminist perspective to succeed in the course. By extension, this misconception comes to be understood as "if a teacher proclaims herself a feminist and is aware of gender issues in her classroom and curriculum, she is engaging in feminist pedagogy." Another common misconception about feminist pedagogy is that it is touchy-feely or lacks rigor. I make a distinction between feminist pedagogy and feminine pedagogy, the latter where the model of teacher as nurturing mother seems to dominate. With my research, I offer a much more complex view of feminist pedagogy. Being "a teacher who is feminist" is not enough to constitute feminist pedagogy.

Some teachers who are feminist operate under masculine models of power and pedagogy that are decidedly not indicative of feminist pedagogy (Morley, 1999). Teaching based on masculinist models where the teacher represents an uninterrogated body of knowledge that is passed to the students whole-cloth is not feminist pedagogy no matter who uses it. That is not to say that masculinist models are bad teaching; I have learned wonderful things in classrooms where this model of traditional teaching style reigned supreme. Rather, I argue that even if a teacher identifies as a feminist, if she employs masculinist models of teaching, even if they are effective, this is not feminist pedagogy.

I argue that feminist pedagogy is a theory of teaching that moves far beyond feminist identity and gender issues. Similar to liberatory pedagogy, which sprung from Paulo Freire's experience with the underclass of Brazil during the social and political revolutionary of the 1950s and 1960s, feminist pedagogy arose from the North American women's movement of the 1960s. Since that time, feminist teachers and scholars have been creating clearer and more comprehensive definitions of what it means to be a feminist teacher that extend beyond self-identification as a feminist, concern for gender issues, or a push towards social action external to the classroom. There are feminists who are teachers who do not implement feminist pedagogy, and there are teachers who are not feminist who practice feminist pedagogical principles. Feminist pedagogy has evolved into a method of teaching that can be applied by people (both men and women) regardless of whether they are feminist, just as one does not necessarily have to identify as a Marxist socialist activist to implement liberatory pedagogy. In other words, form *can* be separated from content. A class with feminist content is not necessarily feminist pedagogy at work.

Roots of Feminist Pedagogy

When feminist pedagogy was first named as a school of teaching theory in the late 1970s and early 1980s by scholars such as Kathleen Weiler, Carolyn Shrewsbury, Janet Miller, and Margo Culley, and in the articles published in journals such as *Women's Studies Quarterly* and *The Feminist Teacher*, the core description reflected a Freirian approach to teaching that foregrounded issues of gender as opposed to socioeconomic class. Culley (1982) defines feminist pedagogy as subverting the teacher role as a source of knowledge, integrating women's work and words as course texts, and creating connections between the lives of women in the course and the community external to the academy. Miller (1982) echoes these themes, seeing feminist pedagogy as breaking a silence by integrating the voices and perspectives of women in curricula. With Shrewsbury's (1993) definition of feminist pedagogy, the influence of Freire's liberatory pedagogy is more evident. When Shrewsbury

(1993) defines feminist pedagogy, she focuses on integrating critical thinking in course work with concerns for gender justice.

Further solidifying the connection between feminist teaching and critical thinking, in her definition of feminist teaching, Weiler (1988) writes that feminist teachers use critical analysis and reflection as a centerpiece for their teaching, committing themselves to seeing students as individual learners and thinkers. In addition, Weiler writes, feminist teachers provide strong, competent models for girls *and* boys of women in the world. Weiler also addresses issues of conflict in the feminist classroom and between feminist teachers and the institutions where they work, stating that feminist teachers work to change standard curriculums to reflect students' realities and to name sexism and other silences. For feminist teachers, Weiler writes, critical analysis and critical reflection are important, but there is also an underlying commitment to making the classroom less about memorizing facts and more about developing critical consciousness. The objective of teacher and student critical consciousness is not unique to feminist pedagogy; pedagogical schools such as liberatory or critical pedagogies also embrace this goal.

In addition to a focus on critical consciousness, attention to teacher power and authority also became a cornerstone of feminist pedagogy. Shrewsbury (1993) articulates this by defining *teacher power* as energy, capacity, and potential, not domination. Although Miller, Culley, Weiler, and Shrewsbury all echo Freire when including dialogic learning, where students and teachers are all learners and educators within the classroom community as part of feminist pedagogy, these three feminist teachers focus more carefully on the nuances of power complicated by gender, race, and class. By the end of the 1990s, theorists and teachers such as Frances Hoffmann, Jayne Stake, and Elizabeth Tisdell offered more concrete definitions of feminist pedagogy. In their 1998 article "Feminist Pedagogy Theory and Practice," Hoffman and Stake identify four elements of feminist pedagogy: participatory classroom communities, validation of personal experience, encouragement of social understanding and activism, and development of critical thinking skills. Hoffman and Stake are writing about feminist pedagogy within the Women's Studies classroom, but Tisdell opened up feminist pedagogy as a teaching practice for adult learners in other disciplines. In her article "Poststructural Feminist Pedagogies," Tisdell (1988) defines the common elements of feminist pedagogies as attention to gender and women's emancipation, and emphasizing connections between learners and the world outside the classroom and course material.

More than individual articles and scholars, however, the collective voice of *The Feminist Teacher* journal continued to clarify and refine the definitions of feminist pedagogy from the early 1980s through today. *The Feminist Teacher* began publishing in the early 1980s; as the name suggests, the articles focus on how feminist teachers are practicing their theories of teaching across the disciplines and at various educational levels. In *The Feminist Teacher Anthology*, a compilation of selected essays from the first 10 volumes of the journal, the editors provide a definition of feminist pedagogy. In their introduction, the editors "propose several tenets in feminist pedagogy" that reflect the evolution of this theory and practice of teaching at the time the book was published in 1998. These tenets include: builds an orientation toward social transformation, consciousness-raising, and social activism (thought into action); stresses the subjective and communal reality of knowing; shows concern for women; addresses race, class, and gender as "crucial categories for analyzing experience and institutions"; confronts forces of sexism and heterosexism; and explores issues of sexuality honestly with students (Cohee et al., 1998, p. 3).

Most recently, Fisher (2001) defines feminist pedagogy as evolving from consciousness-raising (CR) methods and feminist theories of discourse. In her book *No Angel in the Classroom,* Fisher articulates various themes that she believes are derivatives of CR models: awareness of women's relationship to the world, awareness of power, risk taking to "reveal something about [oneself]," collective and cooperative activities, orientation toward action, and focus on critical thinking skills. Fisher sees a student's access to and an understanding of academic discourse as a foundational element of feminist pedagogy because, without access to discourse, students feel disempowered and excluded from academic arguments. Again, she relates this to CR models where "many women who were hurt, angered, or disappointed by consciousness-raising have testified, the dominant assumptions, vocabulary, and expressive style of any discussion easily excludes those who do not share them" (pp. 46–47). In a feminist classroom, teachers need to be acutely aware of language practices, thus teaching the power and politics of language as an integral element of feminist pedagogy.

The way in which Fisher (2001) stretches CR models to feminist pedagogy does not include self-critique by the teacher, although teacher self-critique *is* part of the discussion. Fisher writes that she talks to herself about teaching practices "for deeper and more continuous discussions of what I am doing" (p. 213). She believes this strategy is crucial for feminist teaching, but these discussions also have to extend to others. Talking with other teachers of feminist teaching practices is the political work of feminist pedagogy. In her book, Fisher describes how talking with other faculty members about her Women's Studies courses evolved into a seminar for students and faculty about teaching practices. The seminars are successful, Fisher writers, only if there is mutual vulnerability among participants, meaning they feel they can be honest and respectful with one another. She writes that, although these discussions may reveal substantial differences and disagreements among approaches to teaching, "we may weigh truths differently as we seek to develop politically and pedagogically sound judgements" (p. 217). This points to an awareness between the philosophies of feminist pedagogy and how individual teachers enact feminist pedagogy in their own classrooms.

When looking at all these definitions, from the earliest to the most recent, I find themes emerging and overlapping, such as: challenges to teachers to be aware of power and student identity in both microstructures (classroom and student–teacher interactions) and macrostructures (sociocultural institutions like racism, classism, homophobia, etc.). Feminist pedagogy is a theory and practice of teaching that is separate and distinct from liberatory, critical, or other radical pedagogies, although feminist pedagogy shares some principles with all these theories.[12]

THE TAXONOMIES OF TEACHING

In doing research for this project, I found that many scholars and teachers neglect to make distinctions among liberatory, critical, and feminist pedagogies. I have come to understand all three of these pedagogical schools to be distinct from each other, although they are all types of radical pedagogies (i.e., pedagogies that wish to radically transform the standards of education as a way of transforming the culture to dismantle systems of oppression). Liberatory pedagogy, as defined by Freire, focuses on student-empowerment with attention to socioeconomic class. The object of liberatory pedagogy centers on making students active participants in changing culture to a more socialist model. Class inequities, and the awareness of these inequities, as well as moving students to critical consciousness by incorporating connections between the classroom and their lived experiences are the primary tenets of liberatory pedagogy. Likewise, critical pedagogy focuses on teaching critical thinking skills and moving students toward critical consciousness. The distinction for me between critical and liberatory pedagogy is that the latter is more aggressive and overt about focusing on socioeconomic class inequities, power structures, and systems of oppression. Critical pedagogy's dominant theme is working on critical thinking, understanding that once students have the skills of critical thinking they will be able to see the inequities of the oppressive systems and work to change them. In other words, critical pedagogy forges a more indirect road to change than liberatory pedagogy. Feminist pedagogy incorporates foundational principles of both liberatory and critical pedagogies, but also addresses issues such as teacher power, teacher self-critique, and attention to traditionally marginalized voices and perspectives both in the curriculum and the classroom.

Although scholars and teachers often conflate or fail to distinguish between these three schools of pedagogy, they each offer different approaches to teaching. That is not to say, however, that they have not informed each other or evolved together. Freire consistently revised his theories of pedagogy, and toward the end of his life many of the elements of feminist pedagogy can be found in his own theories (see *Teachers as Cultural Workers*). I maintain that this evolution does not change the fundamental definition of liberatory pedagogy. Rather, it shows how feminist pedagogy and feminist scholars influenced Freire's own ideas on education and integrated Freire's liberatory theories on teaching into principles of feminist pedagogy.

Besides liberatory and critical theories of pedagogy, another primary influence that helped create feminist pedagogy was poststructural theory. Poststructural theory connects knowledge to power, works to decenter power structures, and deconstructs hierarchies, all of which appeal to feminist teachers. In the classroom, this translates into teachers subverting their own power whenever possible. Whether it is coming out from behind the podium, sitting in a circle, charging students with the responsibility of discussion topics, or creating other strategies that shift the focus away from the teacher, feminist teachers are working toward applying elements of postmodern theory in their classroom practices.

One of the ways that feminist pedagogy embodies poststructuralist theories is in how feminist teachers question and subvert the norms of a classroom (teacher authority, empowerment of students, creating connections between classrooms and social action). Worsham ("Critical Interference", 1999) uses the metaphor of *jamming the machine* to describe these subversions of standard pedagogy. This type of teaching attempts to create new models of power and bring the ideological machine to a screeching halt. But by 1999, Worsham questioned whether these teaching strategies are still disruptive, arguing that they may have become so familiar as to have created another ideological machine that is not necessarily radical.

Another force that helped shape feminist pedagogy was the relationships between academic and activist feminists during the 1970s. Approaches to grassroots activism moved into the academy in the form of feminist theory and Women's Studies courses. As feminist teachers created the new discipline of Women's Studies, they redefined classroom processes to reinforce relationships and connections between the activist and academic worlds. By integrating processes used in the grassroots women's movement, feminist pedagogy emerged. One primary model taken from the grassroots political movement and transplanted into the pedagogy of Women's Studies was Consciousness Raising (CR) groups. CR groups sprung up in the 1970s, a staple of the burgeoning feminist subculture. These small communities of women gathered together to talk about their experiences, make connections between their lives and the political and social climate of the culture, and discuss what action they could take, both personally and politically, to contribute to social change.

CR groups became the stronghold of the feminist movement of the 1970s, where "housewives"[13] and other disempowered groups of women found strength, validation, and purpose in the company of other politically and socially involved feminist activists. These small clutches of "women's space" fed the streams to local and national grassroots activist groups where personal consciousness became political action. The CR groups mimicked Margaret Fuller's Conversation Groups of the mid-1800s in that there was no authority represented; authority rotated among the women present. Personal experience was validated by the group, and the end goal was action, either within the public sphere or one's personal life. CR groups provided a way to connecting the personal and the larger community and then create political action (Weiler, 1988). From the CR groups sprung the now famous feminist slogan, "The Personal *is* Political." The strategies of the CR groups—deconstructing authority, validating personal experience, creating goals for action—when applied to the classroom formed some of the primary themes of Women's Studies pedagogy.[14]

Personal Journal; July 29, 2000

[The Multicultural Leadership Program] class went well today, although everyone was so low energy. They bring these students [first generation college bound high school juniors, primarily African American] to campus for a week of college life and then pack their schedule so full they are absolutely spanked by the end of the week. But what a great group of students. It was 9 a.m. and they were still rubbing sleep from their eyes, so I had them get up and we played musical chairs (people sang!). It did the trick; after that we all kicked in with a lot more energy to talk about writing. One young woman refuses to talk, even when I call on her. Today I asked her to read. She refused. After class I took her aside and asked her what the problem was. She said she just didn't like to be called on. I said that was fine; I wouldn't call upon her anymore as long as she made an effort to participate. I gave her my run down of reasons about why it is so important to use one's voice, especially when one is a woman and an African American woman at that: if she is silent she will not be seen; if she is silent no one will understand her perspective; verbally articulating one's ideas is important to developing critical thinking skills; when she is silent no one can learn from her and learning from each other is part of being a member of the community; by offering her ideas and perspectives to the group, the group will respond to them and her ideas and thoughts will grow as a result. I warned her that tomorrow everyone is reading part of their project to the group, I have been building up to this all week: the Stand and Deliver part of presenting one's ideas. I asked her whether she felt she would be able

to do that, to participate as a member of the community, taking the
risk to share her work with others. She said she would try.

When I talked about the situation in the feminist pedagogy class,
the instructor said she thought I had made a very bad decision. I
was immediately thrilled with the dramatic reaction in this class
where no one has been questioning/confronting, but only "validating." Great! I enjoy hearing criticism about teaching choices; I
want to be challenged and sometimes I can only go so far with my
own self-critique. I brought the issue to the group because I was
hoping to get a response. The instructor said that as a white
woman, a teacher with power, telling an African American young
woman/girl to speak up was unfair. African Americans, especially women, have historically been punished for speaking up, so I
shouldn't demand it. I countered that I understood that perspective and in fact struggled with it, but ultimately believe that my job
as a teacher is to help these students practice using their voice so
they feel more comfortable taking those risks. And the student has
the choice, but she also has been told why I believe participating
is so important. Yes, African American women who speak out will
be punished occasionally, the dominant culture always extracts a
price for speaking out against it; I have been taxed in that regard
myself more times than I can count. So all the more reason to
work on strengthening their voice and confidence and ability to
articulate their ideas in a group of people. How is a young African
American woman (indeed all women, or any persons reflecting a
traditionally marginalized location) expected to ever speak out if
she does not practice or is not encouraged and nudged? The ensu-
ing discussion was one of the most productive we have had in
that feminist pedagogy class, encompassing issues of power and
silence. The discussion also spoke directly to the dramatically different ways we (the instructor and I) envision feminist pedagogy:
nurturing and "safe space" as opposed to seeing discomfort as a
place of growth.

The prior journal entry exemplifies one distinction between Women's
Studies pedagogy and feminist pedagogy. In feminist pedagogy, conflict is
not seen as damaging to the individual or the community, but as a power
source for growth. As Women's Studies pedagogy evolved into feminist pedagogy, and as feminist teachers began adapting this teaching style to courses
other than Women's Studies, definitions and discussions of feminist pedagogy flourished. The logistics of integrating feminist pedagogy in the composition classroom have been part of discussions in the field since the 1970s.
Feminism and composition intersected in a way that called for a redefinition
of composition (Ritchie & Boardman, 1999). This redefinition includes a
focus on writing process instead of product (helping each student define his

or her own writing process), attention to identity issues in the classroom (race, class, gender, and sexual orientation, among others), confronting the politics of language, and using collaboration as a strategy for producing work. But shifts in composition also incorporate many other feminist pedagogical themes, including those I pointed to in the journal entry (addressing issues of conflict, paying attention to voices and silences, being overt with pedagogical choices, engaging students in active learning[15]). Focus on writing process instead of product, giving careful attention to identity issues in the classroom, confronting the politics of language, and using collaboration as a strategy for producing work points to changes in the field that have resulted from a shift in the culture of education. I attribute many of these shifts to responses to the women's movement as well as other progressive social movements of the 1960s and 1970s. Although these changes in composition pedagogy reflected a back door integration of feminist ideas into the field, feminist teachers more overtly changed composition by writing about issues of conflict in the writing classroom, attention given to voices and silences, and attention to gender issues (as well as race, class, and sexuality). These theories and practices are those more specifically associated with feminist pedagogy, brought to composition by feminists in the field who wanted to apply these pedagogical themes to the writing classroom. These practices have become more mainstream in the field of composition and are no longer seen as exclusively feminist.

Throughout the 1990s, as more women in the field of composition and rhetoric openly identified as feminist, and their teaching practices as reflecting their feminist viewpoint, the field began to view feminist pedagogy in the composition classroom as a site of change and activism. Brodkey and Fine (1992) write, "The future of academic feminism is activism and activism begins with pedagogy" (p. 70). As in Women's Studies, feminist pedagogy became the logical extension of feminist activism within the field of composition.

FROM THE WELLSPRINGS
OF FEMINISM

Feminist pedagogy has been at work both overtly and covertly in composition scholarship and practices over the past three decades. Without naming composition practices or the general philosophies of contemporary composition pedagogy as feminist, we erase the important work and change that feminists have brought to the field. The acceptance of feminist theories and use of feminist practices are directly related to the status of women in composition. As women and, by extension, feminists gained more *ethos* in the field, other teachers and scholars more readily published, read, adopted, and adapted their theories of writing instruction.

The first overt discussions of integrating feminist principles into the field of composition related to feminist literary criticism and teaching literature by and about women in the composition classroom.[16] During the 1960s and 1970s, composition teachers used writing about literature as a primary method of teaching academic writing. At that time, feminist literary criticism in the form of discussions of the role of gender in texts and integrating women writers in course curriculum provided a logical first step in bringing feminist themes to composition. Although discussions of teaching texts by women were prominent in composition journals during the 1970s, these articles emphasized feminist theories of literature, not writing pedagogy. The first time the "f" word appears in a scholarly article within a composition journal, Ira Shor argues teachers should apply feminist literary criticism to composition course materials. In the May 1973 issue of *College English,* Shor published his article emphasizing feminist theory, but he is not writing about composition pedagogy. The article offers suggestions on how to use feminist theories to teach woman authors in an English classroom ("Anne Sexton's 'For My Lover . . .': Feminism in the Classroom"). Connections between feminism and writing pedagogy did not begin to appear with frequency until the late 1980s. In a field that has been dominated by women since the 1970s, it seems odd that overt scholarly discussions of feminism arrived relatively late to the pedagogy of writing.

As the women's movement gained momentum during the early 1970s, more female scholars began publishing, or their work was accepted for publication, in scholarly journals; this corresponds to a proliferation of women's caucuses in groups such as the Modern Language Association (MLA) and Conference on College Composition and Communication (CCCC). One can easily see evidence of the burgeoning presence of women scholars when reviewing the 1970s and 1980s publications of the two most prominent composition journals, *College English* and *College Composition and Communication.* In 1971, there is only one woman published in *College English,* but the first issue of the 1972 volume is filled with the voices and perspectives of women. This issue of *College English,* devoted to the status of women faculty and students as well as the presence of women in curriculum, marked the beginning of an increase of women's representation in subsequent issues of the journal significantly.[17]

In the 1972 "status of women in the field" issue of *College English,* the conversations center on the burgeoning field of feminist criticism and how it applies to women in English departments and literature curricula. In this issue, the editor (Hedges) wrote, "As they (women) rediscover what has been lost and as they reread and reinterpret what has been misread and misrepresented, women critics, scholars, writers, teachers, students are also *inventing.* They are inventing new classroom procedures" (p. 4). These new classroom procedures are the beginning of feminist pedagogical practices.[18] Hedges briefly noted the focus of these new classroom procedures: confronting the male model of pedagogy where the teacher is the active knower (traditionally male) and the student is the passive learner (traditionally female). Hedges stated that part of these new pedagogical practices demanded confronting gender issues in the classroom, primarily in course material. Hedges wrote that awareness of gender issues extends to those between students and bridging the gap between classroom experiences and students' own realities. These changes to classroom practices were a dramatic departure from the traditional university classroom. Hedges believed that radical change, at the behest and sweat of women, was on the horizon: "And what goes on in the classroom will be different from what has gone on the in the past, as students increasingly bring to the literature and other material they read their own personal experiences as women, or men" (p. 4). Hedges pointed to the pedagogy used in Women's Studies as a model for these changes, acknowledging that "we are still at the beginning" (p. 5).

It would be another 12 years before a scholar detailed specific pedagogical practices for the composition classroom as feminist. In 1985, Pamela Annas published an article on feminist pedagogical principles in *College English* entitled "Style as Politics: A Feminist Approach to the Teaching of Writing." In this article, Annas began the overt integration of feminist pedagogy into the field of composition by defining specific teaching practices as feminist. These practices included attention to standards of style and the limits that standards imposed on students, especially women. Annas called for a subversion of or deviation from standard style templates of the academy. Annas believed that female students were especially at a disadvantage when standards forbade the integration of personal experience. Although Annas' theory ended up essentializing gender characteristics (boys do not want to write about personal experience, girls do), her article represented the first overt naming of feminist pedagogy in the field of composition. Focusing on the feminist pedagogical theme of *creating connections*, Annas argued that academic standards prevented students—in her argument, specifically women—from integrating their lived realities into their writing.

Although Annas was the first within the field of composition to name these teaching practices as feminist, themes of feminist pedagogy proliferated in composition scholarship during the 1970s and 1980s, although not identified as such. Editors published many theoretical articles during the 1970s and 1980s about student-centered pedagogical practices that easily fit into the historical definitions of feminist teaching. Although Annas was actively working to integrate feminist pedagogy into composition, I am not suggesting that all composition scholars of the 1970s and 1980s who pushed for more radical pedagogical reform in writing were feminist scholars or teachers. Instead I am arguing that both overt moves by feminist teachers and more general changes that resulted from the feminist social movement of the 1960s and 1970s created a climate where teachers and scholars integrated more feminist pedagogical theories into the field, even if the authors of those theories did not identify them as such. As was the case across the curriculum in the 1970s, radical, student-centered pedagogical theories emerged with prominence in contemporary composition theory.

Despite strong feminist voices and perspectives such as Hedges and Annas, the first women composition scholars (those who wrote specifically about the teaching of *writing*) did not initially envision their work as feminist. Mina Shaunessey, Linda Flower, Andrea Lunsford, and Lisa Ede, all prominent women scholars in the field, did not originally define their scholarship or their own perspective as feminist. Although many of these women would later identify as feminists and write about feminism in the field of composition and rhetoric, if these women did identify as feminists when they first began publishing they did not overtly mention this identity in their scholarship. They did not identify their theories as feminist, but their theories still reflect feminist themes and contribute to the integration of feminist pedagogical practices in the writing classroom.

BEGINNING TO NAME FEMINIST PEDAGOGICAL PRACTICES, THE 1980s

Throughout the 1970s, as feminist theory and attention to the status of women in the subculture of the academy, and specifically in the field of composition, gained momentum, the presence of women increased in scholarly journals. The diligent, tireless work of feminists in the field, and of the coalitions these women formed in professional organizations and at conferences, created opportunities for publication. Because of this increased opportunity, books and articles by women on strategies of how to become better writing teachers proliferated in the 1980s. These texts focused on teaching, but the politics of language and the climate of the classroom were large pieces of these discussions. Extending poststructural theories to composition, much of the scholarship published in the 1980s theorized that knowledge is socially constructed and writing is a complex act involving several different axes of social identity for the writer, teacher, and audience. The classroom was seen not as a politically neutral location, but a site of learning where the teacher could help students see that the personal is connected to the larger culture, and that gender, racial, and other differences are not based on personal perspectives and beliefs, but at ideological forces and socialization processes.

In 1987, Caywood and Overing edited the text *Teaching Writing: Pedagogy, Gender, and Equity,* providing a precursor to the proliferation of feminist essays on pedagogy of the 1990s. Caywood and Overing compiled essays that clarified feminist discussions of writing instruction. Today the book reads as a primer for what are now considered the basics of feminist theory in composition. In their book, Caywood and Overing gathered together women authors who created a preliminary definition of feminist writing pedagogy. The theories of the book focused on a feminine "ethics of care" model where achieving political equity for students in the writing classroom was obtained through accommodation and nurturing of differences. The anthology represents the relationship between feminist theory and writing theory, seeing writing as a process, not a product, and focusing on revision and allowing students to write in their own voice.

In the Caywood and Overing (1987) book, the goal of the contributors' pedagogical strategies is clear: not to create feminist students, but to use feminism to move students toward critical consciousness. The anthology also attempted to confront the question, "What writing classroom practices create an inequitable climate for each student?" They used a feminist pedagogical approach to counter what feminists saw as traditional tyrannical practices (e.g., teaching Standard English with little regard for the political issues involved and ignoring individual needs of students and their cultural and personal locations). The principles of feminist pedagogy as applied to the writing classroom outlined by the book's contributors include:

- creating CR group models of discourse that focus on dialogue and not confrontation or hierarchy (Annas, 1985);
- recognizing silence as a transformative space, but moving students from silence to speech, from ignorance to knowledge (Annas, 1985);
- helping students connect their writing problems with their personal location and the location of their audience; seeing writing problems as issues of discourse, not lagging cognitive development (Goulston, 1987);
- drawing on the life practices of a student's first language (mother tongue) to understand our role as teachers (Daumer & Runzo, 1987);
- bringing to the class the voices and perspectives of women (Daumer & Runzo, 1987);
- using nonsexist language and teaching students to be sensitive to nonsexist language in their writing (Freed, 1995); and
- creating writing assignments that are meaningful for students and that allow students to make choices about their own work (Fuss, 1987).

During the 1980s, another direct influence of feminist theory on the field of composition came in the form of feminist reading practices. Reader response theory, used by many writing teachers, integrated feminist theory so readers would consider race, privilege, and gender of the author and reader (Schweikart, 1986). In the spirit of deconstructionism, a school of thought that refutes the belief that there are truism or foundational structures on which knowledge, identity, or culture is built, Schweikart wrote that neither the author nor the readers can supply all the meaning in a text. She argued that teachers could not simply change the curriculum to incorporate women's voices; teachers needed to integrate critical discussions of gender, and other identities, into classrooms. To do this, students needed new reading strategies. Schweikart outlined a feminist reading strategy that recognized the duality of interaction between the text and the reader. This strategy also recognized that, because the author is absent, reading is subjective. Using this approach, teachers would recognize each interpretation not as valid or invalid, but as one way of looking at the text.

In her theories, Schweikart (1986) connected feminist reading and writing: "Feminist reading and writing are grounded in the interest of producing a community of feminist readers and writers in the hope that ultimately this community will expand to include everyone" (p. 56). Schweikart argued for a feminist ideology to replace the patriarchal ideology. Is the goal of the feminist teacher to create classrooms full of feminists, or just feminist readers, defining a feminist reader as one who uses the strategy outlined by Schweikart? Unlike the Caywood and Overing anthology, where the teacher's objective was to help students become better thinkers and community members, not necessarily feminists, the role of the feminist teacher as described by Schweikart seems less clear. One could read Schweikart as advocating for or privileging a feminist ideology (see earlier quote), not in the form of feminist leadership or facilitation, but in the form of a feminist political agenda ultimately adopted by students. If her definition of a *feminist reader* refers to one who reads critically and carefully, analyzing the ideological power and personal bias existing in and between the reader and the text, the goal of helping students become feminist readers encourages critical thinking and analysis, not the indoctrination of a feminist political perspective.

CONTEMPORARY FEMINIST WRITING PEDAGOGY IN THE 1990S

Between the early 1980s and late 1990s, the definition of feminist pedagogy evolved and solidified as feminists wrote about their teaching. In the middle to latter part of the 1990s publications such as *The Feminist Teacher* and *Meeting the Challenge* showed that feminist pedagogy was not just a teaching method for Women's Studies courses. By the 1990s, composition theorists were naming certain pedagogical practices as *feminist*, solidifying a definition of feminist pedagogy for the composition classroom. Although the naming of feminist pedagogy in composition came late in the decade, throughout the 1990s, elements of feminist pedagogy were clearly delineated in composition scholarship. As previously outlined, some composition scholars have been writing about feminist theories and pedagogical themes since the early 1970s, but these themes and practices were overtly named as feminist most prolifically during the middle to latter part of the 1990s. There are themes of feminist pedagogy running throughout composition theory since 1971.[19] I am distinguishing between overt discussions and specific naming of feminist pedagogy as it manifests itself in the composition classroom during the 1990s and describing classroom strategies that reflect feminist pedagogical themes, but are not overtly named as feminist, as happened in the 1970s and 1980s. Even today, many teachers are reluctant to embrace the moniker of *feminist* pedagogy, instead describing pedagogy that integrates the themes outlined in later in this chapter as *liberatory* or *critical* pedagogies.

Feminist pedagogy is more complicated than a pedagogy practiced by feminists, foregrounding a feminist agenda, that is, a syllabus that foregrounds issues of gender, and sometimes race, class, sexual orientation. Feminist pedagogy embodies many more complexities. Many teachers in the field are practicing feminist pedagogical principles. The field of composition is a model of how feminist pedagogy can be assumed by a field in such a way that it is practiced as a dominant approach to teaching. Why do some teachers and scholars shy away from using the term "feminist pedagogy" as it applies to their own work? Perhaps it is because they do not understand what feminist pedagogy is, thus the importance of this project. Perhaps it is because there is an anti-feminist bias that exists, erasing the contributions of feminist pedagogy in composition. Regardless of the reason, many theorists and scholars use rhetoric such as *democratic, liberatory*, or *critical* in describing what other scholars, especially those within Women's Studies but certainly some in the field of composition, name as feminist.

One example of this appropriation or renaming of feminist pedagogy is Mike Rose's "democratic pedagogy." In his book, *Possible Lives*, Rose (1995) describes the ideal composition classroom as a site for democratic ideals, and that democracy[20] in the classroom will lead to civic action. "To imagine a vibrant democratic state, you must have a deep belief in the majestic of common intelligence, in its distribution through the population to become participatory civic beings" (p. 432). Although Rose creates an idyllic and patriotic view of the power of pedagogy, and I would argue even creates a model where democracy and social action seem to spring organically from simply believing in the intelligence of students, his belief that a "good" classroom environment leads to social action is grounded in feminist pedagogy. Rose describes the idea of a "good" classroom community creating social action organically, and outlines what he believes are "good teaching practices" that will lead to this result. "Good teaching," Rose writes, "is almost defined by its tendency to push the borders of things" (p. 13). Pushing borders and breaking boundaries, feminist rhetoric used by Gloria Anzaldua (1987) and Mary Daly (1987) in the 1980s, creates a more tenacious, yet unspoken or unattributed, connection between feminism and Rose's democratic pedagogy.

Even without naming his philosophies on teaching as "feminist," Rose (1995) evokes veiled connections with feminist theory and pedagogy. Another example of these oblique references is his attention to authority in the classroom. Authority, described by Rose as a management style employed by teachers, comes from care for students, acknowledgment of students' realities, constructing a classroom environment where students are "safe" from insult and diminishment, and where students can take risks. In a democratic classroom, Rose wrote, authority is shared between the students and teacher, marking another prominent theme of feminist pedagogy. Rose's list of "good teaching practices," even as he resisted a final list of 'good practices," included themes of feminist pedagogy that extended beyond shared authority, social action, and pushing borders:

- affirmation of students' experiences and realities,
- focusing on student energies and channeling those energies toward work that is meaningful to them,
- engaging in the local community to understand students' realities and also make connections with parents and other teachers as they create a community, and
- knowing students well—having individual knowledge of students and their cultures and traditions.

Each of these points directly corresponds to 1 of the 16 themes of feminist pedagogy that emerged during my historical research. Does Rose intentionally hide the similarities between feminist pedagogy and his democratic version? Is he oblivious to radical pedagogical theories, ignoring connections and unwittingly borrowing from feminist pedagogical theories to construct his democratic pedagogy? Considering how thoroughly Rose's description of democratic pedagogy overlapped with themes of feminist pedagogy, not a single mention of feminist pedagogical theories in his book feels like, in the most gentle terms, a suspicious exclusion.

Also using the rhetoric of democracy to describe composition pedagogy, Lunsford, (1989) in her speech to CCCC (Chair's Address), called for a postmodern pedagogy that was "radically democratic." Lunsford defined this postmodern pedagogy using themes of feminist pedagogy: (a) nonhierarchical, (b) intensely collaborative, (c) dialogic, and (d) heteroglossic/multivoiced.

As with Rose, Lunsford did not describe these practices as feminist. I am not faulting Lunsford as she is one of the strongest and most consistent voices for feminism within the discipline. Nonetheless by naming the pedagogy as "democratic" as opposed to "feminist," the field of composition missed the opportunity to give credit to feminist scholars who have named these themes as part of feminist pedagogy.

The conflation of postmodern and democratic pedagogies with feminist pedagogy, without naming it as such, is worth examining. Although postmodern pedagogy stresses social construction as its core, democratic teaching centers more on political elements of equality without questioning social structures. Even more interesting is how Rose, Lunsford, and others seem to fold these definitions and approaches into theories of pedagogy, creating definitions that are both postmodern and democratic, but never feminist. That these theorists talk about feminist pedagogy, a pedagogical theory that had been evolving for over 30 years, but avoid using the "f" work, creating new rhetoric to describe it, reinforces the reason for this project.

Some would argue that there is no need to name these practices as feminist any longer because they have become part of the status quo—part of the general belief of what creates a "good" classroom community and pedagogical approach to writing. These practices, once radical, are no longer considered to be disruptive or subversive. I believe that some feminist pedagogical practices *have* been accepted to the point of no longer being radical, but naming these practices as feminist is still radical rhetoric. Most scholars prefer to use words like *critical, liberatory, postmodern,* and *democratic* to describe pedagogical themes and principles that other scholars defined as feminist. This avoidance of the "f" word may also speak to why use of the word *feminist* evokes deviant concepts and disruptive models. These pedagogical practices labeled as *democratic, radical, critical,* or *liberatory* reflect feminist pedagogy. However because of the stigma, stereotypes, or ambiguity about what feminist pedagogy is, some scholars and journal editors use alternative rhetorics of naming. It is because of the ambiguities, stigmas, and stereotypes regarding feminist pedagogy in composition that we need to give more credit to how feminist pedagogy has shaped contemporary composition pedagogy.

Chapter Two

A Historical Representation
of Feminist Pedagogy

The Sixteen Themes

I am sitting in my office with a student. To describe him physically seems beyond the point, but somehow there is a connection between his physical manifestation and the reason I am writing about him now, so here goes. He is tall and lanky, quiet, docile and passive, but, I am to find out, passively aggressive. He wears glasses, small, black, and rectangular, and these give him an intellectual, arty look.

Am I describing him in a negative light? What picture do you have of him now? How will this physical presence you have conjured inform your reading of this story? How have I created him in order to support my version of this tale, this pedagogical moment that frustrates and puzzles me enough to write about it, using my encounter with him as a way to kick off a chapter about feminist pedagogy in the writing classroom? What is the purpose of teachers, of me, telling these stories? To justify our responses to students, to work through teacher angst, to work through how we helped or did not help *this* student so the next time we will do better? My fear is that most of the time we tell these stories to make ourselves feel good and look good. The student is the antagonist and the teacher is the hero. I am aware of this as I tell this story and it makes me nervous.

This student has come to visit me during office hours to have me read his project draft. He tells me he did not get any "good" feedback from his peers, that it was all vague and unhelpful. This student comes to me a week before the final draft is due, complaining of unhelpful peer feedback. As he sits in my office, digging through his cluttered green folder to find his draft, I search my mind to remember his project proposal. I remember something about boys in the classroom, or boys in the educational system, and how they are at a disadvantage. I remember telling him one book he needed to read, at least in part, was *Failing at Fairness: How Schools Cheat Girls* by Sadker and Sadker (1994). The student locates the draft in his folder and slides it across the desk to me, like a secret offer that can not be spoken. As I start reading his draft, I quickly discover that his research focus is more pointed than I remember, more accusatory. The research question, it seems to me, is more along the lines of, How have feminists changed the institution of education so as to favor girls and discriminate against boys? In his paper he cites statistics that boys have higher dropout rates than girls, are more likely to be diagnosed with attention deficit disorder (ADD), have a higher suicide rate than girls, and are less likely to go to college. The reason, he writes, is because of feminists. They made such a fuss about how girls were neglected in school that everything has now changed to favor girls, the pendulum has swung wickedly in the other direction, knocking young boys to their knees in the face of biased feminist teachers.

As I read I feel an emotional response equivalent to frustration and anger. I check this emotional response. I am his composition teacher, after all. What about the writing? The argument is ill-constructed. He quotes statistics without giving any sources. He makes general statements like, "I have never seen a teacher favor a boy in class" without any specific data presented as evidence. I read on, making notes in the margin, stopping occasionally to say, in what I think is a gentle tone, "You can't really say this without backing it up somehow. Where did this information come from? Cite the source, set up the quote, explain why you are using it."

On page three of the five-page draft, he brings in two specific examples from his personal experience of feminists whom he has had as teachers. At first I look up and say, "Good! Specific examples! This is what you need more of!" However, as I read on, I can feel frustration rising in my chest. The first example is of a feminist teacher who ignored the men in the class and only spoke with or talked to the women. The second example is of a feminist teacher who, in talking about the use of nonsexist language, drew a pig saying "Oink!" in the margin of her handout as a symbol of a "male chauvinist pig."

The second example is one about me, but so hugely misconstrued that I almost do not recognize it.

Here is my side of the story.

I had written a handout about nonsexist language use for the class. I wrote that it was perfectly okay for people to use *their* as the gender-neutral third person even when the verb is third-person singular. I had written on the class handout

I know some teachers will cringe and circle in red pen if you write, "The student was asked to bring *their* notebook to class" because they will say the pronoun (their) doesn't agree with the singular subject (student). That's hogwash in my book. Language is changing and one of the most interesting ways language is changing involves use of nonsexist rules. As a result, the standard is changing so that it is acceptable to use "their" as a pronoun for a singular subject because the English language doesn't have a singular pronoun that is gender neutral." In the margin of the handout, I had put a squiggly line under "hogwash" and had drawn a cartoonish picture of a little pig with a bucket of water being thrown over it (the pig was saying, "OINK!").

When I realize what I am reading in this student's paper, my little pig drawing and my paragraph on nonsexist language being twisted into a comment on "men as pigs," using my teacher power to exercise feminist dominion over and discrimination against males, I stop and look at the student. I wonder if my face is red. I smile and ask, "Is this supposed to be an interpretation of *my* handout?" The student smiles back and nods. I sigh, look down to collect my thoughts, and then launch into a short lecture on misinterpretation and what the *intended* reading of the pig drawing is. I am not sure he is convinced, this bespectacled young man in my office. I only feel worse, delivering the lecture, defensive—even as I am checking my tone—and as if I am trying to rationalize a mortal sin.

After my spiel, I spend another 35 minutes with this student, re-reading his paper, talking with him, giving him pointers on how to create a stronger argument, and reminding him that his *audience* is a feminist, so he needs to be aware of that dynamic when writing a paper about how feminists persecute male students. At the end of it all, we have worked through a detailed outline of his paper. I feel exhausted. I have a headache. I feel relief as he finally rises from the chair to exit. He leaves my office nodding "yes" as I ask him, "Do you feel you have a clearer direction than when you came in? Do you feel you know where you are going with this project?" When he has disappeared around the corner, I lay my head down on the wood desk, smelling the dirt ground in from various teacher hands and, more than likely, drool and tears. My first thought is "How in the world am I going to objectively evaluate this paper?" The second thought is, "Goddamn it! If I weren't so overt about being a feminist, and using feminist pedagogy in my class, would he have read my (witty and clever) pig drawing as a vicious man-bashing slam?"

Herein resides one of the many rubs when applying feminist pedagogy, a teaching method designed and evolved from Women's Studies courses, to other disciplines. My composition students do not expect a feminist teacher. In fact, many of them do not *want* a feminist teacher. That is to say, the moment I identify as a feminist, many of them see me as man hating and prejudiced. For this student, my efforts to be overt with my political location created a dynamic, where he could not get beyond what he felt he knew a feminist is (man hater), and therefore he felt oppressed, dominated, and often persecuted in my classroom.

Because few (if any) other teachers reveal, at any point in time during the semester, their political and social locations, when a feminist teacher does, she is immediately suspect. Her mere confession of a political or social location is interpreted as a bias. She is not objective or neutral, something the ideology of traditional education convinces students that good teachers are. Feminist teachers know there is no such thing as objectivity and neutrality, so one must be overt about where one stands; because feminist pedagogical practices are still not the norm, students do not know what to do with these overt discussions of teacher location.

There are also other dynamics, negative consequences, or at least they feel negative—playing out in this example of feminist pedagogy in the writing classroom. In my composition classroom, I enact other tenets of feminist pedagogy (giving students choice in the work they do) by allowing students to create their own research questions. We, as a class, collaborate on goals of major projects, but they decide how that work will be created and engage in work that is not only challenging, but fun and meaningful to them (at least that is the hope). The danger of this is clearly represented in the prior example: a student who decides to write a paper on how feminist teachers are responsible for increased suicide rates, lower test scores, and fewer males in college. Of course this project will elicit a strong negative emotional response from me, a feminist teacher. As a result, I will be hyperaware of the comments I make and how I evaluate the work. In an effort to be unbiased, I am likely to award this student a higher mark than he deserves, both to prove to myself, and to him, that I can be objective and fair. Evaluating papers is excruciatingly subjective, even more so in a composition classroom where the students design their own projects/questions as opposed to the teacher assigning scripted research questions that allow little wiggle room for students to create their own work. To minimize this subjectivity, I use the goals we establish as a class as a rubric for evaluating the papers. Even so, it *feels* subjective. It is up to me to decide whether, as one ubiquitous goal states, "evidence is clearly presented and cited to support the claim."

Another element of feminist pedagogy playing out in this scenario is my effort to embrace conflict instead of working to avoid it. It is simply easier to not reveal that I am feminist, or committed to feminist pedagogy and what that means to me, because even the act of doing so creates conflict in the classroom. In the prior situation, the conflict is local and specific: The student is using as evidence in his argument a misrepresented example of my feminist teaching strategies. I confront the student by attempting to explain the intention behind the "OINK!" drawing, but he may or may not have been convinced. Beyond this confrontational moment, now I *do feel* a bias against this student. Because he has judged me as male hating, I now have judged him from this one encounter as ungenerous; I see him as a student who is interpreting strategies I use in the classroom in the most negative light so as to fit within his model of what feminist teaching is (domination and oppression of male students). I also feel a sense of panic: What if other people in the class have interpreted the drawing in the same way? Should I bring this issue up to the class as a whole? Should I attempt to argue that nonsexist language is not necessarily a feminist issue? But it is, isn't it? How can I embrace this conflict without making the student feel embarrassed, betrayed, or targeted? In this story, I am not the hero; instead of feeling heroic, I feel resentful and frustrated.

DEFINING FEMINIST PEDAGOGY

The complexities of *how* feminist pedagogy is practiced surface in the earlier example of my own teaching. The reflections, and the actions that are the fodder for those reflections, spring from the definition of feminist pedagogy outlined next. In the following tables, I attempt to map out the history of feminist pedagogy and the connections between Women's Studies theories and composition theories on pedagogy. In each table, the first column represents one of the themes that emerged as I was doing my historical research. The second column outlines the Women's Studies scholars (and, on occasion, scholars from other disciplines outside of composition) who have specifically defined and refined the theme as part of feminist pedagogy. The third column represents composition scholars who have written about that theme in the context of the writing classroom. Sometimes the composition scholars identify their theories of teaching as feminist, other times not. Even if the composition scholar did not specifically identify as feminist, their theories are represented on the table. By showing the connection between Women's Studies scholars' efforts to shape a definition of feminist pedagogy and the parallel theories that were emerging in composition, the tables show the intricate connections between composition theories of pedagogy and feminism. Through the tables, I show how composition theory has borrowed from feminist pedagogy in such significant ways that it seems imperative to see contemporary composition pedagogy *as* feminist pedagogy.

One of the major conundrums of this project is creating a list of themes while trying to avoid creating an essentialist definition of what feminist pedagogy is. These themes are not a list of mandatory practices that define feminist pedagogy. As with most things feminist, many scholars and teachers will cringe at a specific definition of feminist pedagogy, seeing it as a way in which something invented to resist the hierarchy of the patriarchy as it manifested itself in the traditional classroom is, in this project, reduced to a list of themes that will suggest a teacher who does not do these things is not practicing feminist pedagogy. I answer these critics with my commitment to only recording what the historical documentation shows. I am trying to compile a sense of what scholars over the past 30 years have named as feminist pedagogy so that we may better understand what feminist pedagogy is and how it has contributed to contemporary composition pedagogy. The 16 themes should be seen as a way to document the history and create a point for discussion, not the definitive answer to the question "What is feminist pedagogy." I want to show how *complex* feminist pedagogy is and how many ways a single theme can be interpreted and practiced in any given classroom.

Following each table, I elaborate on each theme. In these sections, I outline the major theorists who contributed to this collaborative definition of feminist pedagogy, showing how they have expanded on or added to previous theories of feminist pedagogy since the 1970s. I realize that these sections offer only an abbreviated summary of how each theorist discusses the theme. These are concise and in many ways reductive representations of the theorists and their work. Due to the number of theorists represented, and given publishing constraints, I can only include a sentence or two to represent how each theorist is writing about each theme. That means often reducing a complex, theoretical article on pedagogy to a few words that strive to represent the spirit of the theorists ideas. I am quite certain that there will be readers who will respond by saying, of some of my distilled summaries, "How did she get *that* theme out of *that* piece of scholarship/scholar?" I am willing to face these critiques, but hope—in the end—the scholars will find I am not misrepresenting the spirit of the work.

The following is a summary of the 16 themes, a preview of what I discuss in detail in the next sections:

- Confronting sex biases, both the teacher's own and others';
- Embracing conflict instead of working to avoid it;
- Being overt with one's political and social location (self-disclosure, often with strategic stealth);
- Reconstructing power so that it is empowering, not oppressive and checking teacher authority;
- Teaching with the whole self;
- Integrating theory and practice;
- Critically reflecting on teaching through a teaching journal or other consistent method of critical engagement of classroom dynamics;
- Creating connections between learning and knowing and connections between classroom and community issues;

- Working toward student critical consciousness;
- Considering dynamics and issues of race, class, gender, sexual orientation, among others;
- Engaging students in active learning;
- Considering each individual student's realities and needs;
- Giving students choice in the curriculum and in the work they do;
- Bringing passion, joy, and fun into the classroom;
- Being aware of voices and silences in the class;
- Recognizing that each classroom community and student is unique; avoiding making assumptions.

A Clearer Look at the History of Feminist Pedagogy: The Sixteen Themes

I have rather loosely grouped the 16 themes into three categories: teacher critical reflection, classroom strategies, and student concerns. The problem with these categorizations is that few of the themes fit neatly into a single category. Is the theme of "engaging in active learning" about teacher critical reflection (the teacher making sure he or she is creating an environment where active learning is possible) a classroom strategy (small-group work and student-led classes), or a concern for students (making sure students have power to engage with other classroom community members)?

Consequently, many of the themes, one can argue, span all categories. This can be evidence of the interconnectedness of feminist pedagogy: Boundaries and categories blur. This messiness or inaccuracy can also be seen as one of the major downfalls of such a project. The decision to place themes within specific categories is one of organizational presentation. These categories should not be seen as rigid or fixed taxonomies. These groups will make sense to some, but not to others. There are a great number of ways these themes could have been labeled and grouped.

In the tables that accompany each category, I list the themes in that category and, in chronological order, the educational theorists who have written about each theme. I chose to include *these* theorists because of their focus on a particular theme of feminist pedagogy in their scholarship. Because most feminist teaching strategies were adapted by English studies (teaching writing, language, and literature) after they were defined elsewhere, the second column in these tables highlights the scholars who first wrote about or significantly extended discussion of the themes. The third/last column reflects feminist pedagogical theory as it specifically manifests itself in the field of composition and rhetoric, listing scholars who have adapted feminist pedagogical principles for that discipline.

The dates next to the names indicate when the author(s) published the article or book focusing on that theme. Following the tables, I elaborate the descriptions of each theme and the scholars' contribution to the theme. The themes named in each of these categories represent general teaching strategies, but a teacher interprets and implements these strategies using many different practical approaches, as the ethnographic chapters demonstrate.

Themes of Teacher Critical Reflection

The themes in this category point to pedagogical practices that demand teacher self-awareness and critical attention to classroom dynamics. Teacher critical reflection is a category that distinguishes feminist pedagogy from other schools of liberatory and critical pedagogies; no other pedagogical theory insists so strongly on the centrality of teacher self-reflection of pedagogical choices. Throughout my historical research, this theme of teacher self-critique popped up repeatedly. Once I noticed it, I began to understand this theme as the cornerstone of feminist pedagogy. Liberatory and other critical pedagogies focus on moving students toward critical consciousness. With feminist pedagogy, turning that critical eye not only toward students and classroom dynamics but back on oneself is imperative to creating a classroom that meets specific needs of students. The themes included in this category are: confronting sex biases, embracing conflict, being overt with issues of authority, reconstructing power as empowering instead of oppressive, teaching with the whole self, integrating theory and practice, and consistent critical reflection of classroom dynamics.

Because contemporary writing pedagogy makes strong connections between writing and thinking and between language and power, composition course curricula often include political discussions and readings that encourage students to examine the politics of language or the intersection of language, politics, and cultural ideologies. The themes in this section relate to how the teacher creates a critically conscious and socially connected writing environment through his or her own critical awareness of the classroom community. Themes of Teacher Critical Reflection also ask the teacher to be aware of his or her physical presence and voice in the classroom.

Historical Tables of Feminist Pedagogy

Confronting Sex Biases (Both The Teacher's Own And Other's). Attention to gender issues within the classroom community and course curriculum is a primary theme of feminist pedagogy (Tisdell, 1998). Feminist teachers are aware of how gender biases play out in the classroom and continually check their own behavior to make sure it does not fall into typical patterns of calling on males more than females; responding differently to

THEMES OF TEACHER CRITICAL REFLECTION	WOMEN'S STUDIES THEORISTS (in chronological order)	COMPOSITION THEORISTS (in chronological order)
Confronting sex biases (both the teacher's own and other's)	*Confronting sex biases (own and others):* Culley (1982), Weiler (1987), Rothenberg (1988) *Considering race, class, sexual orientation, not just gender:* Shrewsbury (1993), Sattler (1997), Tisdell (1998), Cohee et al. (1998), Gusfstafson (1999) *Integrating multiculturalism:* Mayberry (1999)	*Confronting sex biases in curriculum and course materials:* Hedges (1972) *Considering race, class, sexual orientation, not just gender:* Smitherman (1986), Malinowitz (1995)
Embracing conflict instead of working to avoid it	Weiler (1988), Deay and Stitzel (1991)	Jarratt (1991)
Being overt with one's political location (self-disclosure) and checking teacher authority	Maher (1987), Rothenberg (1988), Bleich (1989), Bensimon (1992), Omolade (1993), Shrewsbury (1993), Bauer and Rhoades (1996), Sattler (1997), Tisdell (1998), Weiler (1988)	Hedges (1972), Harold (1972), Elbow (1973)
Reconstructing power so that it is empowering not oppressive	Culley (1982), Shrewsbury (1993), Omolade (1993), hooks (1994), Damarin (1994), Bauer and Rhoades (1996), Sattler (1997), Cohee et al. (1998), Tisdell (1998)	Hedges (1972), Elbow (1973), Malinowitz (1995)
Teaching with the whole self	hooks (1994)	Roskelly and Ronald (1998)
Integrating theory and practice	James (1994), hooks (1994), Cohee et. al. (1998), Hopkins (1999), Mayberry and Rees (1999)	Strotsky (1990)
Critically reflecting on teaching through a teaching journal or other consistent method of critical engagement with classroom dynamics	Bell, Morrow, and Tastsoglou (1999), Gustafson (1999), Fisher (2001)	Rose (1985), Marshall (1997), Cooper (2000)

student comments, questions, or work in ways that reinforce socially constructed gender differences; and paying attention to female silences, encouraging females to practice using their voices in class discussions. By doing so, teachers challenge their own sexist assumptions and actively work to resist them (Weiler, 1988); Shrewsbury (1993) names this as a concern for "gender justice" in the classroom. Rothenberg (1988) extends gender justice to include rigorous self-critique of the biases that teachers carry with them into the classroom. Even feminist teachers can be inequitable with female students, Rosenberg writes, and therefore they must come clean with their class on their own racist/sexist assumptions, modeling risk-taking behavior with students. With their students, teachers must examine gender with explicit critical analysis (Gustafson, 1999). This extends not just to the community dynamics of the classroom, but to the course curriculum as well. Feminist teachers include voices of women and minorities in their course curriculum and talk about sex-based stereotypes in the curriculum and classroom (Sattler, 1997).

Attention to gender stereotypes also applies to potential teacher biases regarding issues of race, class, and ethnicity. With movements toward multiculturalism[21] in the 1980s, teachers were advised to acknowledge the cultural differences of their students. Mayberry (1999) wrote that feminist teachers needed to move beyond multiculturalism to looking at individual realities of students, an integration of Freirian theories and theories of multiculturalism. Mayberry challenged feminist teachers to look at difference on an individual level instead of generalizing from historical or social groups.

Awareness of biases that exist in the composition classroom began as a discussion of women's voices and the representation of women in course curriculum (Hedges, 1972). The concern for how and whether teachers of writing were incorporating the voices of women is the focus of the special issues of *College English* in 1971 and 1972, devoted to the status of women on college campuses. Although the articles in these special issues discussed more general concerns, such as the publication rates of women scholars and tenure rates of women in the field, many of the essays argued for integrating women's voices in the curriculum (Olson, 1972) and paying attention to women's voices in the classroom (Rich, 1972). As the discussion of gender in the writing classroom evolved, scholars began documenting research regarding how men and women approached different writing tasks, challenging teachers to be aware of the type of assignments they asked students to create and whether those assignments privileged one group's skills over another.

Although contemporary feminists see this earlier gender-based research as lacking in discussions on gender construction or essentializing femaleness, at the time these articles were published (in the 1970s and early 1980s), the mere mention of gender distinctions and awareness of how different social locations influence a student's response to a writing task was groundbreaking. An example of the evolving awareness to issues of gender construction and the complex interrelationships between various social locations was presented in Peterson's (1991) article on autobiographical essays and Kraemer's (1992) response to that same article. As is the problem with quantitative research applied to classroom situations or groups of students, Peterson neglected to complicate her research by taking into consideration dynamics such as race, class, and sexual orientation. Kraemer wrote a response to Peterson's research pointing this out, challenging composition theorists to reject easy taxonomies. In his response, Kraemer challenged composition scholars to complicate their research by considering class and race and other locations influencing a student's classroom and writing experience.

Evolving from discussion of gender, composition scholars began discussing both class (Villanueva, 1991) and sexual orientation (Malinowitz, 1992; Sloane, 1993) in the 1990s, relating these issues to how students approached writing tasks or how language and cultural expectations hindered students who belonged to communities outside the dominant culture.

Embracing Conflict Instead Of Working To Avoid It. The feminist classroom has always been a site of conflict because it resists hegemonic forces of traditional classroom environments (Weiler, 1988). Feminist teachers do not try to minimize conflict, but instead strive to create an environment where students and teachers relate conflict to critical thinking, examining an issue from all angles. Deay and Stitzel (1991) wrote that conflict could lead to anger and defensiveness, but teachers needed to see those dynamics as a natural response and to look for positive examples of conflict as well. By taking responsibility for negative dynamics in the classroom, teachers could help students work through the tension points, using them as a spring board to growth and critical consciousness.

During the early 1990s, when writing teachers began creating curricula where the politics of language and cultural practices were part and parcel of writing instruction, the potential for conflict in the writing classroom increased. Students in the writing classroom often resist political discussions claiming these discussions have little or nothing to do with writing. By extension, students (and others) can also reject the theory that writing and language are political. Attention to dynamics such as race, class, gender, and issues of sexual orientation in texts, both the student's own and those read as part of the course work, bring potential for conflict into the composition classroom. In response to this conflict, feminist composition teachers called on students to discuss these issues as they related to writing or the politics of language and the dominant culture.

The theme of embracing resistance also extends to writing teachers who enact pedagogical strategies or curriculum that run counter to institutional norms. In her book *Women Teaching for Change*, Weiler (1988) addressed both types of resistance: resistance by students because they are being asked to confront ideological and cultural beliefs that previously have not been questioned and resistance by administrations or institutions who are not committed to confronting gender or racial stereotypes in the curriculum. The writing classroom should always be a site of conflict, Weiler wrote, because engaging in counterhegemonic practices leads to critical conscious-ness. Because of this potential for conflict, coupled with the commitment to self-disclosure, feminist writing teachers realize that they can be "an affront to students and their families" (Weiler, 1998, p. 127). This conflict is not bad, Weiler stated, but teachers need to be aware of it and help students work through the tension. Jarratt (1991) located her discussion of conflict specifi-cally within the composition class in her 1991 essay. In "The Case for Conflict," Jarratt (1991) challenged composition instructors to embrace conflict in the classroom as a site of growth and critical consciousness instead of seeing it as a negative dynamic to avoid. Jarratt saw conflict as an important dynamic in classrooms where critical consciousness is one of the goals. Without conflict, teacher and student ideas, locations, and positions cannot challenge their own and others' ideas, locations, and positions.

Teaching Journal: September 25, 2001

> We haven't even been in class for five weeks and already I am at wit's end with the ENG201 course. There seems to be a hostility (towards me?) with two of the male students that is poisoning the discussion space. They call out answers and step all over the female voices; they engage in intimidating body language like rolled eyes, scoffs, and glares when they hear something they don't like. Today I talked to these young men after class, asking them to articulate their frustrations to me in person. The offered that "everything we talk about is male bashing." I pointed out that only two of the ten essays we have read so far have had to do with gender (and only one of them would I consider to be "femi-nist"). I then challenged them to think about how their body lan-guage and discussion points are shutting down other students in the class. I invited them to think of the class as a cocktail party: you have to make room for everyone to talk; you have to listen to other people's points of view. They seemed to understand this analogy. Tomorrow I am going to have to address the issue as a class and talk about who is silent and why and how to make space for more voices.

What happens when conflict becomes destructive to the classroom commu-nity? Allowing conflict to fester, unchecked, quickly creates an environment that shuts down the community. A feminist teacher, acting as mediator and facilitator, names the conflict and attempts to resolve it, working with the community to air out the issue and move on. Conflict can have a corrosive quality if left unchecked. A feminist teacher overtly addresses the conflict by talking about the dynamic *with* the class, offering an opportunity of learning in the resolution of the tension.

Being Overt With One's Political Location (Self-Disclosure). Self-disclosure refers to revealing one's own agenda, location, and political beliefs while also working to not privilege those beliefs (Weiler, 1988). Feminist teachers are not afraid to take risks and exhibit their own viewpoint, but are careful to communicate that they are not privileging their views (Rothenberg, 1988; Sattler, 1997). In addition to making room for all perspectives, the teacher recognizes that perspectives are never static. Both students and teacher realize that opinions and perspectives, and even social and political locations, change with experience and knowledge (Tisdell, 1998).

Naming personal locations and ideologies often forces teachers and students to confront dissent in the classroom community. The acknowledgment of differences, including the teacher self-disclosing her political/social location(s) to the class, moves students toward critical thinking as they challenge their own beliefs and assumptions. Overt discussions of political issues educate students towards critical consciousness (Bauer, 1990). Weiler wrote that teachers need to reveal their own sexist assumptions to students so that students will take risks and confront their own biases. By doing so, teachers show students that every member of the community, including the teacher, is a multilayered subject. As a result, students can more clearly see connections between culture and identity, between ideology and language. These disclosures, however, often cause much conflict as students feel betrayed when the myth of teacher neutrality is shattered before their eyes (see earlier discussions on conflict in the classroom).

Through self-disclosure, teachers not only open themselves up to student critique but to larger student protests against discussions of the personal and political in a writing classroom. Because the dominant culture does not see writing as related to politics or power, students are not the only group that often resists this theme of feminist pedagogy as it manifests itself in the writing classroom. Parents, community leaders, and administrators can also raise their fists in outrage against strategies of overtness in their many forms (talking about one's own location, addressing the politics of syllabi and selected texts, integrating texts and discussions of traditionally marginalized perspectives), arguing that these topics have no place in a writing classroom.

Opening up one's teaching and syllabus for critique is part of feminist pedagogy. However, because students give more weight to the opinions of the teachers, feminist educators have to work diligently to encourage student questioning of their authority (see next theme on Reconstructing Power). The practice of placing oneself, as a teacher, into classroom discussion by asking students to voice their feedback and concerns regarding the course implies that the teacher will be overt with students about the decisions she or he has made about the course and his or her political, social, and personal locations.

In 1972, Hedges began this discussion of teacher self-disclosure in the field of composition by stating that writing teachers needed to model for students how texts and course material intersect with personal experiences. Elbow (1973) furthered the belief that overt reflections regarding one's identity as a writer, not just as a teacher, were imperative for a composition classroom. In his book, *Writing Without Teachers,* Elbow placed teachers in the role of student, asking students to see the teacher as a peer writer and not as an authority figure or expert writer.

The issue of subverting teacher authority becomes complicated when the teacher is not read as White, heterosexual, older, and wiser. In the early 1990s, scholars like Omolade (1993) and Bensimon (1992) began writing about how feminist teachers who are not marked as White tackle the complex issues of authority in classes where the student population is largely different from that of the teacher. These same scholars also wrote about classes where the teacher and student are marked similarly, but have different locations and experiences. In classes where the student population physically reflects the markings of the teacher, female teachers are more often awarded authority that they can then subvert. However, when the teacher is marked as different, the act of subverting authority becomes complicated (being African American in a predominantly White school or read as a lesbian, regardless of sexual orientation). In other words, teachers who do not reflect what a teacher is supposed to look like have to overcome cultural barriers that tell them, as well as their students, that they are not authority figures. For these teachers, their dress and physical appearance influences their *ethos* with students (Bensimon, 1992). Therefore, some teachers may initially choose more conservative dress, demeanor, or pedagogy in a class, first having to establish authority before being able to subvert it. Black feminist pedagogy foregrounds the complicated issues of power and authority. By overtly examining the source and use of power in the classroom, black feminist teachers struggle with students to create a better university (Omolade, 1993).

Reconstructing Power so That It Is Empowering, Not Oppressive; Checking Teacher Authority. Issues of authority and voice relate to power. Many feminist scholars have written about re-creating the role of the teacher and thereby empowering students to be both learners/teachers within the classroom (Cohee, 1998; Culley, 1982; hooks, 1999; Sattler, 1997). When Culley named feminist pedagogy in 1982, she wrote about a literature course where students brought in diaries and letters of their own relatives, or other women not included in canonical lists. Doing so re-created the authority in the class, shifting it from teacher to student. "The nature of the course changed the authority structure of the classroom, the modes of research and strategies for sharing knowledge, even the relationship between the classroom and the local community" (p. 88). By redistributing power, the teacher models a construction of power that is positive instead of oppressive. Omolade (1993) described her approach to sharing power as acting as "consultant to the learning process" (p. 38). Damarin (1994) wrote that teachers needed to be overt with students about the power the teacher has in the classroom as well as the teacher's own disempowerment within the educational system. Together, she wrote, students and teachers could unpack the baggage of power and create new meaning.

Through empowerment, students learn to use their voices, both within classroom discussions and in community action (Bauer & Rhoades, 1996). In this way, power is redefined not as a destructive force of oppression, but one of individual action and strength. Power becomes associated with energy, capability, and potential instead of domination and control (Shrewsbury, 1993). Later, feminist teachers recognized that silence could also be a source of power (Tisdell, 1998). Refusing to speak, in the context of classroom discussions, can be a way that students empower themselves in the face of teacher authority. The problem with silences as power, however, is that the person to whom this action is directed can misread the silence not as resistance, but as disempowerment, and therefore the silence loses its intended meaning.

By subverting teacher authority, feminist classrooms open themselves up for student voices. Through this subversion of teacher authority both students and teachers help to create knowledge (Weiler, 1988). One way to subvert teacher authority involves creating a model of knowledge that is dialogic: "What dialogic teaching does, then, is to negotiate the public/private split, a pedagogy that constitutes feminist political strategy as part of the classroom" (Bauer & Rhoades, 1996). Feminist teachers strive to create a mutual exchange for better understanding, considering contexts and cultural ideologies. In this way, teachers and students share the power source of the classroom, where students are active partners in learning (Shrewsbury, 1993). When a classroom subverts teacher authority, the students and teachers are learning from and teaching each other (Sattler, 1997), freeing students to challenge and critique the teacher and the institution. This does not mean that feminist classrooms lack authority or that authority or teacher power is

bad. Sometimes exerting the power of authority (e.g., in regard to class policies) is necessary to create a productive community (Maher, 1987). However,
feminist teachers are aware of when they are using authority and have very
clear reasons for doing so, communicating these reasons to their students. In
composition scholarship, both Hedges and Elbow believe teachers must be
vigilant about the use of power in the classroom, working to shift that power
to students. In the writing classroom common manifestations of this theme
create collaborative projects between students (Bruffee, 1984) and show
teachers working alongside students as peer writers (Elbow, 1973). Training
students on how to give meaningful feedback to their peers and peer review
workshops also helps reconstitute power so that all writers, not just the
teacher, are legitimate sources of advice and guidance.

Teaching With The Whole Self. Feminist teaching demands that
teachers give their whole selves to students, emotionally, intellectually, and
spiritually (hooks, 1999). By teaching with the whole self, teachers show students that learning is connected to living, intellect is connected to life, and
the personal has social and political implications. An extension of hooks'
definition of *engaged pedagogy*, where teachers bring their spiritual, emotional, and intellectual self into the classroom, is reflected in Roskelly and
Ronald (1998) scholarship. Roskelly and Ronald wrote that composition
teachers must provide an example of "the whole person thinking." This
includes not just being overt with students about personal and political locations, but showing students that work and writing, thinking and writing,
and, for the teacher, teaching and writing are deeply connected and inform
each other. This theory overlaps with the previous theme of teacher authority and extends directly to the next theme of feminist pedagogy—integration
of theory and practice.

Integrating Theory and Practice. Feminist teachers reject the
dichotomy between knowing and doing (James, 1991). Both in their scholarship and pedagogy, feminist teachers blur the lines between theory and
practice. In the introduction to their collection on feminist teaching, Cohee
et al. (1998) stated that feminist teaching gives rise to theory. Put another
way, practice leads to theory and not the other way around. The connection
between theory and practice harkens back to the earliest moments of feminist pedagogy in Women's Studies courses when political or social action
was linked to personal experience. By extension, feminist teachers continue
to ask themselves and their students "So what?" and "Who cares?", searching for answers that connect to the world external to the academy. One way
teachers connect theories to practice is by bringing in guest speakers who
create a direct link between the theories of the classroom with community
action (Hopkins, 1999). Another way is by allowing students to work in

small groups or produce collaborative work that creates a balance between theories in the class and personal experience of the work they do together (Hopkins, 1999). Other feminist educators use service learning or practicum projects as a way of connecting course work to community issues. Through such strategies as guest speakers, community service work, service learning, and collaborative projects, feminist pedagogy connects theory practice, personal experience, the larger community, and culture (Mayberry & Rees, 1999).

These connections between communities and class inform hooks' belief that there needs to be a direct and tangible connection between women's lives and feminist theory. Composition teachers adapt hooks' philosophy to the classrooms when they create relationships between composition theories and the practices of students learning to write. Teacher research in the field of composition, especially observing and theorizing about one's own or colleagues' classes, offer a method by which to ensure practice and theory are inherently interwoven. Teacher research, a methodology often used in composition scholarship, offers a way for feminist teachers to engage in teacher critical reflection, holding up their own classroom practices for public scrutiny and as the foundation for scholarship, a connection with the theme of Critical Reflection.

In the field of composition, the merging of theory and practice manifests itself in a unique way. Some composition theorists borrowed social science human development theories to analyze student writing practices; doing so wedged theories that do not spring from composition into writing classroom practices. Strotsky (1990) warned composition teachers that they should not rely on borrowed theories from other disciplines (primarily referring to theories of cognitive development) for application in the writing classroom. She challenged composition scholars to create their own theories that could be revised through practice. Theories, she wrote, need to be complicated with practice. Theories guide teaching practices, but theories are not static; teaching practices revise theories, creating a reciprocal relationship between theory and practice.

Critically Reflecting on Teaching. Feminist pedagogy embodies reflectivity/self-criticism (Gustafson, 1999). Strategies such as interrogating gender issues in the classroom; overtly confronting one's own sexist, racist, classist, and homophobic assumptions with the classroom community; and actively working to decenter the power source of teacher authority are impossible without teacher critical reflection. Giving conscious attention to teaching practices and adapting them for each student and each classroom community demand critical reflection by the teacher (Bell, Morrow, & Tastsoglou, 1999). The use of teaching journals, teaching partners, or open letters to students that reflect on classroom decisions and dynamics helps facilitate teacher critical reflection. Fisher (2001) moved this element of teacher critical reflection beyond simply writing or talking about one's own teaching practices and choices in critical ways. She suggested facilitating seminars between teachers and students who want to talk about their own teaching practices, bringing teacher self-critique to a public forum. However, this method is not without problems. In such seminar settings, analysis can be used to discredit, and relations of authority can undermine equality and trust.

In the 1960s and 1970s, teacher critical reflection was not prominent in composition theory. During this time, attempts to simplify theories of writing into neat taxonomies removed teachers from the responsibility of critically reflecting on how best to teach each individual writer. Shaunessey, (1977) a pioneer of and advocate for theories on "basic writers," was the first to demand that teachers look analytically and individually at error patterns in an individual student's work. Adapting the same careful, critical attention to every student in the writing class, not just struggling or emerging writers, Sommers (1998) challenged teachers to move beyond the ease of teaching a static process to every writer (prewrite, write, rewrite) and help students discover their own individual writing processes. However, Sommers made generalizations about writers, separating them into a binary of experienced and nonexperienced writers, contradicting her desire to see students as individuals.

In 1980, Rose wrote that taxonomies of writers, developed from applying cognitive development theories to composition, were acceptable only as long as they were diverse enough to accommodate a wide variety of student writers. Like Shaunessey and Sommers, Rose also believed the teacher's primary role was to look closely at each student and analyze his or her writing patterns, helping each writer individually. No formula works for every student, so teachers need to be critically reflective for each individual. In 1989 Ritchie, wrote that teachers need to resist the idea of a unified voice in the composition classroom, instead seeing writing classes as "multi-faceted, shifting scenes full of conflicting and contending values and purposes" (p. 153). This theme of critical reflection manifests itself in teachers' understanding that learning to write and teaching writing is an individual endeavor, calling for critical reflection and analysis of each student and classroom situation.

Also addressing this theme, Margaret Marshall challenged teachers to be aware of the assumptions they make about their students. Marshall believed there is no "majority" of students. Because teachers often see types of students or generalize characteristics from a general demographic of the larger student body, they must be vigilant about checking those assumptions. Marshall argued that one avenue to achieving this goal was better teacher training. She advocated for more comprehensive and careful training of graduate students in using critical consciousness when approaching teaching so they could be more analytical and reflective about teaching practices.

Teacher critical consciousness is important, but just as important is communicating what the teacher sees going on in the classroom community to her students. Recently, Cooper (2000) asked that composition teachers "explain to students *why* we're doing what we're doing in the writing class" (p. 186). The act of explaining to students classroom strategies and goals subverts the authority of the teacher, ensures that the teacher has critically reflected on the decisions they are making for the class, and invites students to offer feedback on these decisions, all elements of feminist pedagogy.

Personal Journal; July 30, 2000

I am exhausted to the bone. What a full day and a full week, but I loved teaching the Multicultural Leadership Course. After agonizing over my "talk" with the silent student yesterday, she came to class today and volunteered to read part of her paper almost immediately and did so with a strong, confident voice. She not only read from her project, but talked about her work with articulation and insight. I was deeply impressed. I guess whatever I said to her resonated on some level. My speech about "Why participation is important if not imperative" worked for her, but it could have easily gone the other way. I made the right call this time. But that is just luck, I think. Later in the day I saw the same student in the lunchroom and she was all smiles and cheery greetings, so I really won that one over. You never know . . .

I didn't bring up the success in the feminist pedagogy course. I didn't know how to phrase it so it didn't sound like an "I told you so." Context is so important for the teaching moment, and I mean that in reflecting on both the conversation about feminist pedagogy and the way I successfully handled this particular student.

Late this afternoon I ran into Bob (the director of the Multicultural Leadership Program) and I asked him his opinion on the issue: should a *white* teacher push an African American student to speak out, understanding the consequences that could potentially occur. Bob, holding the life experience of an African American male who came of age pre-Civil Rights, got a bit hot under the collar that a white teacher *wouldn't* push African American students to speak out. His perspective is that their survival depends on them learning to use their voice. He sees it as an imperative skill and by not pushing African American students to practice speaking, white teachers are robbing them of not only an education but an important life skill. Another interesting perspective coming from an altogether different location. His reaction reminded me of Delpit's

rail against liberal white teachers. Of course Bob's response solid-
ly supported my perspective, so that made me feel good. Bob's
opinion plus the student's reaction to my discussion with her
made me feel I had definitely made the right decision. But again,
I have to add, *"this time."* Tomorrow I am bound to do some bone-
headed, insensitive teacherly thing that will make me cower in
shame and put me in the corner with a dunce cap on my head and
a sign reading "Power Monger" hanging around my neck.

Themes of Course/Classroom Strategies

The themes in this category focus on helping students become more critical
learners and thinkers so they can engage in action that will create cultural
change (both within the subculture of the university and the broader culture
external to the academy). To further this larger goal of action, teachers use
strategies that can manifest themselves in various ways depending on the
teacher and the classroom. Some examples of the practices related to the
theme of "engaging in active learning" include facilitating a service learning
component, asking students to help design the course curriculum, or allowing students to collaborate with peers to create lessons for the rest of the
class. The themes named here outline the general strategies, but teachers
interpret these strategies using many different practical approaches.

For the writing classroom, these themes move beyond the simple goal
of helping students become better writers to goals of honing critical thinking skills and making connections between writing and public policy, rhetoric in the public space, and writing about community issues. Contemporary
composition theory creates a strong connection between critical thinking
and writing, reflecting one of the goals of a feminist classroom: moving students to critical consciousness through critical thinking and writing.
Another strategy for the writing classroom is to allow students to write
about personal experience, extending that experience to social action. In
these endeavors (moving students toward critical thinking and community
action through writing), feminist teachers use active learning and student-
centered theories, keeping in mind the dynamics of race, class, gender, sexual orientation (among others), and how these multiple locations influence
the writing tasks being assigned and written and how these dynamics play
out between writers in the classroom. When specifically looking at writing
instruction, the themes in this category relate to *how* the students engage in
the work of composition, how the teacher integrates political and social
issues into writing instruction, and how the teacher draws connections
among students, themselves, course material, and the broader cultural forces
as they intersect in writing.

GOALS FOR THE CLASSROOM AND CLASSROOM STRATEGIES	WOMEN'S STUDIES THEORISTS (in chronological order)	COMPOSITION THEORISTS (in chronological order)
Creating connections between learning and knowing and connections between the classroom and outside issues	*Connection to Action:* Golden (1985), James (1991), Wright (1993), hooks (1994), Sattler (1997), Hoffman and Stake (1998) *Connection to students' experiences:* Culley (1982), Ladson-Billing and Henry (1990), Omolade (1993), Mullin (1994), Tisdell (1998), Mayberry and Rees (1999) *Participatory and collaborative classroom:* Culley (1982), hooks (1994), Gawelek et al. (1994), Hoffman and Stake (1998), Cohee et al. (1998)	Hedges (1972), Whipp (1979), Annas (1985), Brodkey and Fine (1992), Malinowitz (1995), Ashton-Jones (1995), Cushman (1996)
Working towards student critical consciousness	Weiler (1988), Bleich (1989), Deay and Stitzel (1991), James (1991), Shrewsbury (1993), Middleton (1993), hooks (1994), Sattler (1997), Hoffman and Stake (1998), Bell, Morrow, and Tastsoglou (1999), Mayberry and Cronan Rose (1999)	Slattery (1990), Ritchie (1989, 1990), Covino (1991)
Considering dynamics and issues of race, class, gender, sexual orientation, among others	Weiler (1988), Mayberry and Cronan Rose (1999)	Ortiz-Taylor (1978), Kramarae and Treichler (1990), Peterson (1991), Kirsch (1993), Mullin (1994), Ritchie and Boardman (1999)
Engaging students in active learning	Ruggerio (1990), Shrewsbury (1993), hooks (1994), Hopkins (1999)	Lamberg (1980), Bruffee (1984), Brodkey and Fine (1992), Shrewsbury (1993), Bridwell-Bowles (1995)

Creating Connections Between Learning and Knowing and Connections Between the Classroom and Outside Issues. Connecting learning to community action constitutes one of the primary themes of the first Women's Studies courses. In these classrooms, teachers would often bring to class a long parade of guest speakers from the community to talk about their feminist activist work with the students (Hopkins, 1999). In this way, these early Women Studies classrooms built a bridge between the learner and the public sphere of political and social activism. Feminist teachers make the effort to encourage social understanding *and* activism, an extension of the traditional classroom where students are asked to internalize the theory, but not often the practice (Hoffman & Stake, 1998).

This theme also includes connections between learners and instructors and between learners and their experiences (Wright, 1993). Teachers value their students' ways of knowing that extend beyond the classroom, allowing students to create their own meaning (Mayberry & Rees 1999). The knowledge constructed in course texts, individual class meetings, and the larger classroom community helps learners and educators acknowledge which forms of knowledge the class or culture is privileging, attempting to subvert those epistemological hierarchies. This type of connected learning links the course subject matter to the students' cultural roots creating "culturally relevant teaching" (Ladson-Billings & Henry, 1990). For students who come from cultures not represented by the dominant ideologies, the classroom creates a space where their realities are legitimized. Culturally relevant teaching uses students' cultures to help them critically examine educational contexts and processes; teachers and students ask each other what role they take in creating a multicultural society (Ladson-Billings & Henry, 1990). For students who are ethnic, racial, economic, and sexual marginalized, this pedagogy encourages education for survival, not just academic success (Omolade, 1993).

During the early 1970s, creating connections between personal experience and the writing course began by integrating feminist literary criticism and composition. In her 1972 article, Hedges argued that teachers need to bring issues of gender into discussions of literature used within the writing classroom. In 1979, Whipp made connections between the larger culture and the classroom more explicit by arguing that writing teachers need to be intimately familiar with the community from which their students came. Whipp believed teachers needed to be aware of community mores and language use to avoid an "arrogant elitism" that would alienate students not only from their lived experiences, but their community. In the first article to name a feminist pedagogy for composition courses ("Style as Politics"), Annas (1985) articulated the need for a strong relationship between the personal and the political, the private and public. Writing teachers must encourage students to see their own experiences as a site of knowledge construction, engaging in writing that reflects student realities.

Although some may argue that this theme is no different from liberatory pedagogy where critical consciousness leads to social action, feminist pedagogy engages in more overt connections with community action. It attempts to move students to action outside the classroom community as part of the course work, not assuming that action will eventually result if critical thinking is taught (Malinowitz, 1995). In feminist classrooms across the disciplines, action in the form of course work can manifest itself as service learning, course practicums with community agencies, or course projects that focus on public sphere rhetoric of change (writing letters to public officials about sexual education funding or organizing a campus zap action to protest sweat shop labor). Feminist teachers understand that social action leads to critical consciousness more directly than classroom critical thinking exercises (Cohee et al., 1998).

One model of course work as community action was outlined in Brodkey and Fine's (1992) "Presence of Mind in the Absence of Body." In Brodkey and Fine's article, community action becomes part of the course work when students critique the university's sexual harassment policies and ultimately write letters to newspapers and university officials to change the policies. The academic lesson for these students was one of awareness to discourse communities, but the cultural lesson was how to engage in productive community action for change. If students are not taught how to engage in constructive and productive community action, or if they feel their action is not leading to change, they resort to desperate measures (what Brodkey and Fine name *voices of despair*) that are often destructive to their own cause. Feminist pedagogy shows students how to engage in effective community action and helps students become more socially responsible through that action (Golden, 1985). In this way, the classroom community rejects the dichotomy between knowing and doing and approaches learning through critical and activist outlooks (James, 1994).

The natural extension of creating connections between learners' experiences evolved into discussions of collaborative writing projects. Ashton-Jones (1995) argued that collaborative learning is inherently feminist because feminism depends on collaboration to succeed. One feminist working toward change will not accomplish anything, but several people working toward the same goal can make a difference. Ashton-Jones theorized that collaboration moves students toward community action. By figuring out how to work with others on a writing project, students can more easily transfer those skills of group work and collaboration to the community. In this model, writing and collaboration are the precursors of political work.

Malinowitz (1995) furthered this argument by saying one goal of a composition course is to give students experience in engaging in rhetoric that will initiate social change. Echoing this belief, Cushman (1996) argued that the purpose of rhetoric is social change and composition courses should be a primary site for training students how to engage in rhetoric for social change. Resistance to these feminist theories of linking writing projects to community action came from teachers, scholars, administrators, parents, and community leaders who believed that social action has no inherent connection to college writing. These critics argued that the purpose of a composition course was to teach academic discourse, not community or political issues through writing.

These modes of connected knowing and collaborative learning are not just important when considering how students are connecting their work with each other and the world outside the classroom. The theories of connected knowing and collaborative learning are also a challenge to teachers. Using these same theories of collaborative learning, feminist teachers talk about their pedagogical strategies with other feminist teachers and with their colleagues who are not feminist teachers, spreading the concepts of feminist pedagogy through mimicry, co-teaching, and communication (Gawelek et al., 1994).

Working Towards Student Critical Consciousness. Borrowing from Freire's theories on *conscientization,* this theme extends the theories of critical consciousness beyond socioeconomic class. Feminist pedagogy helps students see hegemony and various ideologies as forces in their own lives, encouraging students to investigate how these forces have shaped their realities (Mayberry & Cronan Rose, 1999). Teachers challenge students to see the culture as racist, sexist, homophobic, classist, among other things; at the same time, teachers work to show students they are not being blamed, but rather the teacher is challenging students to work for change. In this process, the class community acknowledges discomfort and resistance, often embracing this discomfort. For many students, the discomfort is real and tangible and threatens to shut down the educational process unless open dialogue occurs. One of the primary ways teachers help students work through their discomfort is by showing them avenues for action (James, 1994). Teachers let students know it is okay to be angry and defensive as long as this leads to further self-interrogation, giving them tools to make this transition to awareness and using field books or journals that focus on critical analysis, not just expressive and emotive writing (Deay & Stitzel, 1991).

Teaching Journal: April 6, 2001

> I began writing my end-of-semester narrative letters to each student. It usually takes me about a month to do that, working on three letters every day. It's a labor-intensive task, a labor of love? Sometimes I wonder if it is even worth it. Do the students even

read the 2-3 page epistles I write to each of them about their work? I keep a detailed "teacher's page" for each student, writing short comments throughout the semester: what they did that impressed or surprised me or made me proud, areas that they need to continue to work on, how I have seen their writing and critical thinking skills evolve and what to keep in mind as they continue to write. It is fun for me to take a careful, close look at each one of those student's work and write them a personal letter about what I have seen. I find myself focusing a great deal on both their writing and critical thinking skills in these letters; the teacher dork in me rises up and claps her hands, I feel excited for the changes I have seen in each one of these students throughout the semester.

In their mid-term reflections I had a few students who wrote, "I've never been asked to critically think before. I've never been graded (sic!) on it until this class." I don't believe that is probably true (other teachers have most certainly called upon them to critically think or have likely evaluated their work in relation to that skill), but I think the students' comments reflect *how* few teachers actually articulate for students, and themselves, *how* they are evaluating student work, the specifics of the rubric, if in fact they even *use* a rubric. I give the rubric I use to evaluate projects to students with their assignment sheet, so they know exactly what I am going to be looking for; there is *always* an item on the rubric relating to critical thinking (phrased along the lines of "How well does the writer ask and answer How/Why questions, offering several different answers to complicate their ideas?"). For many of the students it feels revolutionary to critically think about the critical thinking they are doing.

When it is all said and done, I'll print off over 150 pages of single spaced "end of semester letters" to students, killing trees in the name of better writing. Who knows whether they even read the damned things. Who am I kidding? What a self-deluded teacher-fantasy! Happy writers doing the happy writer dance in white spats, top hats, and canes, kissing and waving narrative letters like winning lottery tickets. Sheesh. I need to get some rest. But perhaps they will remember the part where they see themselves, for the first time, as critical thinkers.

Critical thinking skills are tools needed for social action (Bell, Morrow, & Tastsoglou, 1999). By furthering critical thinking, teachers shun easy binary models of pro/con, right/wrong, and good/bad and instead replace them with models that integrate multiple viewpoints and opinions, encouraging students to see that there are no right answers, only more questions and possible answers (Sattler, 1997). The feminist teacher furthers critical thinking by showing respect for all views, struggling through new approaches to learning and thinking that engage everyone in the class (Shrewsbury, 1993). Other elements of teaching critical thinking include creating connections between biological, cultural, and historical situations and problematizing issues of language and knowledge construction. Through these strategies, the classroom becomes a site not for memorizing facts, but developing consciousness (Weiler, 1988).

Freire's (1987) theories of bringing students to critical consciousness demand an awareness of ideology and political structures. Compositionists adapt Freire's theories for the writing class by teaching the politics of language, the ideological structures imbedded in language, and how language reinforces power structures. Teaching that language is political allows students to think critically about rhetorical choices. To analyze the ideological forces at play in language demands a critical analysis of each rhetorical situation. Part of this approach to rhetorical analysis is teaching students that in their writing there are no right or wrong answers, just different options and perspectives to present to a reader (Ritchie, 1990).

This theme of feminist pedagogy also encourages writing teachers to teach awareness of language standards, the power behind these standards, and when, if, or whether to transgress standards in a specific context or rhetorical situation. Teachers and students need to interrogate the construct of academic discourse as a hegemonic force (Ritchie, 1989). In the early 1980s, a debate in composition emerged as to whether teachers should teach the standards. Some theorists argued that a conscientious composition teacher could not teach standard written English without also discussing the ideological power entrenched in those standards. Others argued that to do so within one composition course was an impossible task. Covino (1991) wrote that there existed a possibility of teaching the politics of rhetoric and language while still meeting the university's expectations for the writing classroom. Teachers can show students that academic discourse reflects the ideological system of oppression without reifying the language system as something to internalize *without question*. Students are taught that they can make rhetorical choices, understanding the risk inherent in making choices that deviate from the expected standards of writing and rhetoric.

Teaching critical thinking leads to more sophisticated writing choices and awareness of the politics of language. Smart and savvy rhetorical skills provide the means by which to negotiate the tricky balance between teaching the standards so that students will not be punished for not knowing them and showing students they can choose *not* to use the standard (although the dominant culture typically extracts a price for such transgressions). The feminist composition classroom uses writing as a road to critical consciousness, working with students as individuals and helping them integrate critical thinking in their writing tasks. In doing so, the teacher abandons theories that link cognitive development to static writing processes or writing skills and adopts more fluid and individual discussions of writing practices that focus on critical thinking, the politics of language, and discourse choices. Working with students to develop their own processes for writing and arranging thought replaces teaching a static writing process with teaching individual processes (Hatch & Walters, 1993). This approach forces teachers to look at the skills of each student individually, thus decentering the role of authoritarian teacher. In this model, the teacher takes cues from the student about how to teach, creating a new and unique community in each classroom situation.

Beyond class discussions and teaching the politics of language, some theorists see connections between how teachers respond to student writing as a way to teach critical consciousness. Slattery (1990) argued that well-written end comments on student work helps students further their critical thinking skills. He theorized that if a teacher wrote questions that asked students to think about their position differently or consciously consider what biases they may have regarding their position, students were more likely to develop critical thinking through writing.

Considering Dynamics and Issues of Race, Class, Gender, Sexual Orientation, Among Others. Feminist pedagogy has evolved beyond the Women's Studies model that focuses on gender (see section on history) to include discussions of class, race, ethnicity, sexual orientation, and other "isms" perpetuated by cultural ideology as they manifest themselves in the classroom, curriculum, and culture. Consequently, feminist teachers integrate multiculturalism in any course they teach (Mayberry & Cronan Rose, 1999). Issues of race, class, and gender are not only discussed in the abstract of how they manifest themselves in the culture, but how they overtly manifest themselves in classroom practices (see theme of "Confronting Sex Biases" in the earlier Teacher Critical Reflection category). Teachers show students how we are all products of a racist, sexist, homophobic, classist culture and that these dynamics play out in all communities, even a feminist classroom. Feminist teachers model, through their own classroom practices of critical self-reflection and rigorous confrontation of their own teaching, how one can confront these cultural forces and minimize them through awareness, honesty, and the commitment to change.

As feminist theories about gender flourished in the broader context of academic scholarship during the 1980s to 1990s, so did composition articles that discussed the way female students responded to writing tasks and how they used language differently from the standard academic practices (Peterson, Mullin, Kramarae and Treichler, Kirsch). Feminists in the field wanted teachers to be vigilant about the equity of women in the composition classroom, but also asked teachers to disrupt and critique hegemonic narratives that privileged a White male perspective (Ritchie & Boardman, 1999). Feminist composition theorists such as Ortiz-Taylor, Kramarae and Treichler, Peterson, Kirsch, and Mullin pushed the field to acknowledge and contemplate how identity issues play out in the writing class.

Engaging Students in Active Learning. This theme of feminist pedagogy helps students create their own meaning, learning from the questions they ask and answer (Hopkins, 1999). Ruggerio (1990) named this approach *open learning*, where students choose how and what to learn, having the class collaborate on the goals for course work, and letting students decide the format for their major projects. Feminist teachers realize that traditional educational ideologies have prevented students from creating their own meaning, and therefore these educators spend classroom time teaching students how to engage in active learning. Because traditional ideologies of education teach skills of passive consumption of knowledge, feminist teachers work with each classroom community to teach students skills of active learning and taking control of their education. They show students that, even in other classroom situations, students should feel empowered to ask for new approaches to teaching and learning. When students ask other teachers to implement themes of feminist teaching, they cause a trickle over effect. Active learning also encourages classroom members to engage with the other people in the class, not just with course material (Shrewsbury, 1993). Creating a classroom community where students know each other's names, use their voice to contribute to class knowledge, understand their peers' perspectives, and respect differing realities are examples of active learning.

In the writing classroom, active learning can take the form of small-group work, peer review writing workshops, and other collaborative writing tasks. Such practices are often standard fare in many contemporary composition classrooms. By using these active learning strategies, where students help each other with their writing and work together to formulate meaningful work in the course, students and teachers integrate feminist principles of collaboration, cooperation, and consensus. Bruffee (1984) advocated for collaboration in the writing classroom because he believed the close interaction of students resulted in collective learning that furthered each student's writing awareness. In the 1980s, peer review became a primary method of collaboration, where students benefited from having their peers critically examine their writing. When teachers guide peer review groups, giving students guidelines on what to look for, students not only become better critical readers of their peers writing, but they also become more conscious of their own writing practices (Lamberg, 1980). Students who take on the role of the teacher in peer review situations enact active learning instead of passive consumption. Other ways that teachers help students become active learners is by creating assignments that allow students freedom of choice, giving them permission to break the rules of standard discourse practices so they can construct work that is meaningful for themselves (Bridwell-Bowles, 1995; Brodkey & Fine, 1992).

Teaching Journal; September 6, 2000

> The young women in this class are so silent. Today, for the second day in a row, I had to say, "OK! We've heard from a lot of the young men. How about some young women?" It's exasperating, especially considering the young women outnumber the young men by about five. When I am overt about it, eventually some do speak up. I am going to stop class the next time I see it happening and ask them why they think it is happening.

Teaching Journal; September 18, 2000

> We started out with the "personal location" exercise today. I wanted to get to a discussion of the term "politically correct" since it keeps popping up in their journals. I challenged them to consider whether the rhetoric of "politically correct" is really a way of *not* dealing with the complicated issues of diversity and power. Instead of grappling with difficult issues and conflicts of race, class, gender, sexual orientation, we can dismiss thinking about, talking about, and discussing them by simply saying, "I need to be politically correct" or "That's not PC." I told them I personally thought the term was imprecise and I wanted them to think through why they are using it; when they are tempted to write it, I want them to stop and ask themselves specifically what it means and why they feel the need to use that particular term.

> The gender issue [of young women not participating] continues. There are one or two very vocal young men who like to call out and engage without being called upon. I want students to feel they can talk without raising their hands (and being called upon), but I also want a gender balance. The way it is playing out now, it reminds me exactly of the theories the Sadkers write about [in *Failing at Fairness*] where they say males seize and control power in the class by calling out their thoughts, thereby gaining most of the talk time and teacher's attention. I copied excerpts of the Sadkers' book and they are going to read them for Monday. I told the students I typically have classes read this later in the semester, but because of the gender dynamics in *this* class I wanted them to read it so we could talk about it. I contextualized the excerpt by telling them about the Sadkers' research. I said, "My experience has been that when students read this, they say, 'Oh,

this hasn't been *my* experience [that girls are called on and participate less than boys].' But *you all* can't say that because this phe-
nomena, of women not participating, is happening in this class!"

Then, lo and behold, when we started talking about the essay that
was assigned for today's lesson (an article on race and class
issues in education by Victor Villanueva), *lots* of the women par-
ticipated. Even the really quiet ones. I was so pleased and I
thought, "Wow. That was easy." But we'll see whether they can
sustain that awareness and effort.

Themes of Student Concerns

Concern for individual student well-being and growth is important to feminist pedagogy. This close attention to individual students' lives, originally
gendered *feminine* because of the association with nurturing and mothering,
manifests itself in a variety of ways. Paying close attention to the gender
dynamics of who is speaking in the classroom, giving room and voice to traditionally silenced females, and, as hooks advocates, seeing students as spiritual beings in need of guidance and care are just a few examples of how concern for students manifests itself in a feminist classroom.

For the composition classroom, this last category of feminist pedagogical themes relates to the individual attention writing teachers give students.
Working to achieve the feminist pedagogical goal of attending to each student individually is a labor-intensive task, but imperative in a writing classroom where attention to each student's writing processes and practices is
essential for success and progress. Feminist pedagogy demands that teachers
not only critically analyze each classroom situation to determine what pedagogical approaches will work best for a community of learners, but to see
each person in the community as a valuable part of the class with unique
characteristics and needs. Theories of individual language instruction such as
those put forth by Shaunessey, Sommers, and Murray criticized models of
writing that attempted to create static methods for writers. Feminist-mind-
ed teachers abandon cognitive theories of writing, such as those put forth by
Flower and Hayes (1981), and linear process-focused theories, for those
which give attention to individual student realities, cultures, and needs.
Feminist teachers understand that static models of writing are obsolete
because no one process or theory can be applied unilaterally to all students.
The feminist pedagogical themes outlined in this section ask teachers to look
closely and carefully at their students, the dynamics of the classroom, and
reflect on how their pedagogical approaches best serve both the individual
and the community.

THEMES OF STUDENT CONCERNS AND CLASSROOM STRATEGIES	WOMEN'S STUDIES THEORISTS (in chronological order)	COMPOSITION THEORISTS (in chronological order)
Considering each individual student's realities and needs	Golden (1985), Maher (1987), Weiler (1987), Ruggerio (1990), Ladson-Billings and Henry (1990), Woodridge (1994), Sattler (1997), Cohee et al. (1998), Mullin (1998), Hopkins (1999)	Elbow (1973), Shaunessey (1977), Delpit (1988), Sloane (1993), Malinowitz (1995)
Giving students choice in the curriculum and the work they do	Culley (1985), Golden (1985), Maher (1987), Weiler (1987), Ruggerio (1990), Ladson-Billings and Henry (1990), Shrewsbury (1993), Woodridge (1994), Sattler (1997), Cohee et al. (1998), Mullin (1998), Hopkins (1999)	Murray (1972), Elbow (1973), Annas (1983), Cooper (1986), Berthoff (1987), Bridwell-Bowles (1995), Jessup and Lardner (1995)
Bringing joy and fun into the classroom	Golden (1985), Shrewsbury (1993), hooks (1994), Woodridge (1994), Damarin (1994)	Elbow (1973)
Being aware of voices and silences in the class	Golden (1985), Shrewsbury (1993), Tisdell (1998), Mayberry and Cronan Rose (1999)	Annas (1987), Spender (1990), Kramarae and Treichler (1990)
Recognizing that each classroom community and each student is unique	Shrewsbury (1993), Mullin, Tisdell (1998) *Leadership development*: Shrewsbury (1993)	Rose (1980), Ritchie (1989), Marshall (1997)

Considering Each Individual Student's Realities and Needs. In the
feminist classroom, the teacher challenges students to critically reflect on their
own lives and articulate their experiences as their lives relate to course material (Golden, 1985). Feminist teachers make room for students to share personal experiences, allowing students to tell their stories in unconventional
ways (breaking standard formats or curriculum expectations; Mullin, 1994).
In the first years of feminist pedagogy, student experiences were integrated in
course material, but largely uninterrogated, a remnant of the CR group structure. Throughout the 1980s, the belief that students should be pushed to contextualize their experience instead of generalizing or universalizing a world-
view began emerging. Teachers want students to interrogate their experiences
and discuss how these experiences intersect with cultural belief systems of
race, class, gender, and sexual orientation, among others (Cohee et al., 1998)
By integrating students' experiences into course material, students engage
with each other in more dynamic ways, confronting their own biases as they
relate to their classmates' experiences. In her research, Sattler (1997) reports
that these strategies of integrating student experiences often create classes that
go against the grain of standard curriculums. She concludes that feminist
teachers resist standard syllabi and course curriculums, instead creating courses that reflect the needs of their students (see "Giving Students Choice").

In the composition theories, focus on student identities and individual
writer's needs emerged with Shaunessey's (1977) theories about basic writers. In her book, *Errors and Expectations*, when Shaunessey challenged
teachers to look closely at error patterns in individual student texts to best
teach each writer, she was advocating a theme of feminist pedagogy. During
the late 1980s and 1990s, attention to individual students and their identity
issues within the writing classroom emerged in composition scholarship.
Scholars wrote extensively about identity issues and power relationships in
the writing classroom. Discussions regarding gender (Flynn, 1988; Kirsch,
1993; Gawelek, Mulqueen, & Tarule, 1997), race (Delpit, 1988), class
(Villanueva, 1991), and sexual orientation (Sloane, 1993; Malinowitz, 1992)
caused the field of composition to reflect on how teachers constructed writing assignments, taught language use, selected course texts, and facilitated
class discussions. Most of these theorists argued that composition instructors must carefully negotiate class dynamics and course work to accommodate the identities and realities of individual students. However, these theories often conflicted with each other. Delpit (1988) chastised White, politically liberal teachers for not teaching or enforcing Standard English usage
with African American students who need those skills to survive and succeed in the dominant culture. Others countered Delpit's argument by saying
students have a right to their own language practices, recognizing the importance of teaching the *politics* of language (see earlier "Working Toward
Critical Consciousness" theme).

Beyond language use, Malinowitz (1991) and Villanueva (1992) wrote that composition teachers need to be aware of identity issues such as sexual orientation or socioeconomic class, working to understand the barriers students may have to assignments or class readings and discussions that potentially alienate them and their lived experiences. For the writing teacher, the feminist pedagogical theme of considering each student's reality and needs extends beyond honoring individual students' experiences. Critically constructing syllabi, facilitating class discussions that embrace varied realities and perspectives, and paying attention to individual students' language and writing needs are all dynamics included in this theme.

Giving Students Choice in the Curriculum and the Work They Do. Relating to both subversion of teacher authority and practices of active learning, feminist teachers allow students to make decisions about the work they do for course credit, encouraging student autonomy (Ladson-Billings & Henry, 1990, Sattler, 1997). By encouraging students to design work that is important to them, teachers help students create their own meaning and learn from the questions they ask. In this way, a feminist curriculum is never static, instead, it allows teachers to create a course that evolves with student questions (Maher, 1987). Because of efforts to shape the curriculum with students, feminist teachers reject standard curriculums, working to subvert them whenever possible (Sattler, 1997).

One way teachers allow students to shape the curriculum is to build the course on the students' questions (Maher, 1987). As an extension of Ruggerio's (1990) theory of "open learning" (see the theme of "Engaging Students in Active Learning"), some teachers use student texts as a bridge between the broader culture and their own world. The student texts provide a translation of course material or cultural narratives into a concrete form that relates to the student's reality (Mullin, 1994). Other teachers incorporate this theme by using small-group discussions and collaborative group work as a primary element in their classes (Hopkins, 1999). These two strategies (small-group and collaborative work) are often used in the contemporary composition classroom.

Ladson-Billings and Henry (1990) make direct connections between student choices in curriculum and honoring cultural diversity. However, there is continual tension between cultural realities in a multicultural curriculum or classroom. Multicultural education, although designed to affirm traditionally marginalized perspectives, can also cause conflict in the classroom when students are asked to consider perspectives their personal value systems reject. When a teacher asks a Christian student to confront her or his strongly held belief that homosexuality is wrong, the student will often feel alienated or angry. To address these conflicts, Weiler suggested teachers create overt distinctions between community values of antiracism, antisexism, and antihomophobia (among others) and individual belief systems like spiritual or family beliefs.

In composition circles, the theme of giving students choice first took the form of allowing students to define their own approach to and process for writing. In 1972, Murray argued that teachers need to let students explore their writing process in their own way (p. 14). Although Murray did not define his approach as such, his argument reflects this feminist pedagogical theme because it allows students to define the way they approach work as well as the type of work they do. The result manifests itself in students creating work that reinforces meaningful connections with their personal experiences and realities. Giving students choice in the "how and what" of their work directly applies feminist theories of student empowerment (Bridwell-Bowles, 1995). Encouraging student choice and empowerment gives students the authority to create connections between the work of the course, their own experiences, and the external community. In the composition classroom, allowing students to define their own work extends to students creating rhetorical situations that connect with the external world, and engaging in real or fictional public debate in the form of writing speeches, letters, brochures, or editorials (Brodkey & Fine, 1992). More specifically, Annas (1985) argued that composition teachers need to not only accept personal experience as evidence in student writing, but teach students how to use personal experience more effectively. By creating a flexible curriculum that allows students choices, teachers reinforce, confirm, acknowledge, and reflect students' realities (Jessup & Lardner 208).

Some composition theorists interpret this theme as allowing students to make rhetorical decisions to write outside the standard discourse or language practices (Bridwell-Bowles, 1995). When teachers encourage students to create their own meaning or use their own language, they further classroom discussions on standards of academic discourse. By allowing students to write in other discourses besides those sanctioned by the academy, students potentially can write projects that are more meaningful to them or more reflective of their own reality. Cooper (1986) wrote that students have a desire to please the teacher by writing in academic discourse, but because they have not yet fully internalized the discourse rules and patterns of academemese, their writing ends up sounding stilted and the students feel caged and stifled. Cooper advocated freeing students from the idea that they have to write within a discourse they have not yet learned. By doing so, students can develop their thinking and writing skills within the institutional context with greater ease, gradually integrating academic discourse as they learn it.

Teaching Journal: April 10, 2001

We had a very lively discussion in class, but it felt like the teacher against the world. We're examining the politics of Standard

English, so I asked them to read June Jordan's "Nobody Mean More to Me Than You." It's a mesmerizing account of a teacher's work to help her African American students understand Black English as a language (as opposed to slang or "improper" English). For Jordan's students there are heartbreaking consequences for taking that stance: Jordan's class chooses to write about a classmate's brother being gunned down by police using Black English and realizes in doing so authorities and the community will not take their appeal seriously because of the language they use. As I have come to expect when I teach this text, most of the African American students in my class were on the verge of anger that anyone would call Black English a "language." They have been very effectively convinced that it is nothing more than the wrong way to talk, an ignorant, unintelligent version of "proper" English. It is interesting that most of the "white" students are willing to at least entertain the theory that Black English is a language as opposed to a dialect or slang; the African American students argue vehemently that it isn't a language. One student even went so far as to say the distinction resided only in pronunciation. "If I can't annunciate my words correctly, how is that a different language? That is just laziness, not language." So, Black English is "improper," "lazy," "incorrect." Overall, though, we had a good discussion, grappling with such issues as teaching "Standard English," the complexities of a teacher honoring many languages within the class, the taxes extracted by the dominant culture when one chooses to transgress language norms, and the connections between language and culture. Still, I felt at the end of the class it was one of those situations where the African American students left class shaking their heads thinking, "White folks crazy." Or maybe that is even too gentle. Perhaps some of them were more angry than that, angry that a white woman teacher had the audacity to argue that Black English was a legitimate language. Perhaps to some students that sounds like a condescending commentary on the inferior intelligence of Black folks, if one has been indoctrinated to believe that Black English is inferior, ignorant, lazy, slang.

Bringing Joy and Fun Into the Classroom. The theory that rigorous intellectual engagement can also be fun was first brought to feminist pedagogy by Golden (1985). In her "Seven Point Plan," the first point is bringing her excitement to the classroom; Golden wanted her excitement for teaching to infect her students. Because feminist teachers often deviate from standard curriculum to teach issues and texts that excite them, these teachers show their students how exciting and challenging different ideas can be. hooks (1999) expanded the commitment to excite learners by articulating her desire to bring passion and joy into the classroom. Making learning and the evolution to critical consciousness a pleasure zone engages students more quickly and fully in course material (Weiler, 1998). That is not to say that there is not discomfort or conflict in the class, only that the teacher works to integrate pleasure as well. Feminist teachers fight passionately to create a space for joy and laughter (Damarin, 1994), viewing laughter as revolutionary.

Although some composition theorists associate attempts to make writing pleasurable for students as an indication of rigorless play, teachers such as Elbow (1973) and Shrewsbury (1993) wrote that, without a sense of joy in writing, students will not engage fully in smart rhetorical processes. By bringing delight into the writing classroom, students discover positive connections to writing.[22]

Being Aware of Voices and Silences in the Class. In conjunction with the theme of "Considering dynamics of race, class, gender, . . ." (see earlier category of "Goals for the Classroom"), teachers must be attuned to the voices and perspectives that are missing from class material and discussions so they can integrate these perspectives (Mayberry & Cronan Rose, 1999). Taking a cue from feminist activist work, teachers encourage students to use their voice, seeing the connection between voice and empowerment. In her poststructural definition of *feminist pedagogy*, Tisdell (1998) wrote that teachers need to make sure all voices are heard, and that all silences are questioned, asking, "Who is not speaking and why?" Feminist teachers not only realize where the gaps and silences are, but question the reasons behind those silences. These teachers strive to help students to feel comfortable speaking out, thinking for themselves, and integrating their opinions and observations in discussions (Golden, 1985). Helping students find their voices is also part of developing students' independence so they can confront differences and make connections with others in the class, creating real relationships instead of just interactions and conversations (Shrewsbury, 1993).

Teaching Journal; September 27, 2000

We talked about the gender split (or absence of female voices in class discussion) today, within the context of the Sadkers' excerpt. There was a very lively and engaged discussion. A lot of the young women spoke for the first time. Many were offering excuses for why they don't speak out in class: "I like listening to other people;" "Everyone always says what I'm thinking so I don't have to say what I think"; "I only talk when I am really passionate about something." I have heard those responses countless of times in conferences with female students when I ask them why they are silent. I gave my rebuttals to those reasons: other people can learn from you; everyone has to be an active member of the community for the community to be productive; we all have very unique and specific perspectives so even if you think you are in the same camp as someone else, chances are they would like to hear that you agree with them; honing verbal skills is part of becoming better writers and critical thinkers; by not participating you are not only robbing yourself of an education, but you are letting down your peers and relying on them do to the difficult work of speaking out for you. There were also some young women who owned up to feeling self-conscious or having low self-esteem, feeling intimidated by others because participating seemed so much easier for them. We ended the class by making a commitment that more people needed to participate, and that the more vocal members of the class (in this class three very vocal male students) would try to make space for those who wanted to talk, but who took longer to formulate their ideas (silent spaces would be not seen as dead, but productive think time). After class I felt very good. We'll see how this pans out, though. It does take a lot of extra energy to push oneself to talk in class, especially if that skill has been effectively squelched after thirteen years of traditional education. The early morning hour of this course only compounds that problem.

Attention to silences in composition scholarship sprang directly from feminist research that showed women are silenced in both the academy and the curriculum. Because of these silences, women are invisible or absent to many students and teachers. In the early 1970s, when feminist theories came to composition, these early articles about the relationship between feminist theories and composition challenged women to speak out and to express their ideas and challenged teachers to alter curricula to include women authors/writers. In similar ways, feminist scholars studied voices and silences of female students, looking closely at socialized language practices that separate women and men (Kramarae, 1980; Spender, 1990). These discussions of gendered silences evolved to include students who are outside the dominant culture for various reasons (ethnicity, race, religion, sexual orientation, socioeconomic class).

Silence is not always seen as disempowerment. Annas (1985) saw silence as potentially transformational, a way to claim power in a moment of reflection. For Annas, silence represented a powerful moment before speech. But her theory related to *moments* of silence, a significant distinction from the systematic silencing of a population or erasure of perspectives from curricula or discussions. Feminist theories on silence and voice challenge composition teachers to pay close attention to the voices and silences not only in the classroom, but in the curriculum, including as many perspectives as possible. It takes a finely tuned critical eye to *see* silence. Without close self scrutiny, teachers do not observe the gaps of silence in their classes or curriculum. Also problematic, especially in regard to inclusive curriculum, is the reality that not *all* voices will have equal representation. Feminist pedagogy asks that writing instructors work toward multiple perspectives and diversity, being cognitively and critically aware of the inevitable choices and silences, and communicating those to students.

Recognizing That Each Classroom Community and Each Student Is Unique. Paying attention to voices and silences forces teachers to examine the dynamics of the classroom on a student level. Who is speaking and who is not? Why? Who is engaging well in the writing tasks and who is struggling? As stated earlier, theories that brought individual student differences to the foreground have a major role in contemporary composition theory. From writing process theory to a student's right to his or her own language (1979), individual identities and locations play a significant role in the contemporary theories on the teaching of writing. A feminist writing teacher looks closely and analyzes each writer and community individually (Rose, 1995). Because students write in "unique and varied responses to their experiences," a writing teacher sees each student as an individual with different writing needs (Ritchie, 1989). Therefore, a teacher resists making assumptions about classrooms, students, and student locations and perspectives. Showing an example of how assumptions can be quickly codified as truth, Villanueva (1991) wrote about the assumption in composition that race and basic writing are linked. In his essay "An American Freirista," Villanueva critiqued the field of composition for creating a direct correlation between basic writing and people marked as racially non-White. Through his own research, he showed that "basic writers," those who have not internalized the rules of Standard English, are not necessarily those students of specific racial locations, but are children whose primary language did not reflect Standard English, most commonly associated with, but not exclusive to, socioeconomic status (SES), not race. Marshall (1997) reinforced this argument by pointing out that there is no majority of students in any category, so teachers cannot make assumptions about literacy practices of any group.

To honor the uniqueness of each learner and each community, the feminist teacher envisions herself as a leader/facilitator instead of the ultimate power broker. Creating a model of positive leadership means acknowledging that everyone acts on their beliefs, but the choices they make in how they do that determines their effectiveness as leader. This style of leadership encourages autonomy of and mutuality of others, articulating one's needs while at the same time negotiating with others to incorporate their needs. Feminist teachers articulate their needs and goals for the course, negotiating with students so the course reflects the students' objectives as well (Shrewsbury, 1993). In this way, leadership is clearly a form of pedagogy.[23] When students and teacher negotiate course goals, each classroom becomes a unique community honoring the desires of both teacher and students. In situations where a teacher must exert her power, such as when consensus cannot be reached, the teacher is overt with why/how she is making decisions on behalf of the class, modeling responsible leadership.

An extension of positive leadership involves developing leadership qualities in each student. Shrewsbury (1993) wrote that it is not enough for the teacher to model effective, positive leadership, but she must work to help students develop their own leadership skills by placing students in locations of power and leadership. Examples of how some teachers choose to accomplish this are student-led classes, assigning discussion group or project leaders, and allowing students to plan and execute lessons for their peers.

In conjunction with honoring the uniqueness of each community, the teacher also extends this philosophy to each student. The teacher analyzes how each student learns best and adopts teaching strategies that work for the individual (Mullin, 1994). One way many teachers do this is to evaluate not by giving exams or other subjective means, but by allowing students to design their own projects or determine their own contract for course work. Because not all learners come into a class with equal chances or equal life experiences, teachers recognize that each student will offer unique perspectives, but the teacher must allow each student to create work that is meaningful and important to her or him (Tisdell, 1998).

SKEPTICS

The themes used to describe feminist pedagogy are not a handy set of instructional techniques; instead these themes offer a glimpse into how feminist scholars have documented their approach to teaching. This is a pedagogy of liberation (concerned with politics and power), explicit gender analysis, self-criticism, and reflexivity that values ways of knowing that extend beyond the classroom space, with a focus on critical consciousness (Gustafson, 1999). This definition is not without complications.

There are within the field of composition vocal critics of feminist pedagogy; some of these critics identify themselves as feminists. There are scholars who bristle at any attempt to codify a definition of feminist pedagogy, but there are also scholars who reject even the spirit of feminist pedagogy as no more liberating or progressive than more traditional theories of education. Skeptics of feminist pedagogy believe there is no way to measure whether feminist pedagogical practices further critical consciousness (Gore, 1993). Critics like Gore believe that feminist teachers privilege a feminist political perspective and therefore do not encourage critical thinking, but instead actively work toward indoctrination; in this model, the dominant ideology is replaced by a feminist ideology that is no less oppressive or less rigid.[24] This seems a short-sighted interpretation of the scholarship on feminist pedagogy and reflects a criticism leveled against the early years of feminist pedagogy as it manifested itself in Women's Studies courses, where the agenda of the course was education in feminist beliefs and activist movements. As feminist pedagogy has evolved and become more interdisciplinary, the focus is no longer education toward feminist beliefs so much as considering all perspectives, honoring student differences, and being overt about one's own belief systems.

Another general critique of feminist pedagogy is that it is too focused on specific practices (like sitting in a circle or coming out from behind the podium) and not focused enough on teaching strategies. It seems, however, that few feminist scholars prescribe specific practices they believe are inherently feminist. Rather, they describe the goal (empowering students) and suggest ways in which that goal can be achieved (coming out from behind the podium, sitting in a circle, allowing students to lead classes), rather than offer one way or practice that will work to meet the goal in all classroom communities. Because one of the themes of feminist pedagogy is recognizing that each learner and community is unique, it is unlikely that a feminist teacher would implement the same practices in all classrooms or advocate that one specific practice reflects the *only* means by which to exercise a theme. For example, sitting in a circle is not inherently empowering, nor does it work in every classroom. Feminist teachers recognize that sitting in a circle can be inherently oppressive for students who want to hide in the class, who feel exposed, or who feel uncomfortable participating; the logistics of some classrooms (the sheer number of students or lecture halls where chairs are bolted to the floor in rows all facing forward) also create barriers to arranging a class in a circle. If they do use a circle, feminist teachers clearly articulate to the class *why* this is the chosen structure, allowing students to voice their own opinions.

I once taught an Introduction to Women's Studies course where a young man in the class who had panic disorder frequently missed class because he felt overexposed in the circle. In a conference, he told me he had to take extra medication before coming to the Women's Studies class solely because having to sit in a circle, where he felt everyone was looking at him, was too much for him to bear. I asked him for suggestions on how to make the class less stressful for him, but he could offer none, understanding that the circle was important for discussion and seeing the benefits of that simple logistical maneuver in the closeness of the community and the vibrancy of discussion. I felt at a loss to make the class a place where this student felt empowered. He ended up dropping the class largely because his disorder prevented him from being able to attend. Looking back on the situation, I feel as if I did not go far enough as a teacher to accommodate the special needs of this student. It was a humbling learning experience for me, where I failed to follow the spirit of feminist pedagogy in the way I handled the situation.

Fisher (2001) believes that some criticism of feminist pedagogy comes from a feeling of judgment by the word feminist. In our culture, the word *feminist* is often associated with judgment—someone who is pointing the finger at others to say they are not being fair or just to women (specifically, but other TMP as well). Because of this cultural reaction to the word *feminist*, some people may be reacting to feminist pedagogy as a challenge to their teaching credentials (Fisher, 2001. Fisher argued this is uniquely compounded by the nature of how some people view *professor* as a word that implies a right and wrong way of approaching knowledge. She wrote, "If 'feminist professor' is not a contradiction in terms, it is at the very least an invitation to mental and emotional fatigue" (p. 45). From this perspective, feminist pedagogy or feminist teachers are misunderstood as judging those who teach a certain way, pointing the finger and saying "you are doing it wrong." However, the point of this project is not to say one method of teaching is less valid or one practice is less desirable than another, but to more clearly articulate a historical composite of feminist pedagogy so more people understand what it is. Although feminist pedagogy is the theory of teaching I choose to adopt, and that works best for me and my philosophies, I would not suggest it is universally the best for everyone or that the way I practice feminist pedagogy is the way anyone else will choose to practice it.

From my research, when considering the main criticisms against feminist pedagogy as outlined earlier, I believe the skeptics are working from an old model that reflects an outdated definition of feminist pedagogy harkening back to early Women's Studies courses, where the main determining elements of feminist pedagogy were attention to gender issues, subverting the authority of the teacher, and educating toward a feminist perspective. Although there are remnants of these elements in the contemporary definition of feminist pedagogy compiled here, the current praxis and scholarship are much more rich, complex, and comprehensive, creating a definition of feminist pedagogy that can be applied to any course across the curriculum by a teacher who is devoted to student-centered teaching that evolves to critical consciousness and community connection.

Because of the attention to critical consciousness, student-centered teaching, attention to ideological power structures like racism, classism, sexism, and homophobia, among others, a feminist pedagogical approach is particularly well suited for a contemporary humanities course and more specifically a composition classroom. In the contemporary composition classroom, students are asked to see language as a powerful tool of ideology and create connections between their identities as writers and thinkers and the larger culture. Contemporary theories of composition challenge students to be active learners invested in their own intellectual development and writing processes, seeing language as a powerful tool for social action.

THE PRACTICE OF CHANGE

In the next three chapters, I show how feminist pedagogy and scholarship are being practiced by contemporary scholars. Each of the next three chapters is devoted to a case study of a specific feminist composition scholar. These chapters show how each of the three feminist composition scholars are enacting their feminist beliefs in their classrooms, their university communities, and their scholarship. These studies (by Lynn Worsham, Harriet Malinowitz, and Jackie Jones Royster) demonstrate the histories and theories of feminist pedagogy and feminisms in the field. The research of these three scholars/teachers offers dynamic examples of how feminists in the field are enacting their beliefs in the areas of scholarship, teaching, and leadership. Before launching into these chapters, a short interchapter provides some background on feminist research in composition and introduces my methodology for the case studies.

Interchapter on Research and Methodology

Project Journal: August 28, 2000

I'm reading an amazing book by Cheryl Sattler (*Talking About a Revolution*). She interviewed nine feminist teachers, both at the high school and university level, about feminist pedagogy. The very interesting thing is many don't identify as feminists (most of the ones who resist identifying as a feminist teacher are the high school teachers). A couple of teachers tell her they resist categories and labels, one even said "group mentality" was bad and that feminists who are really into sisterhood begin to menstruate together (!!) (71). But Sattler believes some of this feminist-phobia (my term, not hers) may have to do with being afraid, as high school teachers, of identifying themselves with a politically unpopular group, dangerous even, almost as dangerous as being an out lesbian high school teacher (or worse yet, an out gay man as a primary or secondary school teacher, since the prevailing myth is that male teachers are potentially pedophiles, otherwise why would they want to be around small children? Add to that the myth of gay men preying on boys . . .).

My immediate response when reading was "paranoia!" What are folks so afraid of: "a group of women with minds! Run for your lives! They are controlling our children! EEEK!" And then I thought back to the meeting I had with Kate last week. We were talking about the letter I am going to send to Worsham, Malinowitz, and Royster (the people I am hoping to persuade to participate in my ethnographic research). I had given Kate a copy of the letter to read, the questions for me being: Why would they say yes to helping me? How can I convince them to participate? Kate said she was talking with a colleague about the letter and she asked the colleague, a feminist teacher, "What would be your response if you got a letter like this, asking you to participate in some research about feminists in the field?" The colleague's response was, "I'd be afraid I was being set up." "Set up" as in "used in a nefarious way to make me look bad." I was floored by that response. Taken aback. I keep coming back to it in my mind. Why would that be the *first* response when approached by a researcher to talk about one's feminist identity? What *is* that about? At first I wanted to cluck and say, "Well, there is that academic insecurity, that ugly beast, raising its grizzled head. Everything is a competition with/against each other so paranoia runs rampant." But when I think more about it, paranoia runs rampant in activist circles, too. I am thinking of a woman in the Cincinnati NOW chapter who refuses to give the treasurer's report if there are any "new" people in the room. I always think, "What the hell is she afraid of?"

I know I'm different from most people, most women, especially. I tend to spend very little time thinking about what other folks think of me or spending lots of time and energy strategizing how to gain access to systems of power. That often gets me in trouble, manifesting itself in a maverick spirit that pisses people off. So I have a hard time relating to reactions of what looks, at least on the surface, like fear in others.

Why are feminists afraid or paranoid? Or *some* feminists, anyway. Are we still persecuted and punished for being feminists? Individually? After reading Sattler's book, perhaps I can understand the response of Kate's colleague a bit better. Maybe it is coming from the same place as the resistance of some of the high school teachers to identifying as feminist. University women were (in Sattler's study) more embracing of the "f" word because it is more accepted, but they still expressed some nervousness about it. Still, it makes me feel a well of frustration and sadness when the first reaction towards one's own colleagues, fellow feminists, is the assumption, "She's out to get me."

That reminded me of a day last fall in the graduate class I was sitting in on. The prof (a "out" feminist) talked about a young feminist scholar who had "attacked" her work at a conference. It was apparent the prof felt the attack was *not* just about her *work*, but some sort of personal assault. The prof spoke of the trickiness of the rhetorical situation: how to respond to what she felt were misrepresentations of her work by the young scholar without looking like she was defensive, without shutting down conversation. But clearly, she *did* feel defensive.

These situations seem all too common: a replay of the Biesecker/Campbell-Kohrs "cat fight." And how much of this, like the Biesecker/Campbell-Kohrs point counterpoint that became so personal it was painful to read, is staged by journals: "See? The feminists really just *can't* get along."

The Sattler book gave me a lot to think about. But not just about the insecurity and unease many women feel in their academic work. The methodology of her project interested me. She allowed her participants to read and comment on the transcripts of the interviews. She also wanted to make sure her research "gave back" to them in some way. She overtly asked them to try to think of how her research *could* give back to them. I want to make sure I incorporate some of those strategies in my own research, or perhaps take them even further: allowing participants to talk back to not just transcripts, but my interpretation of the interviews.

The Sattler book also brought to my attention the complexities of what I am trying to do: identifying teachers and scholars as feminist and asking them to talk about their feminist work. That could be perceived as a huge risk on their part. And I worry about them feeling "set up." Very problematic. I don't want them to feel that way; I honor their work too much. But can I be completely analytical about their work while worrying about whether they will not like what I am seeing or discovering? How can I know what will make them nervous? I plan to ask each of them that question specifically, "What makes you nervous about this project?" But the more I think about all these issues of honesty and critique and research and feminism, the more overwhelming it becomes.

A project that begins with one question—"How are feminists in composition studies enacting their beliefs in their teaching, leadership, and scholarship?"—quickly blooms into a multitude, a maze, of sticky issues. The number of choices *any* researcher makes about a project is mind boggling, if not infinite. For a feminist researcher, these choices weigh even more heavily because she is pushing herself to be critically *aware* of all those choices and critique them at every turn in the complex labyrinth that is a research project.

The historical compilation of feminist pedagogy outlined in this project is culled from a tremendous amount of feminist scholarship on activism and teaching (see chapters 1-2), but in the end, I was the one who made choices about the sixteen themes and how to articulate those themes. Feminists in composition carry many themes of feminist teaching strategies over to this field from activist work in the community and in Women's Studies. But feminists in composition also create their own theories and practices of feminism specifically in relation to women writers, leaders, rhetoricians, and being a woman scholar in the "publish or perish" world of academia. Their theories and practices focus more squarely on women as writers and rhetors both in the classroom, in the community, and in the field. Over the past three decades, feminists have shaped the field of composition in areas of teaching, leadership, and scholarship. The point of the ethnographic studies in each of the next three chapters is to show how three such scholars/teachers are doing this. The ethnographies also show the connections between philosophy and practice: how these three women are enacting their feminist beliefs in the areas of teaching, scholarship, and leadership. Being a woman, let alone a feminist, in the academy has never been a carnival cake walk, but historically we seem to be at the top of our game. At least I personally feel that way, especially after the ethnographic studies where I saw, first hand, the profound ways in which my experience as a feminist in the field is better, easier, kinder because of the thirty years of feminist work that has preceded my tenure as a composition teacher and scholar.

As a scholar attempting ethnographic research, I am aware of the complexities of ethnography and of applying feminist methods to my ethnographic research. In her book *Ethnographic Writing and Research*, Bishop (1999) defines *ethnography* as taking place in a specific sociological space, celebrating the identity of the people/place that are the focus of the research and incorporating a hybrid of research methods. In her reflective article on her own ethnographic research, "Postbook: Working the Ruins of Feminist Ethnography," Lather (2001) adds to Bishop's definition, writing that an ethnographer uses a variety of methods, collecting data from various sources, and "troubling the very claims" that the data represents (p. 201). An ethnography gains power when the researcher spends as much time with the object of the research as possible, collecting multiple sources of data, while allowing participants to guide the research questions (Bishop, 1999). But feminists realize that every ethnography is, in the end, a fictional representation, regardless of the amount of time spent on site, in the culture, interacting with the participant. An ethnography that is specifically feminist consistently questions the power position of the research subject and the researcher. Feminist ethnography also extends the issue of research power to questions concerning race, class, gender, national origin, and other systems of power. The feminist researcher has to ask, "How am I using my power and my voice? How can I make sure the power and voice of the research subject is foregrounded?"

In her book *Fictions of Feminist Ethnography*, Visweswaran (1994) complicates the idea of feminist ethnography by naming it a fiction; feminist ethnographers understand they are writing a story, a fiction, that will never reflect any one person's reality. Visweswaran writes that the connection between ethnography and fiction "builds a believable world, but one that the reader rejects as fiction" (p. 1). In the same way, ethnography "sets out to build a believable world, but one the reader will accept as factual" (Visweswaran, 1994, p. 1). This definition of feminist ethnography understands that the story told by the ethnographer is just that: a story. The story pieces together what the ethnographer chooses to include. But understanding that the ethnography is a story is not enough. The feminist ethnographer must also rigorously interrogate issues of power and agency (both systemic and individual), situational knowledge,[25] shifting identities, temporality, and silence, and the politics of identity and identification (Visweswaran, 1994).

In Behar's (1993) feminist ethnography of "Esperanza," she attempts to draw the life of her research participant, a 60-year-old Mexican woman, through storytelling, both her own and Esperanza's. In her research, she confronts the issue of histories, the stories told, as "false document[s]" told by various unreliable narrators. What the researcher creates in the text, the result of the ethnographer's pen or keyboard, reflects the power of the researcher. The researcher decides what is included or excluded, the order of things, and the way they are spoken or told on the black and white of a page. Behar writes, "[I]t is not orality versus textuality that I call into question here, with the image it conjures up of the ethnographer salvaging the fleeting native experience in the net of a text. The more relevant distinction for me is [. . .] the contrast between storytelling and information" (p. 12). In my own ethnographic studies, as in any feminist ethnographic study, the awareness of who is *writing* the story and how the writer's story circles back into the center, the focus, is often as important as the stories of those being studied or observed.

Feminist ethnographers struggle to negotiate the complexities of telling someone else's story in various ways. Behar gives us insight into her and Esperanza's discussions on the work of the book, including the power of naming as represented in the title of the book, and how Behar chose what to include and what not to include of Esperanza's story. Visweswaran creates a "play" in three-acts that reinforces her belief that ethnographic research is fiction. The three act play also articulates the power relationship between participant and researcher—how participants gain power by passing their own fictions to the researcher as "truth," and how a researcher confronts these fictions when she discovers them as conflicts to textual evidence. In "Tell My Horse," Hurston (1938) attempted to subvert the power relationship between researcher and participant by inserting herself into the subject's culture or becoming part of the subject.

The frustrations of feminists doing ethnographic research and how to negotiate issues of power, identity, and storytelling lead to creative methods of writing, as is evidenced when fiction is merged with ethnography (Viswesaran, Hurston) and inserting first person narratives both of self and participants into the text (Behar, 1993; Lather 1997). In their book *Troubling the Angels,* an ethnography of women living with HIV/AIDS, Lather and Smithies (1997) wrestle with the issues of power, identity, and storytelling by creating a horizontally split page with intertexts that record the first-person narratives of the participants. The participants' words are on the top of the page in larger text; the researchers' words appear beneath that in smaller font—an attempt to foreground and privilege the narratives of the participants literally "over" those of the researchers.

In her recent article "Postbook: Working the Ruins of Feminist Ethnography," Lather (2001) provides an extremely interesting feminist critique of her own ethnography and the decisions the researchers made in how to create the story and present it. In this article, Lather includes participant responses to the book. Some of her participants critique the book, saying that it was too difficult to read because of the way Lather and Smithies chose to represent their research/story. Lather writes that her critique, and their critique, of the physical text that was the result of the ethnography represented the failures of representation. "Textual experiments," Lather writes, "are not so much about solving the crisis of representation as about troubling the very claims to represent" (p. 201). The most a feminist ethnographer can hope for, she writes, is an ethnography of ruins and failures, one that recognizes limits and misfirings. In this way, "ethnography becomes a kind of self-wounding laboratory for discovering the rules by which truth is produced" (Lather, 2001, p. 202). In the end, a feminist ethnographer needs to track the failures because there is no method that can solve these failures.

In the ethnographies that follow, I attempt to trouble the text by including my personal journal entries. They provide the first-person narrative of the researcher. I also include transcripts of interviews, although the entire transcripts are not included—an omission I feel uncomfortable about, but page limits mandate their exclusion. Although I chose to include each of these three women because I saw them as examples of feminists in the field and I wanted to discover and to record how they practice feminist pedagogy, I let each women steer the interviews in her own direction. I *did* forward each woman questions that I wanted her to answer before my site visit. They all knew my main interest was feminist pedagogy. However, the stories they told me and the conversations I had with them over the phone, over e-mail, and in person went in different directions depending on how each woman chose to represent herself to me. Because of this, one may feel a "tension" in these chapters between a discussion of feminist pedagogy and a discussion of other subjects the participants wanted to include.

Another way I attempted to make sure I honored the participant's story and how she wanted that story represented was to allow her to talk back to the chapter about her, to "interrupt and disrupt." I discuss the process of this more later in this interchapter. Because I wanted to offer the participants "the last word," I did not "rebutt" any critiques they made of the project. I felt it was important to let them explain their perspective, to offer the critique, without me taking the power back by being able to have "the last word."

There are complex politics to writing histories, storytelling, and false histories making the process more challenging than the act of the research and data gathering. I found myself asking, more than once throughout this project, "How do I *write* this?" How does one write about other people's lives and work in ways that are analytical, but also worthy of the astonishing, powerful work these women are doing? How can I bring my voice and style to this project and still write in a way that will be publishable? Is the end result of publication personal benefit (career enhancement) or service to the field (others will learn from my research and become better teachers)? Why do I feel it needs to be mostly the latter to make me feel comfortable doing this work? How do I tell this story and still maintain the voice and power of these women's stories and *their* words instead of mine? What are my words and what are theirs?

In Kirsch's (1993) study of "successful women writers," she found that even as women tried to break gender norms and challenge traditional approaches to research, scholarship, and teaching, there were prices to be paid for such deviations. The women that Kirsch studied expressed a desire to write in a voice different from the standards typically abided by in the discipline. They expressed this by saying they wanted to write for people beyond the academic community. This desire to write to an audience other than their academic peers in the field could also be evidence that these women wanted to create connections between their academic work and the world external to academia, an extension of their feminist belief system.

Kirsch (1993) wanted to find out how women in the academy negotiated issues of professionalization and academic discourse. Do women submit to the standards or create new ones? Because "the material pressure of academia is writing" (Kirsch, p. xvii), Kirsch set out to discover how women academics approached writing, how they felt about academic writing, how they established authority in their writing, and how gender influenced the use of language/writing for women academics. The issue of how a feminist approaches writing and scholarship emerged as a prominent concern for all three of the scholars in my ethnographic studies. In the following three chapters, each scholar articulates, in different ways, the barriers she is working against to publish the kind of work she is passionate about. These approaches and the subject of their research are intricately woven together with feminist awareness and beliefs.

Similar to my desire to research feminist teachers and ask feminist teachers about their research, Kirsch's (1993) interest came from her location as an English professor. Because historically women had not had the opportunity/authority to speak publicly, Kirsch wanted to investigate how women in the academy were claiming that authority. Kirsch investigated the difference between women who described themselves as successful, confident writers and those who did not, although she herself defined all the women in her study as "successful writers" within their academic position. She wanted to know how women writers positioned themselves in the context of academia, how they spoke to specific audiences (and who those audiences were), and how they claimed authority.

Kirsch's (1993) study was significant because for women academics, publication is imperative to academic success as well as furthering feminist theory. In the "publish or perish" world of academia, people who do not publish are at a grave disadvantage when it comes to job security and salary. In their writing, women academics often feel they need to appease the patriarchal hierarchy to be seen as legitimate (Ray, 1993). All three of the women in my ethnographic studies express their desire to bring diversity of language and epistemology to the field. But they also express concern in varying degrees that scholarly work incorporating maverick approaches to scholarship or deviations from the expected discourse practices are often not accepted for publication. All believed that their scholarship points to, as their teaching and leadership does as well, a site of feminist activism in the university. Within all of the discussions I had with these women, the power of feminist language and rhetoric provided a consistent focus.

Project Journal: September 5, 2000

> I am reading about feminists who have been told (by mentors and editors) to "tone down" their work so it isn't so offensive (i.e. unabashedly feminist). I nod. I'm already worried about that. I can feel myself self-monitoring already, holding back my own voice, restraining the hotheaded feminist so the calm, cool, collected researcher can stroll through unassaulted. Is that just audience awareness or self-censorship? I haven't decided.

BESIDES WORDS

Before the physical act of putting words to the page, and my conflicts with how to use language to communicate what I saw, I was first consumed with the logistics of research methodology. Many feminist research methods have been articulated over the past 10 years. Most helpful to me were Ruth Behar (*Translated Woman*), Gesa Kirsch (*Ethical Dilemmas in Feminist Research*), and Patti Lather (*Getting Smart: Feminist Research and Pedagogy with/in the Postmodern, Troubling the Angels,* and "Postbook"). Behar, Kirsch, and Lather all adamantly work to make their research choices as overt as possible to themselves, to their audience, *and* to their participants. In 1991, Lather outlined some basic questions everyone should ask about one's own research, an attempt to be vigilant to feminist ideals:[26]

- Did I encourage ambivalence and multiplicity?
- What was muted/repressed? Shaped? Subverted?
- Did I create a text that was multiple without being pluralistic?
- Did I focus on the limits of my own conceptualization?
- Who are my "others"?
- Did I make resistant discourses more widely available?
- What is my interest in this work (career? power?)?
- How are the data interpreted? How can I keep myself from the center?
- What is the political moment/relationship of people?
- Are data the means by which the story is told (fiction)?

When I first read Lather's list of questions, I scrawled them onto a 3 x 5 card and taped the card to the inside of my project journal, a continual reminder to me of what I should be doing each time I entered the project zone. Eventually I moved the card to my computer monitor; I could not sit down to write without the feminist research fairies tickling my ear with these questions. The two questions that most often plagued me were "Did I encourage ambivalence?" and "Am I keeping myself from the center?" I engaged in constant arguments with myself over the answers to these two questions. No, I was not being ambivalent. I was trying to *argue* a specific perspective. How can I create a good argument and convince people of the dramatic (positive) impact feminists have had on the field of composition by being ambivalent? "Was there anything I can ever remember being ambivalent about?" asked the opinionated, bullheaded feminist researcher.

Quite frankly, I had no intention of keeping myself from the center of this work. In fact, I felt it was my duty as a feminist researcher to constantly remind myself, and my audience, and my participants of where *I stood* in relation to what I was writing. What did Lather mean that feminists should keep themselves from the center? Did she have a 1-800 number so I could call and find out: customer service for feminist researchers? I wrestled with my understanding of feminist methodology. I understood that the researcher (me) is always at the center of the project, shaping and molding it, creating the results she desires, and communicating that to the reader. If I am not in the beginning, middle and end of this project, then who is? Or was Lather suggesting that one must constantly step aside to make room for the participants' voices, to make sure their perspective and reality is given a wide berth, unmutilated by the researcher's meddling ideas? The latter is what I attempt to do with my own research, understanding that all ethnographies are, in the end, a fictional representation from the perspective of the writer.

MY METHODOLOGY

A feminist methodology demands that a researcher be as overt as possible both with herself and her audience about her research biases; she must confront those biases whenever she can, challenging her methods and approaches and being rigorous with what she is "seeing" and what she is obscuring, both from her own eyes and those of her reader. It feels like a mea-culpa: "I know that I am a weak-minded human, a mere machine for hegemony. I privilege my own agenda and ignore those pieces of the puzzle that don't fit. Please understand that this is just a feeble attempt to try and sort something out, even as I know I am not sorting out, rather I am messing up." The following is a list of the assumptions I am *aware* I was making as I approached the ethnographic research.

> *Assumption number 1:* My working definition of *feminist pedagogy* is a definition that is legitimate; that is to say, it is not unique to me, but others would also agree with this definition of pedagogy being distinctly feminist. This is a tricky assumption. The crux of this entire project is an argument that the historical research, the 16 themes, offers a basic shape of what feminist pedagogy is. Yet even when talking to people about my research project (both with participants and others) I had to convince them that feminist pedagogy is distinct from other radical or critical pedagogies *and* that the traditional way they thought of feminist pedagogy (nurturing mother with focus on gender issues) is a throwback from the beginnings of the Second Wave.
>
> *Assumption number 2:* The teacher identifies as feminist and therefore practices feminist pedagogy. What I was attempting to codify with the ethnographies was the legitimacy of the themes. The primary questions I wanted to answer were, "How are these themes enacted? Do they accurately reflect how feminist pedagogy is practiced?" The underlying assumptions are, however, that Lynn Worsham, Harriet Malinowitz, and Jackie Jones Royster[27] are indeed *practicing* feminist pedagogy, and feminist pedagogy specifically (not critical, liberatory, Marxist, or other brands of radical pedagogy). I was not entering the ethnographies to determine *whether* they practiced feminist pedagogy,

but *how*. The classroom observations were a way of testing the rubric to determine whether there were themes missing or redundant themes represented.

Assumption number 3: Feminist pedagogy does not begin or end in the classroom. I assumed that these teachers and scholars would carry feminist pedagogical strategies over to their leadership and scholarship.

Assumption number 4: There is a lot of thinking that goes on about teaching that is not *seen* when observing a class or meeting or analyzing a piece of writing. Therefore, some themes of feminist pedagogy become more prominent than others. For example, the theme of "Confronting sex biases (both the teacher's own and other's)" would likely play out more in planning lessons and syllabi or individual comments on student's papers, rather than in the actual classroom discussion. The theme of "Critical reflecting on teaching" would, by its description, not be readily observed in the classroom or at a meeting. Only through conversations with the teachers about their thoughts on feminist pedagogy would practices be noted.

When conducting my ethnographic research, I tried to incorporate the ideas of Kirsch, Behar, and Lather as much as I could. I incorporated the ideals of these feminist ethnographers by attempting to be as overt as I could with my subject about what I was doing and why. When gathering data, I asked Jackie, Lynn, and Harriet what work they were most proud of or what work of theirs they wanted me to read, letting them establish part of my focus. Although I did forward them questions that I wanted to ask at the site visit, each site visit was different as each woman determined how much time we spent together, what meetings or classes I would attend, what information they would offer outside what I specifically asked for, and what stories they would tell me about who they were as feminists, academics, and teachers.

When writing I incorporated their voices and agendas as well as my own first-person narrative into each chapter in an attempt to mess up the story or complicate the research (Lather, 2001). As much as I could, I tried to represent these women's voices in their own words as Behar, Kirsch, and Lather modeled.

When I first approached each participant, I began by writing a letter telling them about my project and asking whether they would be willing to participate as feminist teachers. Whether the letter I drafted worked well or whether these three women are simply too generous to turn down a young scholar's request, all three said "yes!" immediately and enthusiastically, putting to rest a small edge of my initial trepidation regarding whether the participants would perceive this project with suspicion. I decided to ask these three women specifically because I was impressed with how open they were about their feminist beliefs both in their scholarship and conference presentations. To me, each of these women squarely centered her work on feminist theories, unabashedly using the "f" word in ways that I found refreshing, smart, and exciting. Second, I selected these three scholars as participants— Lynn Worsham, Harriet Malinowitz, and Jackie Jones Royster—because they represented different locations and perspectives within the field of composition and rhetoric. They were also all well-known feminist scholars and teachers.

Lynn, a White feminist, provides the perspective of an editor of a scholarly journal (*JAC*). Lynn's experience as the first openly feminist editor of a scholarly journal in the field provides important insights on the intersections of feminist scholarship and leadership. Her position as editor allows her to speak to how she is using feminist rhetoric and feminist scholarship to change comp/rhet scholarship. Through her work as editor of *JAC*, Lynn has committed herself to furthering discussions of race, class, gender, and sexual orientation in comp/rhet scholarship.

Harriet's work in the area of queer pedagogy and scholarship, and most recently work in the area of critiquing identity politics, provides an important perspective into feminist teaching practices. Harriet has been involved as a feminist community activist, working with grassroots organizations in the areas of reproductive freedom; issues of rape, assault, and domestic violence; and gay/lesbian/bisexual/transgendered concern. Harriet provides important insights on the bridge between academic work and community activist work.

Jackie's most recent research focuses on restoring African American women's rhetoric of the 19th century. She has also published articles on feminist pedagogy and the dynamics of race in the classroom. Her location as a female African American Associate Dean of Humanities at a large state university in the Midwest, provides a unique perspective from which to interrogate issues of feminist leadership.

With each ethnographic study, I engaged in telephone, e-mail, and personal interviews. When I asked these three prominent feminists in the field of composition to let me follow them around for a few days of their working life, the participants decided how to interpret that: how far they would let me into their world, what classes or meetings I would observe, who I would talk with, and how many hours of their day I would be tagging along. I spent 3 days at each site (their home university) and shadowed them, talking with students and colleagues, observing classes and meetings, and talking to them about their work and their lives. Although some may say that spending such a short amount of time on site does not constitute an ethnography, feminist ethnographers contest the belief that amount of time spent with the group or individual will make the ethnography more "true." *Ethnography* is more generally defined as an anthropological method that looks at various sites of data collection and intersection. Although it almost always includes first-person interaction, it also includes textual research and communication between subject and participant that does not necessarily take in person on site. Whereas traditional ethnography was grounded on the belief that an objective observer could learn the most about a group of people by observing them impartially, contemporary ethnography, especially feminist ethnography, complicates the issues of objectivity, impartiality, and observer so that ethnography is reconfigured beyond observation of and amount of time spent in the physical presence of the participant(s). I spoke with the women about their personal beliefs regarding feminism, life in the academy, being a feminist in the academy, feminist pedagogy, feminist scholarship, and leadership. Before each site visit, I e-mailed each participant a list of questions that I knew I wanted to ask while visiting them. E-mailing the questions 2 to 3 weeks before my site visit, I hoped that each participant would have time to think about and reflect on the questions so they could give me more complete, thoughtful answers.

E-mail to Harriet: March 3, 2001

Harriet,

I wanted to forward you the questions I have formulated to ask when we can find a time to sit down and talk. I don't really want to go down the list and ask each question. I envision the site visit as including a series of conversations that will take us most places the questions cover. That being said, I did want to forward you the questions so that you can ruminate on them for awhile.

Here goes
Describe your career path, i.e. how did you come to be where you are professionally?
Thinking back on your career in academia, what were some of the pivotal moments or "forks in the road"?
Who were your mentors and how have they informed your work?
Who are the women (feminists?) you have watched or looked to as examples of your own work or teaching—women in power positions or those who have ethos within the field? Do you have any feminist role models in the field?
How would you define feminism?
When did you first publicly identify as a feminist?
What has been your most radical feminist act?
Have you been involved politically in feminism outside the academy? If so, how/why?

How have your feminist beliefs influenced your approach to your work?
How is your approach to scholarship different because of your identity as a feminist? Your approach to leadership? Teaching? The teaching of writing specifically? Training graduate students to be better writing teachers?
How has feminism changed the teaching of writing or the field of composition? Research? The discourse in the field?
How would you define feminist pedagogy?
What is the difference between feminism and feminist pedagogy?
I know that may seem like a lot of questions, but hopefully we can have a conversation (or more than one!) that touches on most of these issues in one way or another.

k

At each site, I had a number of conversations where I would ask a prompting question, but more often would let the participant begin the conversation and talk about what they were interested in telling me. They spoke about how they believed their lives and work intersected with my research topic (feminist pedagogy). Most of the interviews were tape recorded, taking place in offices, classes, restaurants, and coffee shops. A few of the conversations were not recorded—those we would have while dashing across campus or during class breaks. In those situations, I would try to frantically scribble down any notes I found important to record. At the end of the site visit, the participant and I would have a final conversation where I would look down the list of questions and go over any I thought we did not cover.

With all three site visits, I found that the participants were generous with their time and thoughtful in their comments to me. I left each site visit feeling overwhelmed with what I had learned, but also energized and excited having seen these women in action. During the time we shared on site, I asked them to reflect on their own teaching, scholarship, and leadership, allowing them to lead the conversations and focus on topics that were important to them.

Also at each site, I observed classes the women taught and meetings they attended or facilitated. I spoke with colleagues and students, both in the presence of the participants and often separately. Once again, each participant decided the level at which I would infiltrate their lives, who I would speak with, which classes and meetings I would attend, and how much of their day I would tag after them. I was continually humbled and amazed at how open and giving these teachers and scholars were with their time and energy toward my research project.

After returning from the site visits, I transcribed the hours and hours of tapes from the classroom observations, meetings, and interviews. When I excerpt these transcripts in the following chapters, I use a bracketed ellipses, [. . .], to indicate that I cut some words or perhaps sentences from the transcript. I only cut words or phrases that are redundant or off topic to the point I was attempting to emphasize with the quote. As is the case with any verbal transcription, speech patterns are not as neat and precise as written thoughts. The ellipses are used to indicate that there were some words I cut, but they were not essential to the idea or point the participant was making.

In addition to the personal interviews where the research participants reflected on, and often reminisced about, their own history, story, perspective, and experience, I offer my own rhetorical analysis of their scholarship and language. Through observing them in their classrooms or at department/university meetings, analyzing how they enact their feminist pedagogy, and speaking with their students and colleagues, I observed them in varying contexts. By speaking with their students and colleagues, I gained insights into how others view these feminists' approach to teaching and leadership. I also read and analyzed both published and unpublished scholarship, speeches, and syllabi from their classes, looking for themes of feminist pedagogy and uses of feminist rhetoric.

A large part of the site visits was observing each teacher in her classroom. At Lynn's and Harriet's sites, I observed two classes each. Because Jackie is now in an administrative position, she was not teaching when I conducted my site visit with her. Consequently, my ethnographic study of her work is more grounded in leadership as a site of feminist pedagogy. With Lynn and Harriet, however, observing the classrooms was important to this research because, without it, I would have little access to the actual practice of feminist pedagogy in the more traditional classroom setting. Self-reported data—data that I gathered from interviews with the participants—provide interesting insights that cannot be "seen" by an observer (such as how choices in teaching, scholarship or leadership relate to an underlying feminist belief system). Both self-reported and observed data create complexities the researcher has to address. There are biases in both research approaches. With self-reported data, the bias resides in the reporter, primarily: She talks about how she sees herself, or wants to see herself, which may vary wildly from how an observer (no observer is ever neutral) sees her. With observed data, the bias resides in the researcher: What I saw is what I typically wanted to see, ignoring the pieces of data that conflicted with my thesis or hypothesis. In other words, the data the researcher (me) needs to gather to reinforce her hypothesis is typically the data she finds: What she wants is what she gets. As a way of minimizing these biases, or perhaps in an attempt to complicate them, once I drafted and revised each ethnographic chapter, I forwarded it to the participant for her to add her perspective to my interpretations and analyses of her life and work. I forwarded both an electronic copy and a hard copy of the chapter to the research participant, inviting her to talk back to the text, to interrupt it, and to insert her ideas, reactions, and responses in any way she felt compelled to. This was my way of allowing the participant to get in the last word, so to speak, and to correct or clarify interpretations I had made of the data that perhaps did not reflect their own perspective. Because I wanted each participant to interact with and mess up my ideas, analyses, and observations in ways that were meaningful to them, I gave few guidelines on what I expected from these responses or interruptions. This resulted in three radically unique chapters, with the participants choosing to insert their voice and perspective in different ways. I also did not alter in any significant way the ethnographic chapters after the participant added her thoughts and edits. This was my way of truly allowing her the last word on the subject.

Letter to Lynn, asking her interrupt, disrupt, and talk back to her ethnographic chapter

A Rumbly, Bumbly Rainy May Day in Ohio, 2001

Dear Lynn,

Whew. Here you go. I don't know about you, but when I am this entrenched in a project, I seem to go in cycles: "This is a piece of crap." "Well, this is taking shape." "This is a mess." "Hey. I kinda like what this is becoming." "Oh, this will never come together." At some point, I just have to let it go. I don't know that I am ready to let it go yet (am I ever?), but here it is anyway. The tyranny of time constraints.

Since this is the ethnographic chapter I have worked on most thoroughly (and began first, once again you are the guinea pig) I can't really tell whether the methodology details in this chapter belong in the methodology chapter or are good right here. I've given you excerpts from other chapters so you have some context for what I am trying to do: the introduction, a hunk of the chapter where I describe the sixteen themes of feminist pedagogy, the methodology chapter. You can glance through these for some context and supporting information, but they aren't part of the stuff I am asking for your response to.

I'm giving you both a hard copy and an electronic copy (on disk) of "The Lynn Chapter." The file on disk is a WordPerfect file, I think that works for you, right (or at least I think I remember that was what you were using at school for word processing)? I want you to not only "talk back" to what I have written, but to get into the text and mess it up. You can decide how you want to do this, but the reason I am giving you the file on disk is to allow you an easy way to insert your comments and thoughts within the text itself (rather than as a separate "ending" or essay). I am inviting, in other words, a feminist disruption of my work. I want the "participant's voice" to be an integral part of this. On one hand, that's rather false since I got to choose what to write about, and there are so many things I wanted to write about that I didn't have space to include. I want your reactions to those choices (what I included and what I left out) and how I am thinking about, talking about, and presenting what I did choose to include, and your life, here.

Also, if you are uncomfortable with any of the interview excerpts (or other things) that are included, let me know. If you read something and think, "Did I really say that? I didn't mean that," change it to reflect what you did mean, or let me know that you feel misrepresented. I am very concerned that I don't misrepresent conversations, thoughts, and ideas. So, please, please, please let me know if you are in the least uncomfortable with any of the information presented from my site visit.

I've also included disks for Merry and Colleen [graduate students I talked to during the site visit]. Their words are here, too, so I want to offer them the opportunity to read and respond (if they choose to).

Ok. Once again, "whew." [. . .] I don't plan on touching the chapter after you have commented on it, unless it is to relocate the methodology stuff to the methodology chapter or to correct/change things you have instructed me to change. I want your responses to be "the last word."

Thank you, from the bottom of my feminist heart, for being so gracious with your time and energy and helping me with my work. I hope that you feel the chapter does justice to all that you do.

Gumby's Lesser Known Side Kick

I approached and wrote each ethnographic chapter differently because each site visit experience and each participant created a different context and view of the world and her work. I resisted creating a standard format or template for how these chapters would look, instead allowing the themes, structure, and writing style that I used for each chapter to emerge as I worked through the data. The only consistent element of each chapter is that I try to address three prominent sites of feminist pedagogy: teaching, leadership, and scholarship. The emphasis, amount of space, and language used regarding these three sites as they relate to Lynn's, Harriet's and Jackie's lives and work play out differently in each chapter. In an effort to offer consistency and contextualization for who these women are and work they have done, I begin each chapter with a short biographical piece about each of these teachers and scholars. These chapter prefaces, entitled "**Contextualizing the Knowing Subject**," are a way to more traditionally introduce the participant for those who are unfamiliar with her work, to provide a context for who this scholar and teacher is, and to show how her work has added to a feminist perspective in the field of composition and rhetoric. More specifically, through my ethnographic studies of these three feminists, I aspired to uncover and articulate the personal impact feminism has made in their lives; how they negotiate their feminist beliefs within the culture of the academy; how they enact their feminism in their scholarship, teaching, and leadership positions within the university community; and how they are changing the teaching of writing as a result of their and other feminists' work. What I discovered was a tremendous amount of careful, thoughtful, and critical work and self-reflection that these women produce in the name of feminism. I was continually inspired and awed by their self-critique and awareness and the astonishing, powerful work they do. My hope is that the following ethnographic studies will pay tribute to that work and the individuals who generously gave of their time and energy to help me complete this project.

CONTEXTUALIZING
THE KNOWING SUBJECT[28]

Lynn Worsham

I cannot really remember how I came to ask Lynn to participate in my project. It was probably a suggestion offered to me by my mentor in the field. Lynn is a logical choice for this project because she is a feminist and editor of one of the field's prominent journals, *JAC*.[29] What I knew of Lynn before I began close, critical readings of her publications as part of this project, was that she had co-edited a book with Susan Jarratt of feminist essays about composition practices (*Feminism and Composition Studies: In Other Words*). I was charmed by her afterword ("After Words") in that book. To me that one essay represented a model of feminist scholarship that wowed me in writing style, self-disclosure, smart connections, and critical analyses. It was this essay that brought me to Lynn's scholarship and offered me an example of how dynamic and passionate academic writing could be. Plus, the essay is just fun to read. Lynn crafts her words with a deliciousness that is too often absent from academic scholarship. As I read more of Lynn's work, I came to see her love of words and the sculpting of amazing prose as part of the signature of her scholarship.

Lynn premiered her first issue as editor of *JAC* in January 2000. That same year she (and the journal) received the prestigious "Phoenix Award" given by the Council of Editors for Learned Journals. In addition to the book she edited with Jarratt, Lynn has also co-edited books with Gary Olson (*The Kinneavy Papers* and *Race, Rhetoric, and the Postcolonial*). A strong feminist theoretical approach grounds all of her research. She is currently working on two books, *The Grammar of Complex Words: Gayatri Spivak's Rhetorical Theory* and *On the Edges of this Time: Feminisms, Rhetorics, and the Promise of Inquiry*. Lynn has also written a plethora of articles that focus on feminist rhetoric, reading, and writing theories in *JAC*, *Rhetoric Society Quarterly*, and *PRE/TEXT*, among other composition and rhetoric journals.

Currently Lynn is a professor at Southern Illinois, where she teaches graduate and undergraduate courses and edits *JAC*. She designs and teaches courses in pedagogy, cultural studies, women's studies, and rhetorical theory. For 10 years (1988–1998), she was on the faculty at University of Wisconsin, Milwaukee, teaching graduate and undergraduate courses in pedagogy, rhetoric, feminist theory, literary theory, and women's and African American literature. Although not listed on her vitae, Lynn's feminist work has a strong foundation in grassroots organizations, working with victims of sexual assault, domestic violence, and welfare reform.

Chapter Three

Lynn Worsham

Counting Ribs and Other Measures of Story Truths

Project Journal Entry. Friday, November 9, 2000:

There was a Center for the Study of Writing meeting today. Small group. Only three people there from the exec board (myself, John, and Mary). We basically went around the table and people described their research project du jour. I talked about my project, describing it as something along the lines of "a history of feminist pedagogy in the field of composition and case studies of three prominent comp/rhet feminist scholars and how they define and enact their pedagogy." One of the graduate students at the meeting asked why I was including Lynn Worsham since she was all about rhetorical theory, not pedagogy. That caught me off guard. There is that split again: rhetoric or composition, the former seen as foregrounding theory and the latter seen as foregrounding pedagogy. It sounds like the theory/practice split. I feel that, within the field, there are "the teachers of writing" and then there are "the rhetorical theorists" with a hierarchy quickly established where theory is privileged. The question asked by the graduate student got me thinking: why *did* I choose Lynn Worsham? Was it because she co-edited the book with Susan (Jarratt)? Because Kate (Ronald) suggested her? Because she is the editor of *JAC*? Because, more than any other essay in this field, I carry around her "After Words" in my back pocket as writing I want to emulate? Upon reflection, I don't know, but what the graduate student said made some sense: when I think of Lynn's work, I don't typically think of a person who writes about teaching but a person who writes about rhetorical theory.

Interview with Lynn Worsham. February 20, 2001:

Being the first feminist editor [in the field] for me is very symbolic. You know, what you were saying about your focus. That one of
your focuses is pedagogy. I really feel that my pedagogical scene
is much more about the journal than in the classroom. But also
about the field. What I can do pedagogically through the journal in
terms of letting people know what feminism is and what scholarship can be. So it is all inter-related to pedagogy.

My site visit to the University of South Florida (USF) was an amazing 3 days
filled with stories, critique, and observations. Despite having bronchitis fes-
tering in my lungs and zapping my energy, I felt invigorated, although
exhausted, at the end of each day. The openness with which Lynn brought
me into her world astonished me. The care she took to make sure I was, as
she kept putting it, "getting enough" was humbling. But, back home under
the grey winter skies of Ohio, transcribing the tapes from the site visit was
equally gratifying. Revisiting those conversations and listening to this feminist scholar and teacher reflect on her life and work felt encouraging and
uplifting. While I reviewed the tapes and transcripts, Lynn's focus and critical self-reflection impressed me. In her life, she doggedly questions how she
personally and daily colludes with systems of oppression to more actively
resist that collusion. My problem, faced with the physical reality of communicating what I was witness to, was how to create a "chapter" from this
information that was scholarly and also a reflection of the incredible work
Lynn does in the spirit of feminism—and, of course, capture the brilliance
and openness of Lynn as a human being.

Project Journal. April 22, 2001:

I started writing the Lynn chapter today. I was so excited to begin,
but then everything fell apart. After three hours of writing, the
result was nothing but schlock. False start number 1. How to dis-
till 80 single-spaced pages of transcription into what I want to say.
And what do I want to say? On my prospectus I remember Katie
writing, in the margin next to the chapter summaries, "What is
your argument for each of these chapters?" A good place to start,
although I really don't want to "argue" anything if to argue means
to position myself as having decided something definitive about
Lynn's work or feminist pedagogy, beyond proposing a more specific definition of what feminist pedagogy is and showing how
Lynn's work embodies that. I could argue that Lynn is a really
smart chick who writes mesmerizing prose and who is crazy-pas-
sionate about her feminist work. But really what I want to write is
just some sort of tribute, to communicate how important the work

she does is to me as a feminist scholar (sheesh! Why don't I just send her some frickin Hallmark card with pastel butterflies on it and some rhyme-y verse: "Dear Lynn. The card says it all. [smiley face], Kay."). Who is my audience? What do they expect me to argue? Do I write the chapter that carefully shows how Lynn's work reflects my definition of feminist pedagogy? That would certainly serve me well. Utterly pointless, and clearly biased (as opposed to obliquely biased??); in that scenario, I will see whatever I am looking for and ignore the rest, and what researcher doesn't do that? Maybe a feminist researcher? What I really want to write is about how I was inspired by all that I saw Lynn doing, as a feminist, in her work. Ugh. What a mess. So, I took a long ride on my bike. I pedaled furiously for about 20 miles, my brain churning over the long stretches of greening Ohio countryside. The cows seemed exceedingly bucolic today, which made me want to get off my bike and whack 'em, or at least chase them around a bit. Make them bellow startled moos in cow-panic. Back at the computer. No bright ideas. Just more schlock.

After transcribing the 18 hours of taped conversations and classroom observations, I poured over the transcriptions looking for connections to what I had written about in the first three chapters of my project. What I kept highlighting and annotating in these transcripts were sustained discussions of passion, critical reflection, and storytelling—not only as self-critique, but as connection both to the larger cultural systems of oppression *and* with students' realities. It was these three approaches (passion, critical reflection, storytelling) that helped me define Lynn's feminist approach to pedagogy.

The academy is very important, the scene of operation for some people. It has kept feminism alive. Everywhere else this is backlash and bad, bad stuff going on. I do think there is an unfortunate part of academia where feminism—and I have written about this—where feminism is only an academic credential [to make people attractive]. It has become fashionable and so if you can talk the talk—a gender critique or whatever—then you come to be that. That is problematic to me. [. . .] There aren't compartments, like "this is the feminist part and this is the rest of it." It is all [. . .] a way of being. [Some academics] make the distinction between politics and a way of being; that really isn't a distinction that I understand." I am the first "explicitly feminist editor of a journal in r/c"— i.e. someone whose scholarship is explicitly feminist, whose teaching is explicitly, publicly feminist. But in making that claim I was gesturing towards all those people in our field who think that they can go about being feminist in quiet, unannounced, and relatively nonpolitical ways, and it sill counts as feminism. There are those people who say that comp studies has always been feminist. It's like saying that since there have been a majority of women in comp, then the field is and always has been feminist. [. . .] It matters when explicitly feminist scholarship becomes possible in a field; it matters when an explicitly feminist editor is appointed to a major journal.

Central to Lynn's feminist pedagogy, at whatever site she is practicing, is public self-critique and the insistence of connecting her experience to theory and theory to the material reality of women's lives.[30] Often these critiques and connections manifest themselves in the form of storytelling. Although storytelling in and of itself is not necessarily a feminist pedagogical practice, stories told in certain ways can demonstrate intricate strategies of feminist pedagogy. A story told by a feminist teacher, in the way Lynn uses stories, demonstrates self-disclosure and self-critique, interrogates the norms of ideological systems, one's role in perpetuating these systems, and creates connections between classroom communities and lived experiences. Used in this way, storytelling becomes a complex strategy of feminist pedagogy.

Excerpt from The Image of Women in Literature class, February, 21, 2001:

[Reading Maxine Hong Kingston's *Warrior Woman*] I get goose bumps just talking about it. (laughing) I know! I'm weird. It's so interesting and poignant. She can give her mother's story another ending. In that sense, she claims power, the power to narrate. The power to narrate is to live a life that she can claim for her own, no one of tradition or one of a slave. The times we are reading about Maxine, you know, that she wanted to live her own life. It's a struggle. [. . .] She is taking the traditions and integrates them, but notice the way she does it. She does it by telling her own story, too. She is finally in a position that is the alternative to the "No Name Aunt" story. She is another warrior woman. She is about to bridge the difference, to find herself amid her mother's stories. [. . .] By telling the story she claims her own history, she names it, and by doing so, she claims her own story.

Lynn is an expert rhetor, a wordsmith, a spinner of captivating tales. I found it easy to listen to her. Lynn's stories move beyond parables of expected or socially sanctioned behavior. They are precise and careful acts of critical reflection; her stories are connected to her feminism because she believes careful critical reflection and self-critique are imperative to feminism. "For me (feminism) is first of all politics. First of all politics," she told me over dinner the second night of my site visit. "And yes, it is a way of being, but it becomes a way of being as you continually critique yourself and the world around you and understand how it operates to a small degree. And this is a process. It is a process through and through. It is also an epistemology, a way of being, a philosophy, a pedagogy, ethics, and it acts as a politics,

always."[31] This belief in rigorous and public self-critique plays out brilliantly in Lynn's stories.

Through her narratives, Lynn not only critiques her own location, but
calls on others to critique theirs. This strategy extends the typical feminist
critique of larger systems and structures to a personal critique. She uses this
strategy in her scholarship, in her classrooms and in her conversations. Her
stories become axes of politics, ways of connecting the political to the personal and back again: "Narrative is radical, especially when commonplace,
for it is in the interstices of the everyday that identity and experience are
produced" ("Worsham, 1998, p. 345). Lynn uses radical narrative as a way to
enact her feminism. Through her stories, whether she tells them in her classrooms, conversations, or writing, she moves students toward critical consciousness, and she pushes herself in that direction as well.

Kay: So when or how did you come to identify as a feminist? Was it
in academia at first or no?

Lynn: I was raised by a feminist. I mean, it wasn't this sort of theoretical type of thing. It was about standing up for yourself, having
economic freedom. My mother was extremely, not obsessed, but
concerned, that I would hear the message, "Do not find yourself
economically tied to anybody." To a man. I grew up, I came of
age consciously in the 1960s when all of this was going on at that
time. So I was very much aware of the larger field, issues around
women and feminist issues. And I think one of your questions
[e-mailed to Lynn before the visit] was "What was your first
public feminist act" or something like that?

Kay: Yes. Most radical.

Lynn: No. That was another question. This may perhaps be my most
radical and my first public expression of my feminism. Four
years old. My mother always had this really ambivalent relationship to being a mother. So, while we were not religious people and did not go to church, she decided one summer she was
going to send me to Vacation Bible School. And she . . .

Kay: (laughs) To try something new, maybe?

Lynn: Yeah. To get the kid out of the house. Mother's day out. So I was
sitting there learning these bible lessons and one of the lessons
was "Eve was created from Adam's rib and therefore women are
lesser." And, I can't remember, they said women have one more
rib or one less rib . . .

Kay: One more because Adam had to use one of his . . .

Lynn: Right. OK. So I proceeded to go out on the playground and
started pulling up people's shirts and counting ribs. I wanted to

have some empirical evidence. I got kicked out of Vacation Bible
School. They called my mother and had her come get me
because I was a problem child.

Kay: You weren't a blind believer. You had to prove it.

Lynn: Right. I couldn't accept the voice of authority. So basically I
have been a feminist since I was four. The academy has been
very important to me to sort of articulate, to raise my own consciousness, and articulate the importance of feminism, but it was
really much more of a community-based, social activist kind of
thing in my history. [. . .] I like activist work because it is really
where you remember what you are doing and why you are
doing it. I mean, I was only half kidding when I said my first
radical feminist act was when I was counting ribs on the playground when I was four. You know? It is the only thing I got
kicked out of!

Within this story of Lynn's first public feminist act of counting ribs,
there is another story imbedded: one of the biblical tale of how woman came
to be, from a piece of Adam's rib. The patriarchal story that dooms woman
to inferior status (made not from God, but from the mere mortal, Adam) is
the fodder for Lynn's own feminism and, consequently, her story. The other
story peeking through is one of her own mother, and her "ambiguous relationship" to the patriarchal institution of marriage, communicated to Lynn
overtly and repeatedly in stories, maxims, and the hard evidence of her
mother's own lived experience. It occurs to me, as I think about the stories
I have read or heard Lynn tell, that this embedding of stories is not uncommon. In her "After Words" she tells the uncomfortable story of her childhood caretaker, "Blue Betty." The story pricks uncomfortably my White-
anglo-saxon-liberal consciousness because "Blue Betty" is a nickname given
to an African American nurse maid by her petite White charge, the power of
naming assumed by a small girl-child. Within that story is the story her
mother tells others of how "Blue Betty" got her name. Through the telling
and retelling, both by Lynn's mother and now by Lynn, the public display
of shame, and the interrogation of that shame, is laid open, a way of not
allowing the wound to fester any longer, but to lance it and analyze one's
own role in the infection.

"LET ME TELL YOU A STORY . . . "

The centrality of storytelling as self-critique points to a significance in first-
person accounts that moves beyond the romantic to the political. In a story

that Lynn tells her "Image of Women in Literature" course the day I observe, she describes how her mother's method of oral history was passed to Lynn, an example offered to the class in how to critically reflect on the role of storytelling in their own lives.

> Excerpt from Lynn's The Imagine of Women in Literature undergraduate class, February 21, 2001.
>
> What is the role of storytelling in your lives? This is important. I want you to think about that. What stories did you mothers tell you about who you were or the people in the family? My mother wasn't a greatly organized person. She had all the family photos in these old shirt boxes. When she was working—cooking or ironing or engaged in some other task around the house – I would dig through the boxes and pick out two or three pictures. I would take them to her and say, "Tell me the story." [. . .] It was a way of handing down history and memory to me. And that's one connection I have with this book [*Warrior Woman* by Maxine Hong Kingston].

In her narrative about her mother's photo history, Lynn loops back around to the role of storytelling in the text the class was reading (*Woman Warrior*). In both texts, the lines between histories become fuzzy and unfocused. Whose stories are being told: the mother's? The daughter's? The narrator's? In *The Red Tent*, a novel that reclaims and rewrites the stories of biblical women, the narrator/main character states, "I am not certain whether my earliest memories are truly mine, because when I bring them to mind, I feel my mother's breath on every word" (Diamant, 1997). Stories such as those told by Lynn, Kingston, and Diamant go beyond the mere act of telling tales that teach a single lesson or exemplify the heroic nature of families and kin. Instead they are stories that point to the corrosive effects of patriarchal power and the intersections of race, class, gender, and other traditionally marginalized perspectives.

In "After Words," Lynn asks herself and her audience, "What are the stories that shame us personally?" Stretching those stories across the loom of critical analysis, weaving together the sharp shards and smooth satins of personal identity and history demonstrates the art of storytelling as feminist pedagogical strategy. Michelle Fine and Linda Brodkey (1992) write, "The stories that document our lives tell what we find worth remembering and contemplating and sharing" (p. 77). A story used in the context of feminist pedagogy goes beyond this simple sharing to connections, critical consciousness, and interrogation of both ideology and self. Stories, as within Lynn's classes and writings, critique the patriarchal forces as they play out in the broader culture, in classrooms, and in our lived experiences, giving light to and naming our shame. Through our stories we interrogate the moments when we are the *least* feminist, exercising feminist critique of ourselves and others. "Storytelling is the way we compose our lives; all identity, all social construction, begins with narrative" (Gibson et al., 2000, p. 71).

> *Excerpt from interview with Lynn:* I was raised by a very patriarchal man who didn't believe that women go to college, much less get a Ph.D. I paid my way. My mother helped me. She went to work when I started talking about college so she could. My dad never contributed anything because he did not believe that girls go to school. Girls exist to serve men. And so, even going to school was a radical feminist act—and to stay in school and go all the way. I didn't feel that it was against my father; I felt like I was doing what I needed to do for me, but there was a lot of opposition. When I was working on my dissertation, I was really broke and I asked my dad for $600 to pay tuition—a *loan*, not a gift. And he said no. "If you want to go to secretarial school, I'll pay your way. But I will not give you $600, even as a loan." [. . .] It was a crystallizing moment to me. He had long lost his control over me because I had been economically independent from him for awhile, but you could tell there was this kind of glaze over his eyes. He just didn't understand what in the world I was doing. Why didn't I get serious, get married, and have babies like any regular person? But I do think, in a lot of ways, getting a Ph.D. and surviving and doing what I have done is certainly a radical act, given the norm of my family.

Lynn's narratives show her exerting the right to act, to speak, to tell the stories that have the potential for discomfort. Many times her stories portray various positions, thereby complicating the reality represented in the narrative. In her essay "Epistemophiliac," Lynn asks, "How will we *not* fail for those whom feminism would work, if the old, familiar language is impossible and the new does not yet exist? How do we speak to each other now, in the interim, in this strange in-between space?" (p. 42) Her answer, within that essay, is to "jam the machine" and "engage in wild improvisation." Although she does not say so there, her acts of storytelling are ways to do just that, ways of exposing those strangely murky, in-between spaces, and connecting the academic work with the realities of women's lives, creating a feminist epistemology. Rather than "women's ways of knowing," the epistemology that is created is one of "woman as knowing subject," a dangerous move in a world where women are denied the position of knowledge-makers.

Feminist storytelling as an act of pedagogy embodies these characteristics of epistemology. It embodies careful listening and critique, using personal experience as disruption. Consequently, a new site of knowledge-building emerges. New meaning is created from the deeper structures of women's lived experiences. Daly (1989) names the places of deeper meaning "critical memory"—it is where women's realities exist because they have no place in the patriarchal culture's master narratives.

Project Journal. March 3, 2001

> Yesterday I went to hear Jackie Royster deliver the keynote address at the Race and Gender Symposium. She talked about her research to recover African American Women rhetors and their words, and said she was writing their stories. Her research was a compilation of history and theory and all sorts of cross-disciplinary work, but she was also creating their stories: adding their voices to history. Again the storytelling theme. Maybe this will be the focus of the ethnographic studies: connecting our lives to our work with stories; sharing ourselves with our students with stories; the stories that shape our scholarship; the stories we tell in our scholarship. It made me go back and dig through The Red Tent. I found what I was looking for. "But the other reason women wanted daughters [beyond helping them with work] was to keep their memories alive. Sons did not hear their mothers' stories after weaning. So I was the one. My mother and my mother-aunties told me endless stories about themselves. No matter what their hands were doing, holding babies, cooking, spinning, weaving, they filled my ears" (3). So, here is to the stories we tell and the meaning that is gathered from them, perhaps the meaning that is created by them.

. . . OF THE RIB-COUNTER GROWN UP (LEADERSHIP AS PEDAGOGY

Through watching Lynn work and reading her words, I realized there is little separation among teaching, leadership, and scholarship. She sees all three sites as opportunities to enact radical, pro-active, *visible* feminist beliefs. In her work as editor of the *JAC*, Lynn is not only the first adamantly feminist editor of a composition journal, but the first woman editor of *JAC*. She embodies feminist leadership as pedagogy in her work with graduate students, the way she envisions and constructs the journal, and in her approach to reviewing and accepting articles for publication. Lynn wants to create a journal that provides a stellar example of what a scholarly journal can be, not just because she is passionate about writing and rhetorical theory, but because she knows she is providing a model of what a feminist edited journal looks like. She wants it to look as close to perfect as she can get it. As Colleen Connolly, a staff editor of *JAC* and one of Lynn's protégés told me, "As a representative of feminist scholarship, she needs the perfection; the disruption [caused by her overt feminism] makes people uncomfortable. It's Lynn's idea to *change* the conversations. The way to gain credibility with that is the professionalism in the text itself, in the editing. So we are hyper aware of text citations and works cited. Little details like that. That adds to her credibility, the journal's credibility, and the credibility of her feminist politics."

Although *JAC* is not a feminist journal, Lynn has a feminist mission for it: "I wanted to do this because I am a feminist and I wanted an opportunity to publish work that foregrounds the politics of difference." Feminist journals have traditionally been a "crucial vehicle" for the production of feminist knowledge (Secrist, 1989, p. 217). They first sprang from collaborative work between the feminist activist and academic communities, working to maintain the connections between grassroots work and life in the academy.[32] Although today feminist journals are more specific to academic feminist issues and theories, they are still primarily associated with Women's Studies as a discipline, something that makes a feminist editor of *JAC*, or any academic journal, unique. Although Lynn's editorship will not create a feminist journal out of *JAC* per se, her work foregrounds issues of feminism such as identity issues and cultural theory. Because editors act as gatekeepers to new ideas and theories within any given field, having a feminist editor of a field-specific journal is significant. Even more than gatekeepers, editors bring forth new epistemologies. "Scholarly journals [. . .] provide a legitimization of knowledge by the decisions that are made on what to print" (Altbach, 1987, p. 177). In light of this power to legitimize certain ideas and theories, a feminist at the helm becomes even more significant.

Initially I was not considering *JAC* as a site of feminist pedagogy or feminist scholarship. When I embarked on the site visit, I was more interested in teaching, and at that time I defined *teaching* narrowly: what went on in a classroom. Although Lynn certainly is a feminist teacher within her classrooms, practicing feminist pedagogy in dynamic ways, I also saw how she translated those pedagogical beliefs to her *JAC* work. Both Merry Perry, the associate editor of *JAC*, and Colleen Connolly, assistant editor of *JAC*, connected Lynn's feminism with mentoring graduate students. Colleen told me, "*JAC* has to be as perfect as possible, but she is forgiving at the moments when you aren't. She uses (those moments) as a pedagogical experience, not to shame or humiliate. She challenges us to be conscious, be in the moment. Don't just answer, but think about it. She is conscious and she wants you to be conscious, too." In Colleen's comment, one can see that Lynn is asking her students to interrogate the work as she does, self-disclosing her concerns, striving for the highest quality without shaming or casting blame. From Lynn, both Colleen and Merry said, they have learned what feminist scholarship and mentorship is about.

Although Lynn's standards for the *JAC* work are high, both students feel Lynn treats them more like colleagues than graduate students. "She treats me as an equal; she praises me and is very respectful," said Merry. "To me all of these things are feminist because she *does* have more power than me; she's higher than me on the totem pole, but she treats me like an equal." Lynn also encourages collaboration among the staff of *JAC*. "People do what they are good at and what they like to do," Merry said. "We make assignments according to interests. There is no hierarchy of jobs." What makes that style of leadership feminist? Is it feminist even if someone else says, "That isn't feminist. That is just human decency or being a good boss." Many times there is resistance to naming a strategy or approach as "feminist," similar to the resistance of naming oneself as a feminist or naming the practices one engages in as feminist. Most of this resistance stems from the dominant culture's inability to see feminism as anything but one dimensional: gender issues, more specifically women's rights. But anyone who practices or identifies as a feminist or feminist teacher knows that it is much richer and more complex than those flat definitions.

Personal Journal: January 22, 2001

> Ryan [a former student] had Elizabeth and me over for a birthday dinner tonight. Steph [his roommate and also a former student] is such a bullheaded German woman (are we all that way?). We were talking about the election and I was ranting about Dubya's first official presidential act: repelling family planning moneys to international agencies that even whisper the word "abortion." Steph turned to Elizabeth and said, "Are you a feminist, too?" So, I clattered out my little soap box and asked Steph, who doesn't consider herself a feminist, "Do you think women should get the same amount of money for doing the same work as men? Do you think women should be able to decide when, if, or whether to have children? Do you think women should be have equal access to education? So why don't you consider yourself a feminist?" She said, "Yes, but that isn't being a feminist. That is just being a smart woman. I wouldn't mind if all feminists were like you Kay, but most of them aren't. I mean they are out there screaming on street corners. It isn't productive." At which point Elizabeth practically rolled onto the floor in laughter because, indeed, last weekend I was out there on a street corner in SinCity with the local NOW folks screaming anti-Bush slogans while waving a sign that read, "Get Bush Out of My Uterus." I said, "I most certainly am that kind of feminist." Steph only knows me as a feminist because I name myself as such in my classrooms; my "teacher self" didn't fit her definition of what a feminist was (the screaming lunatic variety).

> Steph's response to my question about why she didn't consider herself feminist when she believed in feminist principles or issues was, "That isn't being a feminist; that is just being a smart

woman." Her rejoinder reminds me of people's reaction to my definition of feminist pedagogy. "That's not feminist pedagogy; that's
just good teaching." Both responses seem to stem from the same
problem: negative stereotypes of what feminism is and what feminists are and unwillingness to embrace the label. The dominant
culture certainly has done a stellar job in getting people to men-
tally sprint in the opposite direction whenever they hear the "f"
word.

Early on in this project, while examining definitions of feminist pedagogy, I realized the themes were similar to how I approached feminist leadership or being a facilitator of a feminist activist group. If I substituted
organization for *classroom* and *volunteer/group member* for *student*, the
themes represented a feminist approach to leadership. Pedagogy as leadership may not seem like an earth-shattering revelation, but this connection is
significant to me. As a feminist academic, unlike when I am working with
activist groups, I rarely feel like I am doing enough for the cause—for the
material realities of women's, and other traditionally marginalized people's,
existence. Analyzing the way Lynn approaches her leadership position as
editor of *JAC* reinforced the connections I found between leadership and
pedagogy, between activism and teaching.

. . . MAKING HER MARK
ON THE WORLD/WORDS

At the site of Lynn's *JAC* work, her feminist pedagogical approach with the
graduate students who work with her to create the journal overlap with the
pedagogical philosophies used when choosing the types of articles the journal publishes. Lynn understands that the journal is a site of pedagogy for her
peers and colleagues, where they can read about new ideas and learn what it
means to be teachers and scholars. Because of this matrix where students,
colleagues, new writers, new ideas, and the physical product of the journal
intersect, feminist pedagogical themes emerge not just in Lynn's interactions
with graduate students on staff, but in her work with authors who submit
work to the journal, and in the decisions she makes regarding the content
and form of a journal.

Part of Lynn's passion about *JAC* is creating a scholarly journal that is
not dull or boring. "It [scholarly publication] can be something else [besides
dry and dense]. And that's my attraction to editing the journal; scholarly
writing can be *fun* to read. That's one of the reasons we have the color
cover," Lynn told me. But clearly Lynn's passion goes beyond the dynamic

colors of the glossy covers. The care with which she edits also speaks to her intense delight of writing, words, and scholarship. "I like to get down in the middle of the words and see how they work together, how the words radiate and resonate." Looking at my notes, I can't remember whether this comment was about her own writing or her work of editing other people's writing. In reflecting on Lynn's work, I believe it is both.

Lynn sees her position as editor, and her identity as a feminist editor, as important because she can influence the shape of the field in large or small ways. In fact, her being a feminist editor who is committed to foregrounding feminist issues in the publication she edits is a first for the field of comp/rhet. This historical first—and Lynn's responsibility for shaping the field—cannot be underestimated when it comes to figuring the prominence of feminist theories in composition.

Lynn told me she wanted to be editor of *JAC* because she wanted an opportunity to publish work that foregrounds the politics of difference (race, gender, and class, among others). Looking over *JAC* under Lynn's tutelage (perhaps because the journal is like a student, where dialogues occur and new knowledge is created, both personal and professional), it is easy to see her commitment to "the politics of difference." There are articles on cultural critique, gender, race, activism, and community. The word *pedagogy* appears frequently.[33]

In her introduction to the premier issue, Lynn writes, "The digitally created image you see on *JAC*'s cover references both tool and technique; but, more importantly, it is almost self-reflective in its subtle suggestions of a history of mark-making implements, a history of difference that (as in this image) places one technology (the mezzotint rocker) in dialogue with another (the computer and the pixel) in order to achieve a powerful effect" (p. vii). This metaphor can be drawn out to just as much success when analyzing Lynn's stance as a feminist editor, making her "mark" on the field, using technology of the color cover, to draw new readers in, and the computer to create a focused dialogue that reflects her feminist beliefs of careful critique integrated with personal action.

"I want *JAC* to be a place where women and feminists can publish, and also people of color. That is really important. I also value my working relationships with the people I work with and that is also another pedagogical scene or experience. A lot of these people haven't worked in this type of relationship where they have had a feminist or female professor." Lynn is keenly aware of her role as mentor to graduate students on staff and to young feminist scholars whom she has never met except through a submission to *JAC*. Lynn spends precious spare time to help new scholars become published, to help them hone and polish their work, so that it can be presented by *JAC*. She told me she often works one on one, via e-mail or phone conversations, with young scholars who submit work that needs to be revised. "I get articles in that I think would not even get a look from editors because they are feminist, but they are going to get a look now. It doesn't mean I will automatically publish them, but they are going to get a look. And hopefully a review. I think that is all very symbolically important." Lynn gives these articles "a closer look" because she wants to publish more work by women and because she likes the feminist argument they are making in their work. Still, many of these articles need major revisions before they can be considered. "I am working with women writers all the time who submitted work that wasn't exactly right; they need to elaborate their argument, so I work with them on revision. I help to get them to the point where they can publish." The generosity of mentoring individual scholars when she has never met is even more astonishing when considered within the context of the yeoman's task of putting together a single issue of *JAC* where Lynn plays the part of copyeditor, layout and cover designer, advertising and marketing representative, subscription service, acquisitions and submissions staff, production and typesetting worker, all the while teaching and writing as a full-time professor. "It's like writing a book every six months," Lynn said. In addition to the logistics of putting "the book" together, there is the careful consideration of content. "I want to publish good scholarship. It doesn't mean it has to be feminist, but I really do want to make sure that the feminist scholarship that comes along gets a fair hearing."

Personal Journal: April 23, 2001

> I got my reviews back from *Pedagogy* today [in response to an article I had submitted about feminist pedagogy]. They want me to revise and resubmit, which I am more than happy to do. One of the reviews was very helpful and gave me extensive comments for revision. It was a pleasure to read. The other review, a vitriolic condemnation, consisted of two very short paragraphs. "This piece is unsophisticated, both in rhetorical and practical terms. It is unsubstantiated, uncontextualized, untheorized. [. . .] I know that I am being harsh here, but this manuscript probably represents the worst of the 'teaching stories' that purport some modicum of scientific approach." And on. So very hostile. I actually laughed out loud when I read it, a big feminist bark of surprise. Who is typically so hostile and resistant to the mere idea that such a thing as feminist pedagogy exists? I was very proud of the editors (both of them women) for giving me a chance to revise/resubmit after that response. Even though the first was positive and encouraging, the second was so negative it would have been easy for them to say "bag it!" It made me think of Lynn when she told me sometimes she sees the virtue of a manuscript even if it gets a bad review. And that she wants to help feminist scholars be published. It gave me hope that perhaps there are

other women (dare I say feminists?) who are also out there doing
the same thing.

When an editor gives space and voice to feminist perspectives in a journal, especially in a journal that is not identified specifically as "feminist" or
associated with Women's Studies, she is engaging in a type of activism, albeit
within the privileged sphere of higher education. In her book *Talking About
a Revolution*, Sattler explores the work of feminists within educational institutions. At the beginning of the project, she was skeptical about whether
feminism could even exist, let alone change much of anything, within academia. "I never considered feminism an academic subject. Feminism is what I
did when I wasn't in school" (p. 19). This seems not an uncommon critique
or tension. Is academic feminism working toward feminist change or is it
just colluding with the privileged system of higher education, limited to a
sexy theory that will soon become passé and abandoned for the next theoretical approach du jour? The disconnect between academic feminist theory
and the material realities of women's lives external to the academy concerns
many academic feminists. "As academic feminism becomes respectable, it
becomes less connected, more abstract, and increasingly remote from everyday sexual oppressions. [. . .] One becomes complacent when one lives in
one's head" (Middleton, 1993, p. 7).

Others make the argument that social movements arise from rhetoric
(Kohrs Campbell), and an academic journal could be considered a primary
site of such new rhetoric. Although feminist theories provide a voice for an
empowering ideology that has the potential to change the way people envision the world and (hopefully) work for change, the theories often stagnate
in the academy instead of moving into the lives of women outside that privileged arena. Secrist (1989) asks, "Can institutions constructed by patriarchal
ideology be used to oppose it?" (p. 215). Feminist editors (like Lynn) and
feminist journals hope that the answer to that question is a resounding
"Yes!" Scholars such as Lynn know the often hard road of being "out" feminists in the patriarchy of the academy, choosing when, how, and whether to
enact their feminist beliefs, always measuring, just as grassroots activists do,
what the best approach will be (liberal? radical?) depending on a given context. Lynn passes this lesson on to the students she mentors. Stated one such
student, "One of the things Lynn has taught me is she always says you have
to be really smart with your feminist politics. It goes back to the rhetorical
nature of the world. You have to know, where, and how to name yourself as
a feminist. [. . .] One of the greatest things about Lynn is that she takes a
stand for feminist politics. She is not afraid to say no and stand behind it and
be firm in her resistance" (Connolly). In Lynn's *JAC* work, the interconnectedness of leadership, scholarship, and writing creates a pedagogy that
finds itself modeling change, disruption, and empowerment beyond the
walls of a traditional classroom.

WITH A SHARP EYE OF CRITIQUE,
WEAVING CAPTIVATING TALES

Because Lynn gets no teaching reduction for her work on the journal, she has to juggle her full teaching schedule with the arduous *JAC* work. Still, her passion for teaching and her commitment to her students do not wane. "I am still a full-time teacher, a very committed teacher," Lynn states. She cares seriously about her classroom work and enacting her feminist beliefs within the courses she teaches. For me the classroom observations of Lynn were some of the most important witnessing moments. These were the hours where I could see feminist pedagogy *in action* as opposed to hearing it described by Lynn (her philosophy of editing *JAC*) or her graduate students (reflecting on their work with her). It was during these classroom hours that I caught a glimpse of how Lynn's beliefs of feminist pedagogy translated into classroom work.

But my way of approaching those classroom observations using the idea of 16 feminist pedagogical themes caused me some researcher shame. I was not overt with Lynn, Harriet, and Jackie about the specifics of the 16 themes when I went to the site visits. I did not want them to alter their actions or self-edit conversations due to awareness of how I was trying to articulate what feminist pedagogy was. This lack of disclosure was not a smart move.

To complicate this misstep in my methodology, other people I was depending on for feedback on the project felt uncomfortable with the themes. My mentor, Kate Ronald, was the first to bother me with this issue. After reading a draft of my second chapter where I outline themes, Kate wrote to me, "I am worried that you're going to wrench these three women (Lynn, Harriet, and Jackie) into the 16 categories." This concern of using the themes as a measuring stick with which to whack the feminists when I was studying came back after my site visit with Lynn.

Project Journal Entry. March 28, 2001:

> I met with Kate today to talk about the prospectus. While I was talking with her Kate said she had "heard through the grapevine" that Lynn felt I was using the [16 feminist pedagogy] themes as a checklist, at test to see whether or not she was a feminist teacher. What a crushing blow. Kate was quick to say that the news came through someone else, and that Lynn didn't say anything directly to Kate about it when they talked at 4Cs, but that she thought I needed to know. I felt wretched. Of course I am not using the rubric as a test, but to *reinforce* the themes by noting when/how they are practiced. And, as I have coded the transcriptions (from

Lynn's classroom visits), it's clear the themes do provide a great working definition of feminist pedagogy and in very dynamic ways. It's exciting to see. So, I need to email Lynn. I also need to forward her the themes so she can see what they are like. Oh, ugh!

E-mail to Lynn. March 30, 2001

I met with Kate yesterday to regroup before I head off to see Harriet M. She said that you were nervous about the rubric I was using for the classroom observations. What was passed on to me (via Kate) was that you may have felt I was "judging" you—as a feminist teacher—against the themes of feminist pedagogy.

I feel horrible if that accurately represents your feeling. It makes my stomach hurt! So, I decided that I needed to email and explain the rubric. I probably should have done this when I was there, but I didn't want to show you the rubric before I observed the classes in case you would consciously or unconsciously have the rubric in mind while you were teaching. I desperately want you to understand that the rubric is not meant to "measure" whether the people I observe are feminist teachers. Rather it is to check my definition of feminist pedagogy against what is being practiced. That is to say, the rubric is what is being challenged when I observe classes. [. . .] I compiled the themes to try to get some sort of working (and more comprehensive and collaborative) definition of feminist pedagogy; an attempt at historical representation and organization. Rather than using the rubric to measure a teacher (to see whether he/she is a feminist teacher), I want to discover whether these themes reflect how feminist teachers are practicing their pedagogy. That is to say, I want to test this definition of feminist pedagogy. How does this historical definition represent the reality? To figure out whether the themes accurately represent feminist pedagogy, I use them when I observe classes. I am not only looking at the themes, but also looking for new themes that may emerge. My main questions are:

Are there any themes I am missing in this representation of feminist pedagogy?

Are there themes currently on the list that really shouldn't be?
Are there themes that should be collapsed or merged?
Rather than using the rubric to measure the teacher, I am actually trying to test the themes/rubric. Does that make any sense?

[. . .]

It seems to me that the themes—and the rubric—represent the theory and the observations represent the practice. And of course, the themes are only part of that. They are one tool I am using to ground a part of the research. As you know, I am also looking at feminist pedagogy as leadership/mentoring and feminist pedagogy as scholarship.

I don't know if any of this makes sense — or makes you less nervous (if you were nervous before). I definitely feel a sense of doom when I think of you feeling "judged" by my approach. I have such deep admiration for your work, your teaching, your scholarship, and the way you enact your feminist beliefs. I know that you had to afford me a lot of blind trust to allow me into your life to take notes and examine your work. I can't express how much I appreciate that, how much I admire you for that, how grateful I am. Not just because this furthers my project, but because it also furthers my hope of what it can be like to be a feminist in the academy.

Perhaps I wasn't as overt as I should have been regarding the rubric. In hindsight I should have shared the 16 themes—the working definition of feminist pedagogy—with you after I had observed the classes. How could have I done this differently so you wouldn't have felt nervous or judged? It would really help me to hear your thoughts so I don't screw up as I move on to other site visits.

Project Journal Entry. April 10, 2001:

I got an email from Lynn today [in response to the one I sent explaining the rubric]. What a relief! I had been so nervous. It was a short email. She didn't have time to answer all my questions. But, she assured me she wasn't nervous or upset. Whew. I feel a tremendous weight has been lifted.

Response from Lynn after reading this chapter:

About your project journal entry: You still don't have a representation of my concern very clearly stated. I didn't know anything about your 16 themes while you were here on the site visit. I heard about them after the fact from [a colleague]. I was perplexed that you didn't discuss them with me, if not before the visit then after. Why didn't I tell you that I was nervous about your approach? You didn't tell me what your approach was. I don't know what the "proper" thing to do is, what a researcher is supposed to do about such disclosure. But it didn't feel very "feminist" to me to be kept in the dark about the measures through which I was being interpreted. Again, if it was not proper to tell me up-front, then it might have been a better plan to tell me afterwards just before you left, in some sort of "debriefing" session.

The journal entries, e-mail exchanges, and Lynn's response to my analysis chapter show that not only was there a problem with my research approach, a blunder I am willing to take full responsibility for, but there was trepidation about the themes. The first problem was the skeptical question, "What makes these things feminist?" Even after answering that somewhat satisfactorily ("because the scholars identified them as such, although no one scholar compiled them *all* in one definition; that only has come about after historical research"), the next concern was, "Is this list going to be used to measure whether or not someone is a feminist teacher?" I tried to explain that the list of themes was what I was testing in my research, hoping to document *how* this reflected a more complex definition of feminist pedagogy, not whether teachers were feminist teachers. Nevertheless, the rhetoric of how I talked about the themes caused discomfort. "Was it a checklist?" "No, a rubric," I insisted. A rubric, for some, still implied a sort of evaluation because, in this field, we typically use rubric as a description of how we are going to evaluate student writing. In other words, a rubric typically represents a descriptive list to help teachers make grading more equitable (e.g., "An 'A' paper is one in which . . . A 'B' paper is one in which, . . ." followed by a specific criteria that needs to be present to afford a certain "grade". Because of this, people heard rubric and many times the quickest association was evaluation. However, the actual definition of *rubric* is one of explanation, description, or categorization, not evaluation. There was no hierarchy to any of the themes I had identified. Neither was there any conscious attempt on my part to suggest that "a good feminist teacher" will embody X number of themes in one class. My objective was to see whether these themes measured up when feminist teachers were teaching, leading, and writing. After receiving Lynn's e-mail, I knew I had made a wrong decision in not sharing the themes with her (and others). If I were to do the research again, I would use the historical definition/themes to begin a conversation about what feminist pedagogy is.

SHE SHAMELESSLY AND PROUDLY TOLD

After analyzing the sites of leadership (with Lynn's *JAC* work) and teaching (in the traditional classroom sense), I moved to looking at scholarship, the words Lynn herself had written, as a site of feminist pedagogy. When considering Lynn's own writing, I am compelled to return to the theme of "the stories that shame us," which I mentioned at the first part of this chapter.

With her own writing, in her own words, the richness of her stories are a nimbus over the exacting structure of a strong feminist perspective. In this most personal site of scholarship as pedagogy, the care Lynn takes to reflect on the stories she tells is magnified and illuminated by her delicately constructed rhetoric. Within the stories of her scholarship, there are not only the overt layers of narratives told and examined, but the meta-stories that are the intricately designed paragraphs, weaving theory with practice with intellectual rigor. As with her teaching and leadership, when I read Lynn's writing, I see intense attention to detail, the careful crafting of words, rhetoric, and ideas. Lynn's passion for putting words together in scintillating ways produces some of the most beautiful and powerful prose in the field.

Because of her public identification as a feminist, Lynn understands that her work will be judged, first and foremost, as "feminist scholarship," and therefore she works excruciatingly hard to make her published work a positive, passionate, and proud example. Lynn's commitment to writing from a strong feminist perspective, scholarship that overtly and unashamedly uses the "f" word, results in jarring slams against the dominant culture's resistance to feminist ideas and perspectives. One of the most telling and poignant examples of this was her experience publishing *Feminism and Composition Studies: In Other Words*. She wrote about that experience in her essay "Working Titles and Entitlement(s)," in the form of a careful rhetorical analysis of the proposed title (rejected by the MLA press) and the revised title. Her analysis focused on a critique of the power of naming, extending to the publication board's perceived threat of an uppity and assuming maverick brand of feminism, a threat they felt was spoken in the proposed title (*Between Feminism and Composition Studies: Words Without Shame*).

In this article, beyond the careful rhetorical and feminist critique of the review committee's reactions to the book's proposed title, the act of writing about the experience was a feminist act of self-disclosure. This public declamation exposed the inner workings of the publication process and how a feminist voice, throwing itself against that patriarchal structure, is a radical act of naming. In one of my interviews with Lynn, she offered a broader perspective of this experience of entitlement and naming as well as editorial power and the politics of publication.

[When receiving feedback from MLA after submitting a proposal for the book] there were several comments saying "This is too feminist." The problem with it, and this is a quote, is that it was "listing towards feminism." And we [Susan Jarratt and Lynn] were commissioned to do a book on composition and feminism and the response was that it was too feminist? That is the kind of resistance, backlash. And so if we don't have women who are at least sympathetic towards feminism or men who are sympathetic towards feminism in positions of decision-making, you don't know what kind of work is going to get turned down or never even see the light of day. So that is important. [. . .] But the thing we need to remember is that the book made it into print. While there may have been people who didn't like it and didn't really want it published, it did get published and it got published substantially how Susan and I conceived it. But it was a long, hard process. So just the very fact that the editor of *JAC* is a feminist is symbolically important because I would have liked to have that symbol when I was a student. I want to emphasize that it isn't just a symbolic point, but it is a pedagogical point, right? It's instructive. There is a lot of power in that, and in any editorial position, in that you are pointing to whatever to say "This is significant."

It interests me, after reading the "Working Titles" essay, that *shame* was in the original title that Susan and Lynn proposed for the book. As stated earlier, shame is an issue that surfaces more than once in Lynn's work: in the stories she tells (interrogating shame) and in her work with graduate students (constructing power so that it does not shame). In the "Entitlement" article, and in the story of Lynn's experience with MLA, the issue of shame appears again, but this time with a different twist. Shame in these contexts (the proposed book title and the subsequent article that tells the story of the book title) points to a personal and collective feminist rejection of shame imposed by the patriarchy. In telling the story of how the people at MLA responded to the proposed title, and the proposed title itself, there is a rejection of ideological forces that would impose shame. Instead, the stories are told "without shame," a brazen, sassy even, rebuke of patriarchal propriety: "I/We will not feel ashamed for this work, these voices, these words," is what the proposed title declares.

Sociolinguists and anthropologists have long written about the distinction between shame and guilt, both related to issues of "face" in discourse practices.[34] Shame, they argue, is public, and guilt is private. Both shame and guilt are products of our internalization of ideology and what we are told is normal, proper, and good. When we publicly transgress those norms, we are shamed, in effect enduring a public finger-wagging or humiliation.

Guilt, however, is a personal and internalized reaction to transgressing ideological norms. Guilt is a form of internalized shame, where we self-police our actions and behavior and feel guilty when we do not measure up.[35] Although some argue that guilt also distinguishes itself from shame by relying on a personal belief system, rather than a more public, cultural belief system, those personal beliefs, values, and actions that make us feel guilty when we do not live up to our own expectations come from a cultural ideology.

Feminists, then, not only refuse to feel guilt for, or refuse to apologize for, stepping outside the boundaries of what the dominant culture has defined as female or feminine, but they also work to exorcise shame from their consciousness, a public act of defiance against White supremacist patriarchal ideology. In her words and work, Lynn offers two ways to exorcise shame: publicly picking through with careful critical self-analysis the stories that shame us, and refusing the imposition of shame imposed by the patriarchal status quo for not being feminine enough or female enough, for being sassy, uppity, and vociferous about our feminist beliefs.

Shame is a way that ideology overrides lack of personal guilt. It is when we don't self-police, when we resist ideology enough to not feel guilty, that shame then becomes a check of the ideological norms. Even if someone has not internalized the norms enough to abide by them personally, publicly they will be called on to do so or risk shame. In both the proposed title ("Without Shame") and in her storytelling ("tell the stories that shame"), the end result is to call into question the cultural wagging finger, to protest against it, to interrogate the moment of shame and question what ideological structures have caused the shame *and* what actions have produced the shameful moment. Those actions of naming or writing through shame herald the power of feminist transgression and its threat to cultural hegemony.

In the context of Lynn's proposed title, *Between Feminisms and Composition Studies: Words Without Shame,* shame becomes shamelessness, reflecting an unapologetic feminist approach. In the patriarchal empire, feminism is a cause for shame where "shame pre-positions" people in "a highly stratified, meritocratic social order" ("Working Titles and Entitlements" 1997, p. 25). People in authority traditionally cast those without power as being riddled with errors if they do not march in lock step with the defined ideology. Therefore, avoiding shame or being shameless can be seen as a feminist strategy for transgression. In addition to the title evoking ideas of unapologetic feminism, it can be read as pointing to a conversation *between* equal representatives: a feminist belief system and the world of composition studies, although the latter is traditionally female-dominated, inherently male-controlled (see chap. 2 on representation of female scholars in composition journals). After the colon, the title teases us by hinting that the texts between the covers will engage in a feminist critique of the relationship between the distinct and perhaps opposing viewpoints of composition studies and feminism(s).

"Between" can be the crevices separating the boundaries or borders that have kept women, and specifically feminists, out of epistemology in general and out of composition scholarship specifically. Feminism seizes the power to name the between. The proud, public, shameless claim of feminism or feminist identity does not necessarily mortar up the between, but creates a foot bridge, a path, by which to create conversations over the between. Even in my own project, in researching feminist pedagogy and rescuing it from the stereotype of an overbearing feminist pushing her ideology onto unsuspecting students, I hope to engage in an act of naming the between. I am trying to forge through the thick underbrush of negative stereotypes about feminist pedagogy to articulate a useful and meaningful pedagogical theory.

Project Journal Entry. April 3, 2001

I tried to nail Harriet down today on her definition of feminist pedagogy. She carries mostly negative ideas around about it: nurturing, maternal, touchy-feely. It reminded me immediately of coming across Lynn's description of "feminist pedagogy of maternal nurturance." I think it is in her pedagogical violence article. And then I think of Kate, stating she was uneasy about the term "feminist pedagogy." It seems most people I have encountered have a real hesitancy to embrace "feminist pedagogy." It feels as if there is a dominant understanding of feminist pedagogy as some sort of watered down critical pedagogy with an inherently "feminine" twist (un-rigorous, nurturing, womb-like). Critical pedagogy is good. Liberatory pedagogy is acceptable. Feminist pedagogy is somehow problematic. Even in the graduate level Women's Studies course about "Feminist Pedagogy" that I sat in on last summer, the working definition seemed to be some sort of CR-group model of teaching where everyday we had to "check in" and make sure everyone's ideas and feelings were "validated." It felt like a feminine pedagogy, not feminist pedagogy. But in my definition, an amalgamation of definitions I find outside of comp, there is nothing really "feminine." As a woman, or as a feminist, I have never been accused of being "nurturing" or "maternal" in that way some people think is "inherently female." At least in my conscious memory. I remember, as a child, being chided because I wasn't feminine enough: "Kay! Ladies don't sit that way!" So the idea of socialized femininity, like maternal nurturance, being associated with feminism, even feminist pedagogy, seems foreign to me. Why is that so much a part of how some folks think of feminist pedagogy? I remember Lynn talking about that issue: being accused of not being "womanly" enough as a teacher with the story of the hostile student who commented on her "tits" in a student evaluation. And also her saying that there are several different ways of being nurturing that aren't "feminine," but that people expect female teachers to embody that mommie role of feminine nurturance and when they don't, they are criticized for it. Is there a way to reclaim feminist pedagogy in the field of comp to define it distinctly and clearly from the idea of "feminine pedagogy"? I feel that is what I have been trying to do with these site visits: not only challenge my definition by watching these women in action, but also trying to figure out ways to reclaim a more empowering, accurate definition for the field.

Being shameless, then, is a feminist pedagogical strategy: refusing to feel shame, or guilt, for not being a nurturing mother. It means being out and proud about that feminist identity.

. . . WITHOUT APOLOGIES OR WHISPERS,
THE WORDS AFTER ALL THAT

I am drawn, again and again, to Lynn's scholarship because there is beauty
in the words. Yes, the ideas are smart and she has important things to say,
but it is the beauty of the words that causes me to write down phrases and
keep running over them, like sand through my fingers. It feels good. One of
these show-stopping passages comes from her "Confessions of an
Epistemophiliac" article. When I read it, I hear her speaking to academic
feminists specifically, challenging them to do more, to think more critically,
to challenge their own location of privilege. The message speaks to me, but
the use of metaphor and the poetry of the prose are stunning:

> We live in the neighborhood too, though on the outskirts perhaps, and
> we know it is a dangerous place, with an exclusive address. With this
> knowledge in hand, some of us will continue trying to reclaim and
> renew the neighborhood with the tools at our disposal. Others will
> resolve to move their wild patience elsewhere, to some place as yet
> unspoken in the history of desire. *A few will leave no tracks to follow.*
> Though we may no longer dream of a common language and destiny, I
> improvise with Adrienne Rich when I say there are words we cannot
> choose again, words so permeated with the fibers of actual life as we live
> it now that they have no power to reconstitute the world. (pp. 60–61;
> italics added)

In her work, in her rhetoric, and scholarship, Lynn is making sure to leave
tracks to follow. She is offering a model of other tools, those not of the
Master, to create scholarship that connects the personal with the political
with the cultural with the pedagogical. It is through this work, her scholarship, and her leadership and teaching, that Lynn is taking care to reconstitute the world, cutting a new path. This is what feminist pedagogy can be:
lyrical, political, smart, and bursting with self-critique as well as institutional or hegemonic critique.

   In her path-forging trek, Lynn moves through feminist theories, carefully creating alternative rhetorical practices; she leaves a trail, one not of bread
crumbs, but of bright, enduring sign posts, for other scholars to follow. She
is not colonizing new terrain. Rather she is reclaiming territory ripped out
from under and violently kept from traditionally marginalized people.
Although there is wild(er)ness in her work, she is, as most feminists are,
working against the machine of the White supremacist capitalist patriarchy.
She works to jam that machine with her leadership, writing, teaching, and
rhetoric. She implants cultural, political, personal, and field-specific discus-

sions into the nooks and crannies of that machine, all with a sharp feminist focus that will change the product of the churning machinations of ideology. In her article "Critical Interference," she uses the rhetoric of "jamming the machine" as a way to resist the normalization of language, an echo of the earlier excerpt from "Epistemophiliac," where she advocates new language, new words that are "permeated with the fibers of actual life." It is through the careful personal and critical stories she tells in her scholarship that she weaves these threads of life through theory. The result is a model of feminist rhetoric and scholarship, a model of pedagogy, that departs from the traditional/impersonal/third-person singular model heavy with the tongues of White, privileged class males, the forefathers. Objectivity is named for the ruse it is and in its place is frank personal critique, the teacher and author turning stories, holding them up to the light of feminist consciousness, and examining the prism from all angles, creating new meanings, and reconstituting the world.

Instead of replicating the world with their rhetoric and pedagogies, feminist teachers and scholars struggle to create an altered view of the world, one that exposes the systems of domination. As Virginia Woolf (1966) wrote in *Three Guineas*, "Prevent war not by repeating your words and following your methods by finding new words and creating new methods" (p. 143). Therefore, feminists have to be linguistically creative, rejecting sanctioned discourse, the rhetoric of the snools,[36] as Mary Daly describes it. Although strategies are difficult to employ, as we are all drooling fools for ideology, even small diversions do not go unnoticed. Through her writing, Lynn provides a model of rhetoric that others can further interrogate and follow. "Those who have power to name the world influence reality," and with every article published, Lynn is renaming the world through a feminist gaze (Spender, 1990, p. 165).

While reading Lynn's published work, I find myself scribbling down passages to go back to for inspiration. These passages raise a raw challenge about writing I should be doing as a feminist in this field. Although all her writing offers me nuggets of inspiring and delicious prose that I trace in a journal or notebook in my own hand, feeling the way they spill out of a pen, it is her "After Words" essay that I cannot dissect by dividing into passages. This essay, for me, is holistically an amazing rhetorical moment, a radical pedagogical move, and a wild feminist act. It is the one essay from this field of composition and rhetoric that I cannot be far away from because it shows me what is possible and what to work for: the careful self-critique, the integration of theory and practice, the power and importance of storytelling and connection, and the tangible, palatable, delicious sensation that comes from language carefully and smartly crafted.

The "After Words" was the first essay I can remember that spoke to *my* feelings of discomfort as a feminist devoting less and less time to community activist work as I wrote, thought, talked in these ivied walls. After reading the following passage, I wrote a margin notation in emphatic pencil, "Right. We've got to work outside academy!"

> [W]e may not grasp how limited is the role academic feminism plays as an abeyance structure that in twenty years has become a relatively safe harbor, insulated in many ways from a persistently hostile social and economic climate. With our energies consumed in the day-to-day demands of teaching and service, with our attention focused on the pitched battles in feminist theory, we may misrecognize the true sources of hostility and mistake the institutional changes we have made in higher education, most of which have been only cosmetic, for the revolution itself. [. . .] Many of us may believe, for example, that we are actively resisting the gender genocide taking place around the world through our latest research article presented at an annual professional conference (see Jordan). We who try our luck here, in the college classroom or the academic publication, work a particular corner of the world, *a corner that is not especially important to the overwhelming majority of women throughout the world.* (pp. 347–348; italics added)

Lynn is not suggesting that feminist work in the academy and feminist scholarship are not contributing to the larger realities of women. Rather she is insisting that we, feminist academics, remind ourselves continually of our "exclusive address" in these hallowed halls and critique our own social location, doing work on many fronts instead of just one. We must act publicly and speak loudly as feminists. We must be vigilant about what other feminist work is going on in the world and remember that, because of that grassroots work, we have the privilege of freely naming ourselves as feminists, whereas many women working the private sector do not. In academia, feminism is many times seen as a sexy theory that looks good on a vita. Not so in the private sector where the word has become a contemporary scarlet letter, a mark of shame, on which one can be denied a job or promotion. Perhaps that is also true of the academy and I just have not learned that lesson yet.

My attraction to the "After Words," the significance of it for me, goes beyond the fact that I felt my thoughts and feelings articulated for the first time in an academic forum. It is again the construction of the rhetorical site, the radical departure of what is expected of an "After Words" that Lynn transgresses and reconstructs that offers a model of feminist pedagogy, a site of learning and listening.

Kay: The "After Words" is the piece that I go to where I can see that things can be different. It is so wonderful, but it is also so deeply interrogated. At first when you are talking about Blue Betty, I said, "No! Oh, no!" because I thought, "Oh no! This is a *bad* story!" But at every point that I am nervous that you are telling that story, you interrogate yourself.

Lynn: That is so interesting to hear because that is exactly what I was trying to do. I was trying to put together the personal and the theoretical with the interrogation of what is here [in the theory] with what is here [in the personal]. It was very hard to write because there were so many places where I could just really fall apart, it could all fall apart. At the same time I was undergoing lots of mourning. My father had recently died and I was in a different place than I am now [or] when my mother had died. I grieved for years about her. I was also was doing something different; I had never written a personal [narrative], I had never written that kind of autobiographical criticism. In fact, I don't like most of it that I see out there. I was really taking a risk. I was doing something I was uneasy with, but I wanted to do it, but I wasn't sure I could do it.

Kay: What made you want to do it?

Lynn: I'd been wanting to work out the story of Blue Betty for a long time. I had been thinking about writing it somehow for a long time, but didn't know how. [. . .] I am really trying to take from those essays [in the book] and make them into a critical process that puts me at risk and all of it at risk. I mean, how do you write an afterword? What do you do? "This is a smart article. This is how you apply this article; this is how you apply that article." But that is how an afterword is typically done. It puts into relationship what comes before, either in a congratulatory sense or in an applying this to pedagogical situations. And I didn't want to write the usual afterword. I didn't want to write what people expected. I wanted to do something different. But I also wanted to write something that was about feminism both being self-critical as well as being able to move forward in a political direction and all of that; about [how] we come into feminism at different times, in different places, different moments in history; the point at which we enter the feminist movement. [. . .] But that doesn't have to make us unable to talk to one another; we can deal with each other through our differences and in terms of our differences and in spite of our differences without it being this centralized sisterhood or pressure. We have a lot of different feminisms. So, I am trying to talk about collective subjectivity in a kind of abstract theoretical way. I had a kind of collective subjectivity from my mother and other women in my life who are in here, in me somewhere. I guess it was very important

> to me at that particular moment in my life that I wrote some-
> thing both very theoretical and very personal; that was about
> more than academic feminism, composition studies; [it was] an
> active self-criticism.

The "After Words" nourishes me with the type of feminist rhetoric and feminist scholarship for which I am hungry. In the essay, I see connections between theory and practice; between feminist theory and feminist lives; between lives of women and academic writing; confrontations of race, class, gender, and sexual identity. Before I read the essay I felt starved for all those things and I could not find them in the academic writing that I was reading. The "After Words" essay is also brilliant in its self-reflection and self-inter-rogation, the weaving of theory and lived experiences and *the teaching of writing.*

Project Journal Entry. February 20, 2001:

> I went to dinner tonight with Lynn. Over Indian food, I asked ques-
> tions and listened. But I was really dying to ask her about the
> "After Words" essay; it's the one question I have been itching to
> ask. At the end of the interview I told her how much her "After
> Words" meant to me and how I kept going back to that and
> (Dorothy) Allison (1996) as models for my own writing. The entire
> conversation was amazing. ("Amazing" seems to be the word for
> this visit, but I am getting tired of my own redundancy and lack of
> creativeness; what can I say other than "amazing"?). She was so
> candid and open about her thoughts on the essay, and about
> everything I asked. When I asked her what her most radical femi-
> nist act was, she said without hesitation, not getting married or
> having children. I found that brilliant and, once again, so affirm-
> ing. That is another word to describe this visit. I have felt affirmed
> by her words and work over and over again. The way she articu-
> lates and lives her feminism offers me great hope. It is a way I can
> feel good, instead of guilty, about being a privileged class feminist
> in academia.

Beyond the feminist message of the scholarship—not just this essay, but her published work, which has feminism as its central theme—the passion that is visible between the words provides a model for feminist rhetoric and scholarship. When I read Lynn's work, I see how carefully she puts words together. There is a real passion, a serious art, to it. The words are pleasura-ble to read. I often find myself stopping to read passages aloud to hear how they sound, and they sound *great.* They are words meant to be read aloud, like a public manifesto, full of high spirits and conviction. When I tell Lynn of the delight that comes to me reading her words, she expands on the attention she gives to her own rhetoric.

> I am glad [that passion] comes through because that is what I am interested in. I get a lot of pleasure and intellectual stimulation by working out something through the words. [. . .] I want to be entertained. I can't just sit down and deliver a message. I have to have fun while I am doing it. Even if it is something deadly serious, something that very much matters, I have to be able to have fun with it, be involved in working out the language; that interests me, excites me, makes me laugh. [. . .] I think you can do scholarly work in ways that are not just plodding and explaining. It makes it harder. I think it makes it harder and maybe more time consuming, labor intensive, but I think you need to it that way.

Because Lynn is doing it this way, she is marking the trail. Through her careful counting of ribs and other storytelling measures of lives and words, she creates a feminist pedagogy through her mentorship, scholarship, teaching, and rhetoric. It is a pedagogy of self-interrogation, self-critique, passion, and pure delight.

CONTEXTUALIZING
THE KNOWING SUBJECT

Harriet Malinowitz

I first encountered Harriet not through her scholarship, but through conference presentations at the Conference on College Composition and
Communication. I remember being wowed by one presentation specifically,
although now I can't quite remember what the heck it was about. I do
remember that I walked away from that presentation saying to myself,
"*That* is the kind of academic feminist I want to be." "*That* kind of academic feminist" was one who strongly grounded her scholarship in activist
work, making constant, continuous, persistent, and poignant connections
between the field and life and work in the community.

Now that I have spent time with Harriet listening to her talk about her
life and work, I see that her approach to academic feminism is the logical
extension of a feminist consciousness that was first grounded in community
activist work. Harriet's feminist and activist work began almost at the same
moment, when she marched into a Graduate Committee meeting in the
English Department meeting at the University of Massachusetts and, with a
group of fellow graduate students, suggested a revision to the qualifying
exam reading list to include more women (out of 60 authors, 2 were women;
the feminists proposed adding 6 women to the list). That was in 1978. Since
then she has carried her feminist spirit with her to Central America as well

as into the streets of New York City, working for labor, reproductive freedom, queer rights, and on behalf of rape and domestic violence survivors.

Her feminist perspective permeates her teaching and scholarship, but so does what she calls her "dilettantishness." She has been a student in various programs: Labor Studies, Women Studies, Creative Writing, and Composition. Harriet holds an MFA in fiction, an MA in Teaching English as a Second Language, and a PhD in composition. Currently, Harriet is an associate professor of English at Long Island University in Brooklyn, where she founded the Women's Studies program and designed much of that program's curriculum. At LIU she teaches women's studies, cultural studies, queer theory, composition, rhetoric, and various writing courses to graduate and undergraduate students.

Harriet first and foremost defines herself as a writer. Indeed, she writes in various contexts and genres from short stories and stand-up comedy to literature reviews for *The Women's Review* to academic articles within the fields of Composition and Rhetoric and Women's Studies. She has published scholarly articles in women's studies journals and comp/rhet journals; she has also written for feminist activist presses and popular newspapers and journals in the New York area. In the field of composition and rhetoric, she is best known for her consistent feminist perspective and her attention to queer issues in the field, specifically through her book *Textual Orientations: Lesbian and Gay Students and the Making of Discourse Communities.*

Chapter Four

Harriet Malinowitz

The Writer-Passion
of a Feminist Dilettante

I quickly become overwhelmed whenever I visit New York City. Too many tall buildings. Too much concrete. There never seems to be enough light, enough sun on my skin, enough space, enough solitude. Too many people. Too much thrum and screetch. My heart is definitely one of a prairie woman, yearning for the solace of wide open spaces. When I arrive at Harriet's office at Long Island University (right off the 2/3 subway stop in Brooklyn at Nevins Street), I have been in "The City" (as if there is only one) for 3 days, and the harried pace is beginning to clench my psyche. Harriet is coming in just as I arrive on the fourth floor of the humanities building. We are both scratching through our bags furiously, even the simple task of looking for pens or keys seems fevered. We are busied, individually, in the minute trappings of official business. We cheerfully greet each other and then hurry through the atrium. Harriet stops our collective bustling to introduce me to the administrative assistant as her "trailer who is shadowing me for three days." I feel slightly mysterious or at least vaguely sly and important, a dime store novel detective.

The fourth floor of the humanities building has just been renovated, so it feels new: light, airy, a residue scent of latex paint. The wood is blond. The furniture is low to the ground with soft cushions that one sinks deeply into when sitting. The grit and noise of "The City" are exiled elsewhere. There is the soft, cottony hum of air purification and climate control. The offices have large plate glass windows, even if these windows only face the internal corridors. It seems almost more fitting that they do. This clean, blond, hushed world peers in on itself instead of out onto the honking, hacking, beeping cacophony of Brooklyn. Harriet and I settle into her office. She seems frazzled and rushed. Flustered, almost. She must have a million things on her mind, I tell myself. Or is she just nervous about me being there? I believe the physical reality of me to be an intrusion. There is an awkwardness at first. The bodily presence of me, with my tape recorder, seems odd to us both. Unlike politicians or other people within the public domain, academics are rarely called on to be the subject of a feature-like article. As a former journalist, I am used to these sorts of tagging along story missions. As an academic, I know how foreign they are in this world, where the written word is the more genuine representative of the person, not the messiness of day-to-day working and living.

Harriet leaves her office door open as we talk. Periodically, a colleague walks by and Harriet calls after them so she can introduce me. When one colleague, Celie, stops by, Harriet explains, "This is a visiting [researcher] who is shadowing me for a few days so she can write about all the horrible things about me in her book. It is a total exercise in self-absorption." Celie asks me what my manuscript is about, and I summarize by saying it is about how feminists in the academy translate their beliefs into classroom practices. Celie quips, by way of answering that question, "With a phallic hammer, right Harriet?" Rather, for me, feminist pedagogy is about laying down that phallic hammer (Master's Tools!) and using implements, instead, from a decidedly different tool box or work bench.

Later in the week, Harriet tells me it is colleagues like Celie, and not so much students, with whom she maintains more of a mentoring relationship. The main connection Harriet has with others, she believes, is her passion for writing. "My true mentoring instinct comes out with the writers. [. . .] They know me and are connected with me in some way, and they know I am obsessed with writing. They know I think of myself as a writer."

In Harriet's pup tent of life, the center stake is writing. Harriet first and foremost sees herself as a writer and wants, more than anything else, to write, write, write. Sometimes, in the context of academia and specifically in the field of composition, Harriet is a frustrated writer. Most of the conversations I have with Harriet pivot on writing: her own, her colleagues, how to teach it, how to write with glee and meaning, how to find critical consciousness through writing, how to do the kind of writing she wants to do and get published. Harriet tells me more than once that at various points in her life she has finagled to create a life where writing is the center; in conjunction with this, she has also attempted to create a space where she can do the kind of writing she likes to do, which specifically is not academic writing, but writing alive with personal experience and response to the world. It is this type of writing, which Harriet describes as a personal essay genre, that shows up most often in the articles she writes for *The Women's Review of Books*. This style, what seems to me more of a relaxed, conversational tone that deviates from the stiff, lingo-laden prose of academic discourse, also takes on starring roles in some of her scholarship ("David and Me" and "Unmotherhood," most obviously).

Listening to Harriet talk about her writing life and in analyzing the transcriptions of our conversations, I see a prominent feminist pedagogical approach emerging under the guise of "the writing life." One of these is a feminist consciousness that, although Harriet may not immediately identify as a foundation for her writing, seems central to the end result, the work she produces in the form of text. Another is, of course, the sustaining chord of passion about writing that she carries with her into her classrooms. Through her teaching and scholarship, Harriet creates connections between the importance of writing and critical consciousness. The critical thinking skills that she encourages her students to exercise in their writing are skills she also pushes them to utilize in their own lives.

Harriet tells me that teaching is her "day job," but that writing is her life, the sustenance of her mind and soul. This distinction that Harriet sees between writing and teaching is less distinct for me. What I witness in Harriet's teaching and writing is an integral and overlapping relationship that hinges on feminist consciousness. Her delight in teaching and writing inform each other, enliven and enrich each other, providing intellectual fodder in an infinite loop of kinetic energy. Together these two parts of her life—teaching and writing—create texts and classrooms that model feminist pedagogy. What grounds these twin constellations of teaching and writing is the energy of feminist consciousness.

A SKETCH OF THE FEMINIST MIND AT WORK

To contextualize her world for me, Harriet recounts the story of how she came to Long Island University (LIU). This is the way we begin the conversation in her office, my tape recorder turned on and tested, a quiet, yet telling piece of evidence on the desk: This is not just a friendly conversation. But we both, it seems, want to pretend it is. At least I do. I am genuinely interested in finding out about Harriet. There is no roving reporter on assignment, waiting for the sound byte to squeak out so that she can move on to the next story on the docket. I settle back to hear what Harriet will choose to tell me. Her story starts out, "In the beginning . . . ," but quickly moves into a rather elliptical, stream-of-consciousness monologue that touches on many different stories of how she came to be where she is and how she sees the world as she does. Harriet's narrative begins with her entry into the world of adjunct teaching at LIU in 1984; the linear plot is quickly abandoned for one of cross-association. The plot of this personal story thickens and twists with interesting curves, corners, and intersections around and between writing, critical thinking, feminism, teaching, and social/political activism.

I got my MFA . . . Well, let me go back even farther than that because it all kind of connects. First of all, I sort of had this very, despite being Jewish, a Protestant Work Ethic kind of upbringing. [. . .] I had a father who felt that it was really hedonistic and immoral ever do anything you liked. Or that gave you pleasure. Work had to be unpleasant and also very practical, the kinds of things you have a license [for]. Basically he encouraged me to be a research librarian and my brother to be an accountant. He thought I would enjoy, well, not enjoy, that wasn't permitted, but being a research librarian would be good because I could help other people who were doing very interesting research. [. . .] I loved books. I loved reading and writing. And my brother was more of a math person. So, [my father] sort of thought, "How could you take these proclivities and turn them into something really boring? And practical."

As Harriet talks, my mind's eye creates the image of a wild-haired girl child, tilting her head back to scrutinize the world of her father; he steers her to a quiet, sedate, feminine profession, this man who thinks she should "help others" do interesting work rather than embark on her own adventurous and mind-stimulating path. While Harriet talks and my mind spins new images to accompany the stories told, Harriet is trying to eat her lunch: a bagel with cream cheese and some carrots. Somewhere in the far-reaches of my brain, I feel badly about this. Not the food, but the fact that Harriet is trying to eat and talk at the same time. I watch her struggle to chew, speak, and swallow, and I am pricked by tiny tingles of guilt. But I do not stop her. I could let her finish her lunch before we start the conversation, but I am also acutely aware of time limitations and do not want to waste the short 5 to 10 minutes it would take to yak casually while she finishes her meal.

Between bites and swallows, Harriet tells me she began adjunct work at LIU in 1984 teaching first-year writing courses. "Nobody was supervising what I did. They just gave me an old syllabus and told me to teach." She jumps from this first memory of LIU to reflecting on a future yet to play out: currently LIU is considering replacing first-year writing courses, housed in the English department, with Writing in the Discipline or Writing Across the Discipline (WID/WAC) writing intensive courses in each discipline. Harriet is concerned about this shift because she does not think people in other disciplines have been trained in teaching writing. The intense pleasure she finds in the act of writing and the teaching of writing is at the core of this trepidation. Harriet believes that to teach writing well, one must have passion for writing, a hunger to create text that is interesting, vibrant, and meaningful. Although possessing a sense of deep delight and commitment for what one teaches is not exclusive to feminist pedagogy, this is an example of how the various themes of feminist pedagogy figure prominently in Harriet's approach to her thoughts of teaching and writing. Harriet's concern for having people in other disciplines who are not writers teach writing also reflects

Harriet's deep care for students. She wants them to learn to write, to think consciously and carefully about writing, to be able to create well-constructed arguments, to enjoy the craft of putting words together as a way of engaging minds and audiences, and to understand the politics and ideologies at play in different discourse communities. The WID/WAC shifts at LIU concern her because even if the tenured or permanent full-time instructors receive training in WID/WAC, the writing intensive courses, because they are more labor intensive, will probably be farmed out to adjuncts or graduate students who do not have the writing training or expertise.

These sentiments echo the critique Harriet leveled against WID/WAC programs in her essay "A Feminist Critique of Writing in the Disciplines." In that essay, she wrote that WID/WAC programs caused her grave concern because they took the critical awareness of ideology out of discussions on writing. The focus of WID/WAC programs is to teach students how to unquestioningly ascribe to hegemonic norms, where instructors most commonly ask, "What kind of writing do you do in your discipline?" Instead of critiquing discipline standards and who those standards and structures work to include in and exclude from power, the question of "What kind of writing do you do in your discipline?" hides the power and politics from writing, impeding the work toward critical consciousness. Because Harriet sees writing and working toward critical consciousness inextricably related, especially in her feminist classrooms, she is critical of WID/WAC programs.

> As WID now exists, it doesn't help students critically assess how forms of knowledge and method are hierarchically structured in disciplines, so that some achieve canonical or hegemonic status whereas others are effectively fenced out. In the absence of such a critical framework, students are easily beguiled by the mystique of dominant knowledge systems, which are bolstered by and in turn legitimate asymmetrical social, material, and ideological arrangements. (Malinowitz, 1998, p. 293)

For Harriet, leaning to write in a formulaic way to please a specific discipline, audience, or institution runs not only counter to feminist work, but robs students of opportunities for critical awareness through writing.

Harriet's skepticism regarding WID/WAC courses comes, in part, from her experience as a day-tripping faculty member sitting in on other courses. Because of Harriet's fascination with the offerings and processes of higher education (she refers to herself as a perennial undergraduate), she frequently sits in on classes her colleagues are teaching across the curriculum. "I really like seeing how other people teach and being a student again," she told me. From these experiences, Harriet has observed that instructors in other disciplines do not really teach writing, or at least they do not teach writing as a vehicle for critical consciousness, although the main product of course work may be projects or other major writing assignments. Most typically, Harriet has observed that students create a paper at the end of the course, but there is no discussion about the project or the process before it is due; there is no discussion on how to construct an argument or hone a text. There is no conversation about the power structures at work and the ideologies hidden within expectations held by a specific audience of what is good or appropriate writing.

Perhaps because of her concern about how writing is taught (or not taught) in other disciplines, Harriet prefers teaching writing in her noncomp classes, a version of WID work in humanities courses. Because these courses are not first-year writing courses, Harriet's approach to composition pedagogy feels different in these contexts. In the Women's Studies, Cultural Studies, Queer Studies, and other Humanities courses that Harriet teachers, she feels she is a better writing teacher. This may be due to the focus on critical thinking and cultural critique that are inherent in the curriculum of these types of courses that works so well with Harriet's vision of writing. Also, in her noncomp courses, Harriet feels freer to abandon composition ideology for her own writerly instincts. From Harriet's perspective, composition ideology dictates a process theory (prewrite, write, revise) that often does not work for students. Composition courses also force students to churn out a huge quantity of text (four or five papers using the prewrite, write, revise process), leaving little time for in-depth discussions of writing or careful contemplation of a student's own writing style and habits, as well as the work involved honing, crafting, and fine-tuning a text.

To listen to her talk about composition, one would not immediately define her as a strong advocate of composition theories or approaches. However, even this rejection of what Harriet terms *composition ideology* is a firm connection to feminist pedagogical theory because Harriet is looking for ways to connect with students, bring her passion into the class, and share that part of her life with her students. Also, by resisting disciplinary boundaries and looking toward integrating rhetorical theory, by teaching Women's Studies and Cultural Studies courses with an eye to how to construct a convincing argument and pay close attention to how words fit together to shape an idea, she brings the feminist ideals of creating connections and blurring boundaries to her pedagogy.

BRINGING HER WRITER-PASSION TO THE NONCOMP CLASSROOM

Harriet's resistance to the distinct delineations between disciplines brings writing squarely and centrally into all courses she teaches, even those that are not specifically listed as English or composition credits. With a fewer number of projects assigned in noncomp courses (two instead of four or five), Harriet says she can spend more time talking at length and in detail about writing in noncomp courses. Much more than teaching *composition*, the term laden with the theory and practices of the field, Harriet likes teaching writing.

> "I am more and more teaching my so-called comp classes [. . .] as other kinds of writing courses. I taught a graduate course in reading and writing the personal narrative a couple years ago and I am going to teach it again. That was an occasion where I could have died of happiness. I really was in my element. When I was teaching that class I realized I was drawing on all my real instincts of writing rather than anything I learned in composition." In this writing course, Harriet allowed herself to abandon the composition ideology (process theory, writing assessment theory, teaching academic discourse, contemplating "contact zones") and focus on her own instincts as a writer. This move speaks to the feminist pedagogical theme of integrating theory and practice. When the composition theory Harriet internalized as a graduate student or member of the field did not make sense, she re-created and reshaped the theory from her own practices as a writer, modeling the dialogic relationship feminist pedagogy describes between practice and theory.

Listening to Harriet talk about her passion for writing and finding another way to teach writing, one that feels reflective of her own love for words, one feels the connections between her own practice as a writer and the theories about writing she carries to her students. Instead of doggedly trying to practice the comp theories codified during her graduate studies in composition, Harriet creates theories out of her personal practice of writing, translating her personal approach to her own writing pedagogy. In Harriet's description of her love for writing and her struggles to present her writing experiences to students in ways that are meaningful to them as writers, I am reminded of Schmidt's (1998) introduction to *Women/Writing/Teaching*.

> How did I come to embrace a life guided by a love of words? How did I come to know as a child and as a teenager that teaching and writing together would give my life form and meaning? How did I come to feel that the classroom was a place where at times I felt most 'rooted,' most at home, most alive. (p. 1)

To hear Harriet talk about writing, and her desire to teach writing in a way that is meaningful and delightful to students, I think back to Zlotnik's questions and Harriet's story of herself as a child, burdened by a father who eschewed anything as impractical as a writer's life. How did she find her love

and life of writing despite the patrician's manifesto that pleasure was hedonistic and work should be divorced of delight? In Harriet's case, the answer
to Zlotnik's questions seems to be "The Women's Movement." Through
feminism, Harriet found a way to disrupt the father's messages and seek her
passion instead of hide from it.

Harriet talks openly with her students about her passion for writing, the
antidote to her father's lingering philosophy against anything as frivolous as
a writing life. By talking with her students about her own affinity for writing, Harriet models the feminist pedagogy with self-disclosure and works to
dismantle traditional systems of teacher hierarchy in the classroom. She
positions herself as a colleague and learner with her students, all of them
writers working toward creating a more satisfying and dynamic argument.

> My strength is my instinct about writing, having that instinct about
> writing. Being able to talk about that. I think I am good at talking to stu-
> dents about their writing. There are a lot of things I am not good at, but
> that is actually one of the things that is my forte. And not only [with]
> students, but also colleagues and friends. I definitely do a lot of writing
> mentoring. And I am a slave driver for friends. If they bring a project to
> me, I definitely push them to do more than they wanted to do, but I am
> fanatical about writing really. And that is one reason, paradoxically, I
> feel, that I am not that happy in composition. I don't feel that composi-
> tion is so much about writing or I feel like it is full of people who dis-
> like and distrust writing. [. . .] After I taught that personal narrative
> [graduate level] course, I really started teaching, even my basic writing
> and writing courses last term, more like a writing workshop. Group
> line-by-line readings of their stuff, which I had never done in a comp
> class. I really felt they were developing instincts about writing. Anyway,
> this is just a long-winded way of saying, writing is the central, driving
> force for me, and it is ironic that composition would alienate me because
> it is not enough about writing.

Harriet's desire to share her life-long love affair with writing with her students reflects feminist pedagogy as she creates connections between her life,
the experiences of the classroom, and the learning process. Feminist pedagogy challenges instructors to work toward connectedness between learners
and the instructor, between learning and experience (Wright). By bringing
her delight for writing, and the way she approaches writing, into her classrooms, Harriet connects her life to her students'. She is not only inviting the
students to experiment and find their own way to satisfying, meaningful,
critical writing, but she is carefully explaining how she writes and why she
is passionate about the art of putting words together to convey a message.
By extension, she is also embodying the feminist approach of helping students bring their lives and writing together (Sommers, 1998).

Related to Harriet's fascination with writing and teaching students to become better, smarter, and more critically conscious writers is her commitment to teaching critical analysis. Teaching cultural critique exemplifies a fundamental way in which her feminism intersects with her teaching practices. Her own well-honed skills of cultural critique first came to Harriet via feminism. As Harriet moves through the chronology of her life with me, carefully articulating how she came to see the world, she marks her first moment of critical consciousness as taking place within the context of a Women's Studies course in 1978 when she was working toward her MFA at University of Massachusetts Amherst.

> I am never doing what I am supposed to do at the moment. I am always doing something other than what I am supposed to do. So, in the MFA program, no sooner did I have my life set up so I could write and devote myself to writing, I discovered Women's Studies. I had never encountered anything like that before. My very first graduate course there was called "Lust Fiction of American Women." [. . .] It was a very life-changing thing. And that is what started me on my feminist trajectory. Having started that I became just obsessed and had to take every Women's Studies course in the world. Women's Studies was my entrée to politics in general. From there, that was where, in that area I guess, I began discussing issues of racism, primarily racism in the women's movement, and I was listening rapt, with rapt attention. [. . .] It really, I would say, made me an intellectual. It was my port of entry into the intellectual world.

The subtext of this description of how Harriet came to understand feminism and live feminism shows her making connections between disciplines, connections between systems of oppression, connections between the academic world and the experiences of lives outside the academy, and connections between feminist theory and the political issues feminist activists work for and against. Harriet's feminist trajectory began in a graduate women's studies course, but continues today through every strain of her pedagogy and scholarship.

ESCAPING THE TYRANNY
OF THE COMPOSITION CANON

As we talked about teaching, Harriet described her approach in ways that I immediately identified as feminist teaching. In her eyes, however, her methods have little to do with feminist pedagogy and more to do with her transgressions against how she was taught to teach composition. She talks about composition theories such as process theory almost as tyrannical forces that have prevented her from becoming a good writing teacher.

In her book *Textual Orientations* (Malinowitz, 1995), for example, she takes Peter Elbow to task, writing that his expressivist theories of composition alienate or disregard gay and lesbian students who may not be safe coming out to the teacher of their class by writing about their world/lives. Another example of Harriet's critique or resistance to canonical comp theories is her response to Bartholomae's (1985) "Inventing the University," in which Bartholomae examines students' attempts to use academic discourse and explains ways that comp teachers can help them make the transition from their own discourse communities to those of the university more successfully. Harriet sees Bartholomae's theory as an example of how the field of composition often ignores hegemonic power structures when teaching writing.

> This discursive positioning that Bartholomae favors [not questioning whether/if students understand the ideologies at work when adopting academic discourse] seems to be precisely the contrary of that encouraged by liberatory pedagogy, whose aim is to help students transcend the naive belief that they can, or should, magically enter mainstream culture by "mimicking" its mass discourse and behaviors, as mass media, schooling, advertising, and other institutions encourage them to do [. . .] Might [students] learn something very different if they were to examine the ways in which the privileged discourse of the university represents particular agendas, perspectives, and principles, and contrasted these with the ways other discourses, in which they play a part, represent particular agendas, perspectives, and principles? (Malinowitz, 1995, p. 83)

Elbow and Bartholomae are just two examples of canonized contemporary comp theorists who Harriet feels ignore crucial interrogations of dominant ideological forces that have systematically excluded traditionally marginalized people. Certainly not all composition theories ignore questions of power and hegemony; feminists in the field, like Harriet, Jackie, and Lynn, among many others, have published scholarship where interrogating power structures and ideological oppressions as they play out in rhetoric and the writing classroom are central. However, the composition canon, and certainly the theorists that Harriet read as part of her doctoral studies, represents theories that often ignore the complexities of power and oppression.

It was only after Harriet abandoned what she had been taught about teaching composition—those theories like Elbow's and Barthomomae's that were presented to her in graduate school—and instead configured her own feminist principles with her passion for writing that she felt she was most effective as a teacher.

Harriet: One other thing I do want to say. And again, I don't know how this fits in with the feminist part, but this fits in with all the stuff I had to say about writing. This is one way I would link it more to pedagogy, because I am so much more concerned about writing in life than I am about pedagogy. I mean, I think about it as the center of me, and teaching is just my day job, basically. Something happened in my Basic Reading and Writing class this past year. I might have said this, when I was talking about the personal narrative graduate class and I realized my own instincts as a writer came into play there, and I started doing this in that basic writing class and it really seemed to mean something. And I really just kind of threw over a lot of the usual mantras from composition and decided to bring myself as a writer in there. And take them through a piece of writing the way I take myself through a piece of writing and that often has to do with grappling, trying to figure out what is really the right word here? And why is this one OK, but not good enough? And how can you make sense of this sentence? Just at that really minute editorial level. And it was turning the class into a workshop. I had never taught it like that before and there is so much we have to do in these classes. It involves reading, just a million things. All the assignments they have to do. And I decided to really cut down the assignments and go in depth into that. And I pretty much feel like I would continue to do that. That I liked that. It was a lot more pleasurable for me and they really got it. So.

Kay: So the main difference being that it was something you were excited about or it was a model that you used that you could transfer to the classroom?

Harriet: It was real to me. I almost feel like an impersonator in a lot of these comp classes. I felt like I was doing what . . .

Kay: What people were telling you to do, how to teach comp.

Harriet: Yeah. I even used revision. "OK: First you draft. Don't worry about the grammar. Then . . ." (Laughs) I had really felt like an impersonator. I also felt like there were times that I was having conferences with students but I wish I had a tape recorder and could just present the transcripts and send it into one of these comp journals. They were so hilarious because of the way they would completely manage to avoid, the students, manage to avoid the net of composition. I would have these completely whacko conversations with them where I wasn't getting through to them at all, but they were very enthusiastic. I am often amused a lot by the realities of classes instead of what we usually talk about in conferences. And so much of it is so funny.

Kay: Well, it is the separation between the theory of what you think you should be doing and what you actually end up doing, which is what works.

Harriet: And also how students react to things. So, I don't know how that relates.

Kay: No, it is very important. And it also relates to one of the themes.

Harriet: What do you mean?

Kay: The themes of feminist pedagogy. Like you were saying "This isn't feminist pedagogy" but I think it is. The desire to connect "This is how I do it," or "This is my perception," or "This is what works for me. I am going to communicate that with the students so they can see, they can either feel empowered to create their own way of doing things or that the way I do things will be meaningful to them." That self-disclosure is somehow useful to them.

Harriet: Right. And again going back to the mantras in composition, in so many of those process books they say, "This is how writers really write." And I would pass that on, but it's not how I wrote. I thought, "I am a writer. I can show them how I write. And that is what I really know best." And it works for me, so I am the most equipped to teach that way. It seems to work.

Kay: I think you are right. I think it is important to be passionate about what you are teaching instead of following the formula. If you are passionate about writing, tell them why and how. But I think a lot of comp teachers aren't passionate about writing.

Harriet: Exactly. And a lot of them treat writing as suspicion. As I was saying yesterday, so much of the work is about how can you triumph over the misery of writing. And I always find it amazing that people in composition never talk about people like Ellen Willis, Kathy Gordon, Patricia Williams. Patricia Williams they do because of her books. But I know her not because of her books. I know of her from her column in *The Nation*. Writing like *The Voice* and *The Nation* writing to me is the best writing around, as far as I can tell. How come we don't ever talk about that stuff and who are we reading?

This question, and its answer, of who we are reading and how we are reading with students, with our colleagues, circles back around to the issue of writing and scholarship as pedagogy. Harriet is critically aware of what she is asking her students to read and write. But she also extends that focus to the field. She yearns to make a space for the writing she wants to do, the writing she is passionate about, within the field, integrating the personal essay into her scholarship. That is not to say others are not doing this type of scholarship in composition. Victor Villanueva is a prominent scholar who consistently grounds his scholarship in personal narrative. Harriet certainly is not unique in her desire to integrate personal essay into her scholarship or pursue a style of writing she is passionate about, even if it transgresses the standards of academic discourse. However, this is Harriet's struggle: to write how she desires and still get her work published in the field.

RESEARCHY, FOOTNOTE-Y, FACT-THINGEES

Conversations I had with Lynn and Jackie about scholarship snaked through my mind as Harriet talked to me about writing. All three of these women are passionate about their writing and yearn to change the discourse practices and standards of the field to incorporate the kind of writing they like to do. For Lynn and Harriet, they want their own writing to be delicious for the reader to gobble; they also want to integrate direct, personal connections to lives outside the ivied walls of academia. Jackie's approach brings the realities of traditionally marginalized lives and voices to the field, but in doing so she wants to create a methodology that disrupts traditional epistemologies, creating a feminist approach to knowing. For all three of these women, the passion for writing and feminist scholarship as disruption becomes a site of feminist pedagogy as it teaches and leads others to new ways of teaching, learning, knowing, and creating.

Despite Harriet's frustrations and struggles with what she feels is the field's resistance to the type of writing she wants to do, Harriet understands the privilege of being able to do the work and writing she does. One of the things that thrills her about a life in the academy is that it facilitates a writing life. "I know for a lot of people the pressure to publish is a huge burden to them, but I revel in it. [But] I am increasingly realizing how unhappy I am doing these real researchy, footnote-y, fact-thingee kinds of essays." This discontent—the feeling of using a language that does not represent what they want to articulate—is expressed by many feminist academic writers. Secrist (1989), in her work on feminist scholarship, writes, "Feminist scholars are often in the position of trying to break out of, rather than rely on, the authority of received knowledge" (p. 185). In scholarship, *received knowledge* often embodies the expected standards of the academic discipline, the researchy, footnote-y, fact-thingee models that Harriet resists. Instead, Harriet said, she wants to integrate human drama in her academic writing. Later, in a way that I feel illustrates this point, Harriet told me about an essay she was sending out about choosing not to be a mother, and the rhetoric in "motherhood" and "unmotherhood" discourse communities. Harriet first gave the essay to friends to read, but then revised it before she sent it out to academic journals. "I went back and took something that people outside the academy really enjoyed when they read it and made it into something they probably couldn't enjoy." In explaining why she felt the pressure to do this, Harriet said, "I put it in much broader and subjective terms and I probably took a lot of the joy out of it." How much personal information is unacademic or anti-intellectual? How can academic discourse and intellectual analysis be integrated with personal experience in a way that will be seen as smart and scholarly instead of just self-indulgent brain purge?

A couple months after my site visit with Harriet, I called her to talk about some questions I had as I was pouring over the transcriptions, her syllabi, and scholarship. The phone call happened to fall the day after she received a letter from *The Journal of Feminist Studies* about the "Unmotherhood" article she had submitted for consideration.[37] The "Unmotherhood" essay begins with a narrative moment of Harriet on vacation, encountering an evangelical preacher man and their exchange. Harriet's personal narrative reads easily and wittily, a pleasure to read.

> I told him how, as a Jewish atheist, I had read the bible for the first time while preparing to teach a literature survey course. "My favorite character, without a doubt, was Jesus," I asserted generously and truthfully. [...] I felt myself speaking not only to a person, but to a person framed within the certifying tableau of the American Family on Vacation, while he spoke to someone unframed, the tacked-up edges of a canvas showing. I kept waiting, with a familiar clench in my stomach, for him to ask me, as people often do, if I were married and had children. I had already told him, outwardly breezy, that I was Jewish, an atheist, and pro-choice. Surely that was enough for one afternoon. (Malinowitz, 2002, pp. 2-3)

Harriet's essay moves from this narrative moment to theoretical reflections on the rhetoric of parenthood focusing on reproductive choice, eugenics, sterilization practices, fertility, and teen motherhood. Throughout the theoretical and cultural discussions, Harriet weaves in her personal story talking about her relationship with her mother, and how she formed her definition of motherhood by examining, when Harriet was a child, her own mother.

She chronicles the ways in which she came to her understanding of what motherhood entails, moving carefully from her childhood to her adolescence to her adult life. Through her personal storytelling runs a solid stream of theory that speaks to the connections between femaleness and motherhood. Harriet is brutally honest regarding her own decision to not become a mother. "I like to be alone, and I don't like to be bored. [. . .] I like kids, there are some I love, but the unremitting contact raising them requires would destroy me. This is in large part because I'm unable to get engaged with their culture." The article is balanced between careful cultural and rhetorical analyses, grounded in smart theory, and intelligently candid, often humorous, self-disclosure. The reviewers and editors of *The Journal of Feminist Studies* responded by saying they wanted more of the "research-y, fact-thingee stuff"; they wanted the autobiographical elements weeded out. One reviewer wrote, "This manuscript is way too long (38 pages) for what it delivers. Anecdotal theme setting (pages 1-2) offers nothing new and does not encourage the reader, at least this one, to continue. The essay begins in the final paragraph of page 5." In other words, the reviewer thought the personal narrative, the autobiographical context that begins the essay, the part that situates Harriet as a person within the text interacting in a real way with the issue of motherhood and childlessness by choice, cloys. The reviewer rejected it as "anecdotal," instead of a feminist epistemological approach to theory and scholarship. Rather than trying to understand the subversions, disruptions, and new ways of knowledge-making through personal storytelling, the reviewer seemed to feel annoyed with the disruption to her expectations for an academic essay. I would not say the reviewers in this case are not feminist.[38] They are feminist, but they are working within a decidedly patriarchal model. There is feminism that works within the patriarchal system, and there is feminism working to change the system, to re-create the system. By clinging to academic standards of "it has got to be more theoretical and what is this autobiographical stuff doing in here?", the reviewer was showing her investment in a model of scholarship that was created by the patriarchal academy, designed to devalue or dismiss personal experience as epistemology.

In talking about the reviewer's response to Harriet's "Unmotherhood" article, our conversation began with the connections I saw between Harriet's scholarship and her pedagogy.

Kay: I would say that [as your pedagogy strives to create strong connections to the personal, making it political, that] is true also of your scholarship. I am also trying to make the argument that feminist scholarship is a type of feminist pedagogy where the things you are doing in your scholarship, you may not define as feminist pedagogy, but I am going to.

Harriet: Well, actually, I have a really interesting little addendum for you about that. Very hot off the press as of last night. Remind me, what was it? We had talked about the personal essay form.

Kay: You said part of your real joy in writing was getting to a place where you could do that more. And that you were trying to do that more. So what I am trying to argue is [committing yourself to the personal essay as scholarship], in and of itself, is a feminist move. Because you are trying to integrate the personal with the theoretical and you are trying to shift the discourse standards of the community to make it not something that, as you said, "bores me to tears." Academic discourse, you said, "bores me to tears." So you are trying to shift that, to say, "it doesn't have to be that way." And you are trying to do it in a way where the end result is something feminist. The end result is integrating the personal with the theoretical, to make the personal political.

Harriet: The funny thing is, and here is my little addendum. There are actually two parts, but the more pertinent is that last night I came home and saw my mail and had a letter from *The Journal of Feminist Studies.* I had sent them "Unmotherhood." They have had it for months. This editor sent it to three readers. One reader was enthusiastic about it. Two were not. And this editor seemed to feel that she would like to send it out to more readers. But it seemed, the upshot was, could I get rid of the personal stuff. The problem they had was that the theoretical part wasn't developed enough and "What is this autobiographical stuff doing here?" [. . .]

Kay: I remember that you said that [you had revised the article so that it was more theoretical and less personal and therefore less interesting]. In fact you said that it was less satisfying for you because of that. [. . .] That is the whole distinction I am trying to make. Just because [a teacher or scholar defines] as feminist, doesn't mean they are [enacting feminist pedagogy] in the classroom or their scholarship.

Because I think of feminist pedagogy as a specific type of pedagogy, one can identify as a feminist teacher and not necessarily be enacting feminist pedagogy. That is, feminists who are teachers can be enacting traditional classroom practices, resulting in a pedagogy that is decidedly not feminist. Likewise, a feminist journal can be publishing feminist essays, work that is feminist in content and idea, but not be doing so in ways that embrace disruption to standards. Harriet's scholarship is feminist in message, style, and structure because of her disruption of traditional academic standards and her willingness to die on the sword to do the writing she wants to do, being vigilant and maverick about making connections between theory and practice, between lived experiences and her academic work. Unlike me, however, Harriet does not see her struggles to integrate richer personal reflections in her academic prose particularly as feminist pedagogy or feminist rhetoric. Instead she sees it as a compulsion to quench her nagging thirst for interesting prose in academic discourse. To her, academic writing is typically "just bad prose."

> I think one of worst examples of writing in the world is academese. I think that it is so deadly. And [academics] seem to pride themselves on their deadliness. And a lot of what people criticize as being academic jargon I don't think that is the right word for it. First of all there is so much postmodern language that it has almost become cliche. They were interesting when they first started doing it, but then . . . even things like "situating yourself" and all that kind of stuff. Like anything it just became rote. And it makes you wonder. It makes you wonder about the people writing these things. [. . .] There is such a pressure to publish in academia that it is like a mill. You have to publish, so people just write slop. And then people are forced to read it or they force themselves to read it. I decided I didn't want to write slavish themes. That's why I chose the lesbian/gay theme originally. It wasn't a theme everyone else was writing about. It was something new. If I had to write that book over again, though, I would do it differently. There are still things in there, how I wrote it, that was part of that [traditional academic] model. I was trying to fit into a certain model of how academic writing should be. Now I try to write things that move away from that. Like "The Music Man" or the "David and Me" essays. I am moving more towards integrating personal narrative in my work. Academic writing almost makes me want to cry. I want to write. The emergence of creative non-fiction has been a life saving genre for me. I was dying to write personal essays. That is why writing for the *Women's Review of Books* was so important to me. It allowed me to write those personal narratives and weave them into the book reviews.

The reviews of the "Unmotherhood" essay were not the only disappointments Harriet has suffered recently because of her desire, her need, to write in the way she wants to write, striving to use the personal essay genre as part of her academic scholarship. A couple weeks before the response to "Unmotherhood," another essay Harriet had written about the personal essay and the interdisciplinary nature of mixing genres as a form of academic argument had been turned down by two book editors. In this situation, Harriet was solicited by the editors to write an essay for the book. She told the editors she needed to write a personal essay. They said they were interested in having her contribute and a personal essay would be a dynamic addition to the collection. However, faced with the reality of the text itself, they wrote Harriet and said, after "much agonizing," they felt the essay did not fit within the context of the book. As with the editors of the feminist journal, the editors of the collection invited Harriet to revise and resubmit. In both situations, Harriet politely declined, attempting to argue for the essays as they were written, a feminist transgression of the expected.

BUT IS THAT FEMINIST?

When I suggest that these moves to subvert the standards, by integrating the autobiographical or the personal essay genre into academic writing, are feminist pedagogy and feminist rhetorical moves, Harriet is skeptical. The reoccurring refrain that pops up in this song that is my project is, "Why do you define *that* as feminist?" In an e-mail exchange with Harriet, I try to convince her of the connection between feminist pedagogy and feminist scholarship, in effect arguing that there is such a thing as feminist rhetoric. I believe that the integration of personal narrative reflects a feminist strategy because it subverts the form and standards of academic publication. But these subversions are only feminist if the objective is a feminist message. That is not to say that traditional academic prose cannot be feminist scholarship. Feminist scholars who use traditional rhetoric/standards are indeed engaging in feminist scholarship/rhetoric because their message is feminist. Certainly transgression for the sake of just doing something different is not necessarily feminist. But if one is transgressing the structure to convey a feminist message, "I am messing with the standards because they limit my feminist message and I want to communicate a feminist perspective in a totally different way that speaks to that identity," then that *is* a feminist transgression.

Personal narrative is not always feminist, but when feminists use it because they feel the personal needs to be part of their scholarship as a way to connect the personal to the political or theoretical (feminist), that is feminist rhetoric/scholarship at play. It all slithers back around to good, ole feminist self-reflection: Why am I doing this? If the answer is, "Because it is important to my feminism or my feminist message," then that is feminist scholarship, and feminist scholarship as a form of feminist pedagogy, a way of changing the standards. Certainly feminist pedagogy and scholarship, in all their varying forms, are not necessarily exclusive to feminism. Although Villanueva is communicating, for the most part, a feminist-type message in his work, if he does not see himself as a feminist rhetor/writer, then it would be hard for me to categorize that as feminist scholarship. On the flip side of that Susan B. Anthony Silver Dollar, just because someone plays around with form once in the name of feminism doesn't mean she always will. A good example is Patricia Williams. Her messages are most always feminist, but sometimes she uses the standard discourse/style that is obviously not a deviation from standard discourse practices. Sometimes she integrates self-reflection and critique in the name of her feminist analysis (essays like those in *Alchemy of Race and Rights,* 1991). Sometimes she really outdoes herself by playing with form all over the place to communicate a feminist message (her "Muleheadedness" essay, where she integrates fiction and political commentary with fable/myth and drama). *All* are examples of feminist scholarship, although in different forms.

So, in my mind, it is feminist scholarship/rhetoric if: (a) the message is feminist (even if the form follows traditional patriarchal standards; e.g., Judith Butler or Cheryl Glenn), (b) the objective is to reconstruct or deconstruct the standards because doing this emboldens the feminist message (e.g., inserting personal narrative in an attempt to integrate the personal with political/theoretical; Lynn's "After Words" or Harriet's "Unmotherhood"), and the standards are (c) revised or re-created by way of embodying a radical departure of style/form/function in the name of feminism (e.g., William's "Muleheadedness" essay).

Any piece of writing could be (a), or (b), or (c) and be feminist scholarship/rhetoric; most feminists choose different approaches depending on audience and context, not always using the same tack. Of course, the writer/rhetor has to identify as a feminist, and the message has to be feminist—or all bets are off. But this is a hard theory to sell. I feel as if no one is buying this. I must not be explaining it well; it makes perfect sense to *me*. Maybe I am a polyester-clad sales rep of an incredibly pointless product that no one really has much use for, but in which *I* am ridiculously and pathetically invested. I lug around a big black case of "feminist stuff." I keep knocking on doors and trying to peddle it. My pitch is off, apparently. No one seems to be buying.

But then again, Harriet does consider what I have to say. Because of my argument, she revises her beliefs of feminist pedagogy. She sees that a course's content, containing a calculated feminist perspective that is communicated in complex ways within a curriculum, does signify that there may indeed be such a thing as feminist pedagogy. Perhaps, she tells me, there is nothing that is inherently feminist in form, but there can be in content. This feels like a small victory to me. But I have a difficult time separating form from content so neatly. For me, feminist pedagogy is about form and content, an intricate combination of the two as embodied in various strategies unique to a teacher or an individual classroom. There are, after all, unlimited ways that a teacher can actually practice the 16 themes. For me, the themes represent possibilities for both form and content. It is the awareness of the themes, the commitment to them, all of them, that creates a site of feminist pedagogy, whether that is in the classroom, in scholarship, or as a leader in the department, university, or community.

SHAPING CRITICAL CONSCIOUSNESS THROUGH THE "WHY/HOW"

When I observed Harriet's classes, the themes I heard echoed in our conversations about her teaching (integrating the personal and community in the classroom, teaching critical thinking, subverting teacher authority) played out as dominant themes in her classrooms as well. I observed Harriet teach two courses. One was an introduction to Women's Studies course entitled "Women in Culture and Society." The other was a Cultural Studies course, "Ways of Reading Culture." In her "Women in Culture and Society" class, Harriet emphasized creating connections between classroom knowledge and outside issues. Harriet's teaching also emphasized self-disclosure as she constantly asked students to connect the readings to their personal experience and offered her own life stories as examples. Typically, Harriet's strategy for engaging students and pushing them to critically think involved asking students questions to complicate issues or further their responses. She also used the strategy of asking students to focus on the "How?" questions.

The "Women in Culture and Society" course was extremely small (three students), making the 2? -hour class not unlike an intense, in-depth conversation. There were two young women in the class (one African American and one Middle Eastern American) and one young man (African American). Before we went to the class, Harriet told me a little about the dynamics of the group: The male typically had high talk time, and one of the young women hardly ever said anything at all. This dynamic proved to play out in the class I observed as well, with both Harriet and I actively working to draw both young women into the conversation as much as we could. Harriet said she wanted me to feel free to participate in the class, instead of just observe. I ended up inserting myself in the conversations a great deal. When I was transcribing the tapes, I felt as if I had done too much "participating." The subject for discussion was reproductive issues, so my contributions to the class were often in the form of personal experience as a pro-choice activist in the Midwest trying to reinforce connections between the articles that had been assigned and my own lived experience (theory and practice). Harriet persistently asked the students to relate the readings and issues of reproductive rights to their own lives.

The classroom was large and airy. Long windows stretched along the west wall, and the afternoon sun warmed the room. The floors were highly polished salmon-colored tile, and expanses of blackboards lined the room so that I was not at first clear which was the front or back of the class. Chairs were scattered around in no particular arrangement. Because the class consisted of only five people, including myself, we formed a rather loose group near one side of the room. All of us sat at desks, adding to the casual feeling of a group of friends or colleagues having a conversation.

Although the texts read for this class focused on reproductive rights, the conversation moved from abortion, to motherhood, to insurance coverage, to rape, to mental illness. Harriet let the students lead the conversation, beginning the discussion by asking, "We won't have time to talk about everything, so what do you want to begin with?" Students launched discussions of government funding for social services and the abortion rhetoric used by both pro-choice and pro-life groups, moving back and forth between reading excerpts from the text that caught their eye or furthered their point and relating the text to their personal experience or popular culture. All of us consistently drew from our own stories to deepen the conversation. The Arab American student talked about becoming pregnant and not getting married, much to her Muslim parents' chagrin. I spoke of being a pro-choice activist and clinic "defender" in the Midwest. Harriet talked about her reproductive rights activist work in New York City. The male student talked candidly about his family and definitions of motherhood, his views on abortion, inequities in insurance coverage, and whether crack mothers should be put in jail. This student's opinions typically reflected a conservative social agenda; Harriet asked questions to complicate his perspectives and engage other students in the conversation. She also consistently brought in other perspectives that the students were not considering, such as issues of socioeconomic class and living in rural areas where abortion services are not available.

Laughter and humor were central to these discussions. Although Harriet was challenging some of the student's views, she did so with a light-heartedness that allowed them to avoid feeling defensive or silenced. To draw the quieter female student into the conversation, Harriet talked about a connection she saw between that student's campus activist work and the class discussion.

When I was transcribing the tapes from Harriet's "Women in Culture and Society," I found Harriet continually striving to give students choices and challenging them to make connections between the course material and their own lives. She wants her students to actively engage in the learning process, but also, almost more important than that, wants them to work toward critical consciousness as they make sense of how the course material influences or reflects their own lives and the world around them. Through storytelling, Harriet continuously models these kinds of connections for her students. By doing so, she is also showing the students that she is willing to share her personal beliefs and life with them. She is a co-learner in the classroom community, facilitating and leading in a feminist approach of equity and understanding.

Project Journal Entry. April 4, 2001.

> I am waiting outside Harriet's office before class begins. I can hear her talking to a student. She is telling the student, "You need to closely analyze what you're doing. Unless we learn how to closely analyze what we are doing, we can't do a critique. Focus on the 'How?'" This conversation strikes me because, in teaching any course, I am constantly asking students to focus on the "Why/How?" questions. I tell them that if we are going to think or analyze anything critically, we have to ask and answer these questions from various perspectives. Here Harriet is telling her students the same thing. It seems eerie that we would both come to one of the same strategies for teaching critical thinking. We are both trying to get our students to think critically, giving them the same tool to help them (the "Why/how?" questions).

In our discussions of teaching, Harriet identified teaching students critical thinking and analysis skills as primary goals in any class. "Over the years I have become less and less interested in [having Women's Studies students understand what feminism is] and more interested in offering them material that is a great vehicle to critical thinking. I don't even see critical thinking as a way of getting them towards the material; I see it as the other way around." And that, she said, is her real goal. "If I can help them think critically then I can help people; if they can think critically about things that are just naturalized to them, they can take that with them and whenever they are going to apply it or however they are going to apply it is their business. But that is my ultimate goal now." This goal echoes Harriet's own political awakening; it was through feminist critique that she was moved to action. The critical thinking skills she learned in the Women's Studies courses she took as a student allowed her to see the world in different ways and created the teacher and writer she is today.

THE PRACTICAL FATHER'S GUIDE TO GETTING A LICENSE

Although Harriet was trained in composition and eventually obtained the "license" to teach composition that her father would be proud of (a PhD in composition from NYU), she often feels alienated by the field of composition because of the canonized theories and way some of her composition colleagues talk about writing. This tenuous relationship to composition as a field may also be one of the reasons that she chooses to teach a variety of cross-disciplinary classes such as the two I observed, an Introduction to Women's Studies class and a cultural studies course. As Harriet tells it, teaching cross-disciplinary general education requirements satiates what she calls her dilettantish nature. "It never even really occurred to me to identify with the comp people as a discipline. I think divisions represent [. . .] ideologies, politics, personality. I have never felt that I haven't had friends in other departments. [Through] my work with Women's Studies, because it is interdisciplinary, I feel connected to people throughout the university." This resistance to categories or disciplines that feel limiting to Harriet, and seeing connections between ideas and theories across various disciplines, reflects a feminist maxim of transgressing or blurring boundaries and borders.

Harriet found composition, as she tells it, through purely practical venues. Despite a public rejection of her father's "be practical; get a license to do something" message, his voice continued to whisper persistently in Harriet's ear. During the early 1990s, Harriet struggled to exercise her passion for writing by teaching part time at several schools to pay the bills. At that time, she was resisting her father's mantra by being what she now calls a *subway flyer*. Riding the subway from job to job, often nodding off from exhaustion against the rhythmic rock of the subway car, Harriet realized she was not getting to be the writer she wanted to be. "In New York there are a lot of adjuncts in English departments who are would-be writers," Harriet said. "They really consider themselves writers and this is a temporary thing for them and then their writing careers will take off and it's sad to see how these people spend their life adjuncting. [. . .] I was working four different places and constantly running. I was always just falling asleep in the subway between things. It was just hell." Exhausting herself by teaching adjunct writing and English Language Learner (ELL) courses at various New York colleges and universities, Harriet saw an ad in the paper advertising positions for full-time composition instructors. "I had resolved never, ever to get a PhD. I didn't want to do that. I wanted to write and I knew [a PhD] would ruin me forever." But the prospect of having a full-time job instead of "hobbling this stuff together constantly and living at the edge" appealed to her, so into the PhD world she went.

The PhD composition program, housed in the Teachers' College at NYU, was less than satisfying for Harriet. "This program was the kind of program you could get through with your eyes closed." She is quick to add that this may have been due to the program being associated with the Teachers' College, instead of in a strong composition/rhetoric program in an English department. Serendipitously perhaps, as part of her program of study, she took a graduate-level Introduction to Gay and Lesbian Studies course in 1991 that decided her dissertation focus. The dissertation focused on gay and lesbian students in the writing classroom and was followed by the publication of her book on the same subject (*Textual Orientations*). The book marked Harriet as the preeminent lesbian theorist in the field of composition. "I had this revelation [taking the graduate queer studies course] that I could do a dissertation on [queer issues in the comp classroom]." Her work created a splash in the field of composition. Although her relationship to the field was ambivalent, the discipline of composition and rhetoric glommed onto her as the lesbian spokesperson, and often still does, much to Harriet's frustration.

Because of the recognition the field of composition gave Harriet's scholarship, one of the first ways I identified Harriet as a feminist teacher was through her visibility and voice within the field teaching and talking about queer issues. Her identity as one of the most, if not the most, prominent queer scholars in the field is the primary reason I wanted to include her in this research. Harriet's relationship to that identity, foisted on her by the field, is one she is less than comfortable with. When I originally contacted Harriet to ask her to be part of my project, she sent back an e-mail that made it clear she no longer wanted to be identified as "the lesbian comp scholar."

E-mail from Harriet. October 17, 2000:

Dear Kay,

I got your letter, your [project idea] sounds great. It also sounds like fun, and I'd love to be your research subject! Let me just explain a couple of things, though, so you can be sure that in your view I really qualify for the project.

First, at this point in my life and teaching (as opposed to some earlier parts), feminism and issues of gender/sexuality remain the bedrock on which much else is based, but they no longer figure as spheres of thought and action privileged above all else. Race, class, culture, public rhetorics, many other things, in fact, pop up equally in my courses and in my writing. [. . .] [Right now] my desire [is] to pursue (sometimes, leap among) very varied and wide-ranging interests, which in recent times have included Hollywood musicals, Australian literature, meanings and implications of globalization, personal essays, choosing not to be a mother, oral history, the book review as a genre, social justice in the broad range of contexts, and many other things that have little or nothing to do with compositions (and/or feminism) per se.

The e-mail continues to also disclose her skepticism about feminist methodologies for teaching and writing. During the site visit, we talked about her doubts regarding feminist pedagogies/methodologies and the label imposed on her in comp circles as "the scholar of queerness in comp."

Kay: Do you see [your scholarship] as a form of pedagogy? Of course it is educating people, but how do you see it as a form of pedagogy?

Harriet: Well, it has changed over the years. I started out as an intimidated graduate student. I had a sort of slavish approach to things. Those were the things I *should* do. But I was also influenced by things like, the first thing I ever published and the first conference paper I ever gave was when I was in the Labor Studies program so a lot of my thinking and my ideas came out of that particular context. So I think partly because I was often in different contexts at the same point in time I would use one to inform the other. There was that, but then pretty soon I got into this lesbian/gay writing thing. And that seemed like a great revelation to me at the time. I didn't really even know there was such a thing as lesbian/gay studies and it wasn't really developed. It was just starting to really explode around the time that I had discovered it. [W]hen I thought I would [make this the focus of my dissertation] I thought I was this lone voice in the wilderness. Little did I know that I wasn't.

Kay: But in comp you were.

Harriet: Yeah, but there was the [Gay and Lesbian 4Cs] caucus.

Kay: Right. But I mean talking about how these issues manifest themselves in the classroom. [. . .] Yes, you are right. People in Women's Studies were talking about it, but I think your writing about it in relation to the writing classroom was [new], because you created a relationship to the writing classroom; it was new to the comp field.

Harriet: And when I think back to the time I was doing that, I remember thinking, "I don't remember seeing this, so I feel like there is no place for me. There is no place for me to bring that stuff in." And then I thought that by writing about it I could create a place. I would create a place first for myself and then for others. I was thinking of it quite selfishly. It was just a framework that I wanted to build because I didn't have it. And it really, for me, that worked tremendously. To the point where I am totally sick of being identified that way. Not

identified that way but there are others things that I am
thinking about and I am always supposed to come and be a
lesbian.

Kay: Right. Well, isn't that what Adrienne Rich always said, too?
She was so tired of being asked just to be the spokeslesbian.
She would be on a panel and they would say, "And you're
supposed to talk about the lesbian stuff." Another connection with Adrienne Rich.

Harriet: Right. All roads lead to Adrienne Rich.

ALL ROADS LEAD TO ADRIENNE RICH

Because of the work Harriet was doing (writing about the intersection of
queer theory and composition) in the place she was doing it (the Teachers'
College at NYU), she said she felt particularly lacking in mentors. This was
a steady refrain I heard from Lynn, Jackie, and Harriet. Because of the work
they were doing at the time they were doing it, there were not any mentors
at hand to lead them carefully through the more bramble-y thickets of academia. That is not to say that mentors did not exist, because there have been
feminist academics across the disciplines even prior to the beginning of the
Second Wave. But for these women, doing the kind of research and scholarship they were interested in, there seemed few feminists (if any) close at
hand within their programs or departments when they were younger scholars. Lynn was trying to forge her way as feminist scholar in a program where
there were few women professors, let alone feminist teachers. Jackie was an
African American woman graduate student at institutions where there were
no other African American faculty members and even paltry few colleagues,
let alone Black women who identified as feminist. As a graduate student,
Harriet was trying to find her way as a writer, lesbian, feminist. All three
women dealt with stepping gingerly through the boggy terrain of academe,
looking around for others to help them along the way. To help herself navi-
gate, Harriet invented mentoring relationships in her private mind with
writers she admired. The most prominent of these was Adrienne Rich.

Harriet: Some of my main mentors have no idea they are my mentors.
I tell you one person who inhabited my head for years [. . .]
who I had dreams about and was a huge influence on me was
Adrienne Rich. [. . .] She was absolutely the ultimate mentor figure that I internalized in my head. I loved her writing.
I feel like I have discovered other writers whose work means
more to me now, but for quite a number of years her writing

was kind of the ultimate for me. I loved its seriousness. One thing I realize now that was missing from her work was humor, absolutely. It is very humorless, but I loved it. I loved her seriousness, her thoughtfulness, her use of language. She is a poet, and I am not just talking about her poetry but her essays that I loved. I loved the way she truly cared about things and was not just self-involved like a lot of people. But she took everything so seriously and applied such thoughtfulness to everything. And that she was so smart. I had so many dreams about her that involved some kind of approval from her.

Kay: And they were good dreams?

Harriet: Only when I woke up I was sad. She wasn't really there. And then when I did encounter her in real life a couple times, and when she acted as if she took me seriously as a human being, it was incredible to me then. There were only those fleeting and few times, but she just really helped me in that way without having any idea that she did. And I think I look to different writers for guidance more than the people I have actually encountered. And a lot of the people I think of, the mentors or people who have influenced me, had nothing to do with pedagogy or composition. I would often read *The [Village] Voice* or *The Nation*, some of the columnists I would read really closely because I loved the writing. [. . .] Some were academics and some weren't. It wasn't what we would call creative writing in the old days, but it wasn't academic writing either. [. . .] Some of those writers would be Katha Pollitt, Patricia Williams, Ellen Willis.

Harriet sees herself first and foremost as a writer, therefore her primary mentors were people to whom she looked as writers she wanted to emulate. The care and concern for writing, the integration of personal narrative into the intellectual discussions of cultural issues, and personal self-critique and disclosure were the main qualities that attracted her to writers like Rich and Williams. It was these writers who forged a path for Harriet to follow in her own prose. Williams' (1991) book, *Alchemy of Race and Rights*, became a model of the kind of writing Harriet wanted to do in her academic world. "I loved what she did. I had been trained to write that somehow it had to be fiction and that couldn't come out in the academic part. She really showed me that, when she wrote essays about legal things, that were personal and novelistic and I thought, 'Wow. This is something I could do.'" In addition to integrating fiction-like prose, Williams also modeled for Harriet rigorous self-critique and self-mockery.

> Her students would say something about her to the dean and she would
> say, "What the hell are you doing?" I really loved that she included that.
> And then she would say things like, "I am lying here in my ratty old
> nightgown thinking about . . ." [. . .] I could read [all these women]
> slowly and carefully and drink up the prose. It inspired me to be more
> precise than any editor of an academic journal would ever [. . .] require
> me to be.

This approach to writing, integrating not only autobiographical information, but a careful critique of self, shameless self-disclosure, is a way to practice the feminist pedagogical theme of self-interrogation in the form of
scholarship.

As Harriet was talking to me, I thought of how Lynn, Jackie, and Harriet
all approach their scholarship with their own brand of a careful, critical feminist approach. The attributes that Harriet assigned to Williams, Rich, Pollitt,
and Willis are those I see in Lynn's, Harriet's, and Jackie's teaching and writing. Instead of having a far-flung mentor with whom I have to create a vicar-
ious or fictional relationship, I have the luxury of the living embodiments all
around me. Because these feminist teachers and scholars, as well as others
closer to home, are doing their work, I have models of hope for the way I
want to do mine. The privilege of that is not something I carry lightly.

In the last moments Harriet and I spent together during my site visit,
she said she needed to go back to the subject of mentors. She had been rumi-
nating on her need to fabricate mentors from the public sphere and wanted
to give credit to women who were more integrated into her lived experience.
She told me about a feminist mentor in her first Women's Studies class,
Judith Bransberg, a graduate student who seemed so much more worldly
and well read than Harriet was at the time. "She was six years older than I
was. I was 23 and she was 29. I always felt she was my intellectual mentor.
She encouraged the intellectual part of me to surface." In general, women in
Women's Studies classes showed Harriet a way to be female and not afraid.
"Part of my attraction to Women's Studies was seeing older women say,
'You should take risks.' Seeing that they weren't fearful, that they took risks.
I was taught to *obey* authority because it would protect you. My mother
taught me to respect authority, not question it."

Through these fearless feminists in her Women's Studies courses,
Harriet dove into social activism. Her work surrounding political issues in
Central America in the mid-1980s led her to grassroots activist mentors.
Harriet specifically remembers Francisca Morales, a woman who mentored
her through the Contra-resistance in Nicaragua. In 1985 Harriet was living
with Morales during the heat of revolution. In Morales, Harriet saw an
immediate and important connection between feminist activism and writing,
as well as writing *as* feminist activism, a way of communicating feminist
thoughts to the world.

[Francisca Morales] was so amazing. I learned so much from her. Just listening to her and talking to her. She was this little woman. You wouldn't see her as physically threatening or powerful. But here she was surrounded by 4,000 Contras. It was totally terrifying. There were deaths and funerals every day. I was living with her family. She was the mother, Francisca Morales. She was 51 years old and really active in the radical organizations. Before the revolution she had been illiterate, but it was difficult for me to process that. She was physically little, but so powerful. A real activist, and her activism was centered on reading and writing. I went with her to various meetings. She caught two Contras herself. It seemed like every day I was coming home and she was telling a story about how she nabbed another Contra. Like Adrienne Rich she was incredibly opposite of my mother. I always thought that if she and Adrienne Rich could meet, that would be great. They both had the same small intensity.

Bransberg, Rich, and Morales provided essential mentoring in grassroots activism and feminism, and giving voice to those experiences through stories and writing. As Harriet continued to talk about mentors, she mentioned Jackie Jones Royster as someone within the field whom she has looked to and engaged with in a mentor relationship. Harriet describes Jackie as being "startlingly available" to Harriet and her ideas. She initially contacted Jackie because of a point of contention Harriet had with a piece of Jackie's scholarship. "I disagreed with something she wrote and so she emailed me and we had this really rich email exchange," Harriet recalled. "It was honestly her attempt to try and understand my position and to communicate her position to me. I found it so enriching and positive." Harriet said there are few people who embody both personal warmth and intellectual vibrancy, but she sees that combination in Jackie Jones Royster. "There is a certain openness that comes from her. She has that warm/smart nexus." To clarify, Harriet said she defines smart people as those who engage in self-critique. "That is really important to me, that we aren't just critiquing the work or the scholarship or the culture, but that we are engaging in self-critique as well. Smart people do that." Harriet's definition of *smart* closely reflected how Lynn articulated her definition of feminism, strengthening the connections I see between Harriet and Lynn and their approach to the world and their teaching.

THE FEMINIST TEMPLATE

Through feminism in the form of Women's Studies, Harriet found a port of entry into her intellectual life. Harriet describes feminism not only as the foundation of her beliefs, but "in every pore." "That fundamental layer was through Women's Studies which led me to an interest in race and it was through race that I got interested in class, and it was through class that I got interested in sexuality, in Central America, in environmental stuff; these things just sort of grew, but feminism was the template." Through feminism, Harriet also discovered community activism, the power to change the world one corner at a time. Her first public feminist act was also part of that transitional Women's Studies course in 1978. A doctoral student in the class pointed out that her qualifying exam reading list only included 2 (out of 60) women authors. The class collectively added eight additional women authors to the list and presented the proposal to the English department. Harriet was part of the small coterie of women who went to the English department meeting to argue for the change. At that moment, in a mid-winter English department meeting surrounded by Good Old Boy faculty looking bored, disinterested, and hostile, she realized the influence a small group of people could have on the world. "I didn't know what I was doing, but I realized I was excited to go with [the feminist graduate students]. It was also the moment when I realized I could do something that might affect policy somewhere. Policy always seemed ready-made. I had very essentialized notions of policy and structure of things and really no concept of its making."

After this baptism in the power of activism, Harriet worked on various feminist fronts both in her home of New York City and in Central America. When she became involved in these causes, she turned herself over to them heart and soul. "I tended to get involved in things and become completely consumed, completely active, a maniacal member of the steering committee." Her work with rape crisis centers, revolutionary groups in Nicaragua, gay and lesbian tasks forces, and abortion rights coalitions trained her in grassroots political and social activism. Through these associations, she furthered her critical consciousness. The activists involved in the grassroots organizations showed Harriet a new way to see the world. "They were the type of people who did things in the world in a way that I really hadn't. So I remember being at NYWAR (New York Women Against Rape) and just being befuddled by how the world worked. And for me, being in those organizations was largely figuring out how the world worked." Harriet eventually used these organizing and activist skills to create the Women's Studies program at LIU, developing curriculum, writing and receiving grants, and training faculty in feminist theory.

These activist beginnings find their way into Harriet's feminist pedagogical practices by asking students to take the classroom theories and discussions into their lives. A ready example of this commitment to integrating community and classroom work manifests itself in the form of an "Oral Histories" assignment in the "Women in Culture and Society" class I observed. The students were asked to find a woman in the community who was over 70 years of age and talk to her about her life, specifically in regard to an issue that had been discussed in the class curriculum (reproductive freedom, issues of work equity, race, sexual orientation). The students then had to transcribe the interview and create a narrative around the woman's story, creating tangible and real connections between one person's life and the work of the course.

Harriet's commitment to this theme of feminist connections between the community and the academy, one that began in a Women's Studies graduate course and led to grassroots activism, evolved to feminist pedagogy as leadership: designing and launching the Women's Studies program at LIU. Stepping forward and positioning herself as a leader in the university setting was a seemingly natural extension of Harriet's feminist activism. Her belief system drove this project and touched every part of her life. "[Feminism] was a way that I could enter something that I realized was going to be vital to my life, intellectually, politically, and personally and affect my relationships with people and my sense of happiness." Through Women's Studies, Harriet found a way by which to enter into discussions and ideas that would have been obscured from her without the critical awakening provided by those courses. "[Feminism] gave me a familiar pattern; I *knew* how to enter into something after that."

Harriet applies this feminist template to various sites: activism, leadership, teaching, and scholarship. Because Harriet experiences feminism in every pore, as she says, it is difficult for her to define or describe practices or beliefs that are specifically feminist.

> I think of a lot of things in terms of atoms and molecules. An atom is this totally homogenous thing. A molecule is, too, but it is a compound element. An atom is just this one thing. I can think of feminism, anti-racism, whatever, as these atoms. In a way they exist there, but in a way it is all molecular, too. They are just so totally mixed in together. I know now how many different versions of feminism there are, and because [of that] I don't particularly latch onto one.

Harriet resisted my questions regarding how she would define feminism, eschewing a potentially essentialized, static way of measuring feminism and *feminists*.

To further explain the complexity of settling on one definition of feminism, Harriet uses the analogy of trying to define what it means to be an American.

> If an American is a citizen of the United States, which is also kind of iffy because there are people who are not citizens who are Americans, who have been living here forever. But let's just say you say [an American is

a citizen of the United States], it still doesn't say what kind of citizen. So
when I think of feminism I think of that kind of dispersal of realities.
They all have something to do with women's entitlement to exist as people.

This definition of feminism, "women's entitlement to exist as people,"
comes only after I have pushed Harriet more than once to try to define what
feminism is for her. When I began asking on the first day, she politely
dodged my question. I kept asking, however. I wanted to hear how she
thought of feminism for herself, but she kept hearing the question as my
pressing her to offer an overarching definition of what feminism is in general, for everyone. Harriet relates the way she perceives feminism or her resistance to offering a comprehensive definition of feminism to her geographic
location.

> The fact that I live in New York, that I am here, makes life different than
> if I were in most places. You see yourself and your beliefs relative to
> others and here it is so easy. Sometimes I am out in the country some-
> place and I realize suddenly that the difference is so huge between me
> and other people that. . . . And I know there are people at 4Cs who have
> this problem with me. They think I am a spoiled brat. That I don't
> understand what it is like. That I don't understand what it is like for
> them. And they are right. I mean I understand basically what it is like,
> but I also wouldn't be there. I couldn't be there. I just couldn't. Because
> I really want to live where I want to live. I chose where I wanted to live
> and I chose New York above any particular institution and I have never
> regretted that at all. That again has to do with my concept of feminism.
> My wits become a little dull by lack of having really to face that kind of
> challenge, that truly anti-feminist challenge, in a long time.

Perhaps this is the crux of my pressing Harriet to define feminism and her
resistance: I hail from a geographic location where claiming the identity is
imperative to my activist work. I live in a place where I believe I need to
publicly embrace the moniker so people have a better understanding of what
feminism is. By understanding that I am a feminist, they have to revise the
dominant culture's definition of feminist as a man-hating warrior for female
domination.

Offering a definition for feminism was not the only point of resistance
between Harriet and this project. In an early interview with Harriet, she said
she really did not think feminist pedagogy existed; that is to say, she did not
feel there was a distinct quality to feminist pedagogy that made it different
from other pedagogies. When I asked her to offer a definition of what she
thought it was or what people meant when they used the term, her defini-

tion seemed to hearken back to the earliest models of feminist pedagogy based on progressive education meets CR groups. "Most of the things I have read about [feminist pedagogy] have gotten on my nerves," she said. "They make all these points for being feminist that aren't necessarily. And of course all the touchy-feely stuff. I don't really understand why they have to define certain things they do as feminist. Often it veers into a belief about content and you have to be anti-racist, anti-sexist, anti-homophobic." It isn't that Harriet is opposed to being aware of social and political representation when designing a course or choosing course materials, only that some educators tend to use the tag words without understanding the complexity of the issues involved.

> When I write a syllabus I am very aware and care a lot about creating a syllabus that represents diverse people, but I realized a long time ago that the reason developing a syllabus is so hard is that in addition to that there are a million other forms of diversity you want. So you might want diversity, but in what area? Like in the course I am teaching now (Reading Culture), what culture are we looking at? Are we looking outside the United States?

A lot of feminist teachers focus on diversity, Harriet said, but for them diversity is limited to basic identity issues. Diversity becomes a sexy part of the rhetoric that remains uninterrogated. A teacher who is practicing feminist pedagogy will be more critical of how she is interrogating, integrating, and teaching diversity than a teacher who is simply including diversity because it is part of what is expected. There is a significant and profound distinction between a teacher who includes some texts by women or minorities on the syllabus because that is the standard operating procedure in her enlightened department and a feminist teacher who rigorously interrogates how diversity will be represented and discussed and what kinds of diversity will be represented, always being overt with these choices not only with herself but her students as well.

To illustrate the problematic way *diversity* has become a tag word with little substance or critical reflection behind it, Harriet told a story of buying a house in Brooklyn. The rhetoric that realtors used to describe different neighborhoods proved interesting. *Diversity* became a signifier they used to indicate a neighborhood that was largely White middle to upper middle class with a few traditionally marginalized cultural representatives acting as spice. Many of the realtors spoke about the diversity of the school. "But it usually meant that there weren't even five kids in the class who weren't white. It also wasn't socio-economic diversity. [Diversity] was something that their children had to be exposed to," Harriet recalled. Translating this scenario to feminist pedagogy, the diversity issue is one where teachers feel their students need exposure, but too often the interrogation stops there. Instead of talking about systems of oppression or why having a smattering of readings on the syllabus that represent traditionally marginalized voices does not count as diversity, some teachers use diversity as a way of syllabus design and nothing more. In this way, teachers, schools, and university administrators can talk about diversity without really getting serious about their collusion with the systems of oppression or giving serious consideration to those systems. Instead, a feminist teacher is critically aware of the voices and silences within her syllabus or curriculum and openly confronts those with her students. Harriet's critical awareness of diversity and her critique of the rhetoric surrounding diversity stems from her original feminist training in critical consciousness. Currently, institutions and individuals who are not enacting feminist pedagogical principles have fetishized marks of difference; the identities of traditionally marginalized people or the world perspectives who do not represent the dominant culture become exotic points of intrigue as opposed to sites of critical analysis and change. There is no critical reflection or awareness involved.

For me, this severe lack of teacher critical reflection that Harriet sees in some educators points to a type of pedagogy that is decidedly not feminist. Because one of the crucial elements of feminism is the ability to critically reflect and change one's own reality and collusion with systems of oppression, so is critical reflection of choices and decisions made by the teacher on behalf of the class essential. Smart critical reflection is not a short-term goal, but a skill one works on over a lifetime. Bizzell (1992) compares writing and critical consciousness by saying they are both "a life long practice" (p. 12). Ironically, what Harriet originally named as the elements she most resented about feminist pedagogy (lack of attention to real critical analysis of diversity issues; touchy-feely classrooms where chairs are in a circle, but content is anti-intellectual; and lazy teachers who use the theory of student-centered classrooms to excuse themselves from actual teaching) are descriptors that are very much not a part of the feminist pedagogy I am investigating. Instead, the elements that Harriet articulates as necessary to all of her classrooms (careful selection of texts and topics that cover various perspectives, often those traditionally left out of curriculum; a strong focus on teaching students critical thinking and analysis; making connections between her life and experiences and her classroom, and encouraging her students to do the same) are themes that ground my research.

In e-mail and phone conversations with Harriet following the site visit, she revised the way she saw feminist pedagogy. As I tried to explain and argue for a distinct pedagogy that was feminist, Harriet came to embrace the term as a valid descriptor for a specific pedagogical approach. Although Harriet's definition of feminist pedagogy may not exactly line up with the one I am using in my research, she said our exchanges allowed her to see feminist pedagogy that was not so much about form as it was about content. For her, it was easier to see that there can be content to a course that is uniquely feminist.

> I remember then [when taking the course on feminist pedagogy in grad-uate school in the late 1970s], and forever afterwards, thinking, "So what is feminist pedagogy?" I never really did get it. I guess I am final-ly turning that around and saying maybe there is nothing to get. Something you said, wrote, made me think that feminist pedagogy is really about content and not about form. And the problem for me was that it was suppose to be about some kind of form. But that never seemed exclusive to feminism or feminist pedagogy, nor did it seem par-ticularly always present in feminist pedagogy. I guess my final conclu-sion is that there is no form that is feminist pedagogy, it would really be about content.

Kay: The other thing is that I don't want to wedge [you into my definition], for example, to say, "Well, she is a feminist teacher," which I totally believe and I feel like what I have observed supports that and then to have you say, "No I don't believe there is such a thing as feminist pedagogy. Therefore, I can be a feminist teacher because my ideology of feminism impacts how I teach, but there is no such a thing as inherent feminist pedagogy."

Harriet: But now I would say, something you had said before in an email, did make me rethink it that there is such a thing in terms of content, an ideology, and that does seep into every-thing that I do. It is kind of like a feminist perspective, almost. I guess I feel I have more of a feminist perspective than a feminist pedagogy. Because that somehow has to do more with content and relationship to content. And again, [feminism] is not the only perspective, but it is one very dom-inant one.

Feminist perspective. Feminist ideology. Feminist pedagogy. Although all three ways of describing a feminist approach can generally be interpret-ed in similar ways, my project is about getting specific about what those approaches are. It is only when we have a historical definition that we can be critically aware and cognizant of the work we are doing and how we are furthering, or not furthering, a feminist belief system in our approach, work, teaching, and writing. I agree with Harriet that there is not one *form* that is feminist, but I would change the rhetoric of that and say there is not one *practice* that is feminist. Each teacher will enact any or all of the themes dif-

ferently depending on their own teaching style, their social/political location, their personality, and the context of each specific classroom. Each
teacher will pick and choose themes to emphasize.

THE NATURE OF A DILETTANTE

Harriet's commitment to writing passionately, and teaching her students to
do so as well, demonstrates a connection between scholarship and teaching,
between the personal and the theoretical, between feminist pedagogy and
feminist rhetoric. Her desire to teach from the center of that passion, and to
bring her lived experiences into her writing and her classrooms, provides a
model for her students and colleagues to do the same, thereby subverting the
standards of the field and re-creating a feminist way where a more traditional patriarchal model existed. Using critical consciousness and honest, sassy
self-disclosure, Harriet's writing and teaching merge into a dialogic force of
energetic interactions. Her desire to create connections where she sees divisions, resisting dividing lines and categories of identity and instead explor-
ing many different ways of knowing, being, learning, and teaching, speak to
the dilettante-ish nature she claims for herself. This identity seems to me
inherently feminist in nature, blurring boundaries and resisting neat categorization, seizing the power to name and create new ways, new roads, new
models. Perhaps, in the end, this is why Harriet resists the idea of a distinct
feminist pedagogy. The messing up, the disruptions, seems too important to
be contained in one approach or theory. Her drive to avoid rigidity and stag-
nation is, in itself, I would argue, a feminist pedagogical strategy for making
connections and consistently and carefully reflecting with a critical eye on
teaching and writing and how these two ways of life intersect with lived reality. Although I have a need to see Harriet in this way, I understand and
respect her rejection of parts of my argument that would create a more comprehensive and perhaps neater view of feminist pedagogy as it manifests
itself in her life and work. Perhaps it is inevitable that where I see themes she
sees disjuncture. It is her dilettantish and eclectic nature.

ADDENDUM

Harriet intended to respond to this chapter by inserting her thoughts within the text. I e-mailed her electronic copies of the chapter in July 2001 so that
she could add her comments before my November 2001 deadline. However,
on September 11, 2001, tragedy struck New York City when the World

Trade Centers were reduced to a pile of rubble. As one can imagine, Harriet, a life-long New Yorker, was deeply shaken. To help the community to cope with the event, Long Island University, where Harriet teaches, created courses to examine the rhetoric of "The War on Terrorism," the phrase the press assigned to the war against Afghanistan, declared by President George W. Bush as a result of the September 11 attacks. Harriet fell in and began teaching extra courses to meet the needs of the community. Because of all this upheaval, Harriet was not able to comment or integrate her thoughts and responses into "The Harriet Chapter." Following is the e-mail she sent in response to my last effort to wiggle something out of her. It constitutes her response to this chapter, pointing to how the material realities of teachers' and women's lives affect the work to be done.

E-mail from Harriet dated November 11, 2001.

Dear Kay,

When the lumpy envelope from you appeared in my mailbox, I thought it must be my much-deserved anthrax. . . .

I've been absolutely crazed with overextension since Sept. 11. The two books I was reading—a novel by Stendhal and a biography of two Australian women artists—have been frozen in time on my bedside table, with the bookmarks exactly where they were that day, like victims of Pompeii. . . . Along with several other faculty members at LIU, I'm teaching an impromptu, half-semester, 1-credit, tuition-free, and open to the public course called "Critically Reading the 'War on Terrorism.'" I've been putting all my energy into that, to the point of fairly neglecting my other (real, full-credit, full-term, tuition-fed) courses. In addition, I turned my Miami paper over to that whole subject (Keith did, too), and actually presented the paper just a couple of hours before the bombs started to fall. (I got to watch them on CNN at the airport gate, for quite a while before boarding.) Since then, in addition to everything else, I've been doing a tenure review for someone, adding things like the Koran to my literature course— which of course requires a lot of special, unanticipated preparation—and have turned my Basic Reading and Writing course completely over to that theme as well. There was also a series of teach-ins before the war course kicked in. In sum, the relatively tranquil term I was expecting after the early Oct. conference in your old stomping grounds [Miami University of Ohio] has been non-existent. . . . In truth, I spend a great deal of the aforementioned time immersed in media—the NY Times, CNN and the networks, The Nation, independent media sites on the net, and then at night, obsessing about it all on the phone. . . .

And you know what? I don't feel like my response has been particularly "feminist"! In fact, I remember in my early, tender feminist years, being very influenced by Adrienne Rich's insistence that she would no longer call herself "humanist"; that was passé; now she would claim only "feminist." Of course, I, being a little know-nothing without an intellectual past, had no "humanism" to renounce; I just claimed "feminism" over "vapidity." But lately, I've really taken the opposite tack from her (and I bet she has, too); "humanism" just seems, even if a bit vague and general (!), a more apt description of the orientation of my heart and head. Between despair at the unbelievable and pointless suffering of so many people, and despair at the completely bankrupt rhetoric of Bush et al., which is embraced without question, critique, or investigation by the media and thus by our pathetic populace (I have to remind myself that "they know not what they do"—I mean the pathetic populace, not the media—and thus are not as culpable as people who have not been so relentlessly stupidified—though they could learn more if they really, really wanted to—and some actually are doing just that), I'm in a general state of panic and want to run off to some faraway place, far from flags, God Bless Americas, and the revolting and enduring World Trade Center Smell—someplace populated only by Quakers, Buddhists, and kindly, intelligent atheists. I don't care if they're feminists or not, though I guess if they're not, I'll start caring a lot more about that again.

In any case, CONGRATULATIONS [on being done with the project]. What's happening next? How has life been in Nebraska? I was really sorry you weren't in Oxford when I was there.

So take care.

Harriet

CONTEXTUALIZING
THE KNOWING SUBJECT

Jackie Jones Royster

I approached Jackie Jones Royster and asked her to participate in my project because I believed her to be one of the most prominent, outspoken, and
out-feminist African American scholars in the field. I had listened to Jackie
present at various conferences, including Conference on College
Composition and Communication, Feminism(s) and Rhetoric(s) and
Rhetoric Society of America. I first came to know Jackie as a scholar
through her essay "When the First Voice You Hear Is Not Your Own." In
the essay, she describes the physical reality of being an African American
teacher in the classroom and discusses issues of voice and representation in
a college setting. The bold and honest confrontation of racial and gender
issues, and typically both, are the trademarks of her work. So, what I knew
of Jackie before I began this project was most importantly for me the "When
the First Voice You Hear" essay. In the past few years, I have listened to her
present at conferences and read her scholarship that focuses on her work
restoring the voices of African American women of the 19th century to the
American rhetorical canon.

Jackie's (Royster, 1997) book, *Southern Horrors and Other Writings:
The Anti-Lynching Campaign of Ida B. Wells, 1892–1900*, re-introduced the
rhetorical style of Wells and republished some of her speeches and essays

within the context of the anti-lynching campaigns of the South. As with the "When the First Voice You Hear" essay, the physical presence, the bodily reality, of being African American and female featured prominently in the introduction, where Jackie included editorial cartoons that featured lynchings from *Harpers Weekly* as well as photos of Wells and the people who mentored Wells. The book marks a reclaiming or restoring of Wells to the rhetorical American canon, grounding the scholarship in feminist theory of identity politics as Royster examines how the physical reality of being Black and female manifested itself in Well's life and work. The Wells project led Jackie to more research of African American women's voices lost to the great White male master narratives of dominant history. Her most recent book, *Traces of a Stream*, continues the project that began with Wells, providing rhetorical analyses and historical context for other women, those less famous than Wells, whose voices were heretofore lost to us. Jackie strongly identifies with the women she has researched and written about. Her scholarship in this area began as part of a centennial celebration Jackie was organizing for Spelman College. Through archival research as part of the centennial plans, Jackie discovered women who had been erased. Her passion became resurrecting those women and their voices so they could take their rightful place in the annals of American history.

Jackie was a professor of English, Writing Program Administrator, and Associate Dean at Spelman college for 16 years before moving to Ohio State University (OSU), where she is a Professor of English and now Associate Dean of Research and Faculty Affairs. At OSU, Jackie has been involved with the university's Writing Center and helped to organize the Women's Center on campus where Women's Studies is housed. Her scholarship reflects the intersections of these three areas: composition, rhetoric, and feminism.

Jackie's leadership is not limited to the campuses where she works. She has served on the executive committee for the Teaching of Writing Division of the Modern Language Association and on the executive committee for College Composition and Communication, serving as chair for the latter in 1995. Jackie worked as associate editor of *SAGE: Scholarly Journal on Black Women* from 1983 to 1996. Her identity as an African American teacher, scholar, and leader always figures prominently in her scholarship. Jackie's approach is one of directness, confronting the difficult issues of racism and sexism with frank honesty that provides a model for how we *should* approach such difficult, thorny issues, but often do not.

Chapter Five

Jackie Jones Royster

Radical Pathways of Nerve and Sass

Journal Entry: May 15, 2001.

I want Jackie to have a different office: more spacious, with state-ly furniture befitting an associate dean. In her small office space, a large desk dominates the room; a small table with four chairs is squeezed into the area just inside the door. There is little room left, unless one counts the huge amount of space overhead, with fifteen foot ceilings belying the cramped quarters beneath them. There is hardly room for two people to stand comfortably. When other people entered while Jackie and I are in her office together, I try to stand small and hunch over: too cramped. She definitely needs more room, more space. And she is so insanely busy. It is exhausting just watching her work, and following her around for the day. This project, which has become in my mind "observing feminists in their natural habitat," always slams me up against the material realities of their lives. These women are so intense-ly passionate about their work, Harriet, Lynn and Jackie. And I at least want people to appreciate that and acknowledge that. So that is another reason for this project. In the meantime, I want Jackie to have a different, better, more comfortable and spacious office.

I arrived at the Ohio State University (OSU) campus on a rainy day in May. The building where the administration for Humanities is housed, University Hall, is stately in that academic, brick, "founding fathers" sort of way. It is situated just off "The Oval" (a prominent green space in the middle of the

OSU campus). As I dash to the building under a too-small umbrella, I am confused by bustling students on a campus I expected to be deserted. Because OSU is on a quarter system, students and faculty are still wearily winding down the term, whereas mine ended a full 2 weeks ago.

Once inside University Hall, I find the main Humanities office and chat with the administrative assistant. She is contemplating an Intro to Women's Studies course for the first summer session, and I am trilling the praises of the course, even though I have no idea what the intro courses are like at OSU. "It's a life-changing course," I tell her. "Or at least it typically is for many of the students in *my* classes." I am saved from fully contemplating the arrogance of that comment, as well as my assumptions that this young woman embodies a similar social/political location as my students, clearly she does not as a nontraditional student who is African American, by Jackie trundling me back to her office. I sit down at the small table, piled high with packets and papers, as she finishes up some administrative tasks before we dash off to the first of many meetings that day.

The wall behind Jackie's desk displays prominent portraits of Ida B. Wells and Frederick Douglass. There is also a framed poster displaying concentric circles of carefully arranged Native American beaded moccasins of varying sizes and shapes, toes facing in. The poster advertises a Smithsonian exhibit. I saw the same exhibit in New York City last fall. "All Roads Are Good," the poster declares.

Roads. Pathways. Passageways. Trails. Treks. Traces. Ways. Journeys. I encounter this rhetoric of travel, of guidance, of marked journeys in Jackie's scholarship, leadership, and teaching. The poster's declamation, "*All* roads are good," can be read as a validation for ways typically not recognized by the dominant culture, specifically in the context of the museum exhibit, Native American ways. This reading also works well when applied to Jackie's own work. She is a trailblazer as an African American woman who is associate dean at a Big Ten university. But her work of creating paths for others to follow does not stop there. As a scholar of 19th-century African American women, women who similarly created paths of leadership to follow, Jackie re-forges those women's paths with scythe and grit, paths obscured, and sometimes obliterated, by the asphalted interstates of master narratives. By re-cutting these trails, she offers an alternative route: *all* roads are good. By extension, then, *all* destinations are good. Through her work as a leader in the field and in her university community, as a teacher, as a Black feminist scholar working to reclaim, recover, and restore the paths and journeys of African American women who traveled before her, Jackie creates the possibility of not only other roads and ways, but new destinations.

As I sit at the table while Jackie rummages through the papers on her desk, she exclaims, "I would have so much more time if I could actually *find* things." My first response is to commiserate: There are stacks and stacks of papers everywhere. The table I am sitting at is covered with thick piles of annual reviews for both college of Humanities programs and professors. I stop this train of thought. "Actually," I think, "You do a great job of finding things." Really, it is more about finding people, stories, identities, and places and then creating road maps so others can find them. Jackie would probably protest this analogy: She is not "finding" them at all; she is reclaiming them. They were not lost or undiscovered; these trails have been a part of this U.S. culture all along. They have only been ignored and overgrown because the White supremacist patriarchal superhighway is easier, faster, and more readily available. But it is not better. *All* roads are good.

PATHWAYS AND PASSAGES FORGED, OBSCURED, CLEARED, AND RE-CUT

Before a pathway or road can be traveled, acting as a more expedient way to get from Point A to Point B, it needs to be forged. In the restoration scholarship of 19th-century African American women that began with Jackie's book on Ida B. Wells and the anti-lynching campaign, the paths they forged have been obscured. Jackie has taken it on herself to clear these treks and, in some cases where the overgrowth has obliterated the course, re-cut the trails so others can follow. In *Traces of a Stream* (2000), the title itself describes the clearing work that Jackie has taken it on herself to do. There are only "traces" of a stream to follow, but the records show a stream existed, delivering the water essential to grow lush vegetation and provide sustenance to entire populations or communities. In this book, Jackie's work historically follows the stream, the identities and stories of African American women who helped write the history and culture of this country, and creates, from the traces, a record of what the burbling, thriving, surging water force was before the dominant culture rerouted the life-giving source away from the communities that depended on it for survival. In this way, her work is like remapping geographical and geological terrain. In her own words, however, Jackie names her processes and projects of restoration *historical ethnography.*

Jackie defines historical ethnography as a transdisciplinary and multidimensional approach to history making. "I get to discover little-known people and retell, as I have done today, their stories" (Royster, "Sarah's Story," 1999, p. 47). But this scholar is not just telling stories; instead she is looking closely at historical context, cultural practices, rhetorical moves, and the relationships of the world to these women, the relationship between these women and the world. She fills in the gaps carefully and with deliberate attention to the authority and responsibility she is taking on when she does so. In the spirit of feminism and the spirit of these women whose lives have been covered up with the thick dust of the Master and his narratives, Jackie takes the risk to deviate from standard practices of scholarly research where evidence is presented, not created. The deviation, then, comes not in form so much as approach. It is the *way* she pieces together these histories—from photographs, newspapers, personal letters, essays—that creates a model of feminist scholarship. The stories are not created from documented sources or scholarship, but from a plethora of personal and cultural artifacts where Jackie fills in the gaps as she can. In using this unconventional approach, Jackie acts defiantly; she has the nerve, as she often says of the women she is writing about, to forge a new way. From her work comes an alternate approach to scholarship, another way of seeing the world, a new path to follow.

In her keynote address at the 2001 Race, Gender, and Orientation Symposium at Miami University, Jackie said she wanted *Traces of a Stream* to encourage other scholarship, evidence of her own deliberate, defiant trail blazing. Because the methodology she uses in that text is a deviation from standards of historical data collection and analysis, some have scoffed at her invitation that others should follow, or *can* follow.

> **Kay:**   I think another way of looking at defiance within your work is just the way, the methodology you use. The way you say, "Well, you know, I know parts of these stories, but I am telling the other parts because those voices are lost and . . ."
>
> **Jackie:**   " . . . and so what. We can know a lot of stuff and not know it all."
>
> **Kay:**   And that kind of defiance of, "I don't care what you're going to say about that approach or what the standards are to the approach when there are gaps and how people fill them. I am going to do it this way."
>
> **Jackie:**   And I think it makes sense. And so, yeah. That is the way I see me. I feel a lot more radical than people think I am. In some ways you would think that I have conformed to certain kinds of traditional expectations for how women might proceed. Even this year, someone was saying [. . .] my choices were very different choices, but not everybody can do that. Only privileged people can do that. "So, you are Jackie Royster, you can do that." It took me 15 years to do this book, so you think these are easy choices? They are not. I

have experienced quite a bit of turmoil in having made these decisions and pushed these ways of doing things. If you think people automatically accept what I do, think again. So it is that kind of thing. At this point in my career, after having done things in whatever way that I have, that pushing the boundaries in whatever way I have managed to push, there is the assumption that I am just, everything comes easy. But it is difficult. I can expect that. If you tried to do it, then you would have a problem.

Kay: Well, I think, reading over the stuff I have read by you, I have always been attracted to the way you approach things because it is never in the typical way. [...] You always throw in some surprises. You are always trying to turn it, twist it, shape it in another way that I think is really refreshing. So, for someone to say, when they just happen to pick that last chapter [of *Traces of a Stream*], that you could do that, but they never could, when you look back through your work, you can see evidence of that [maverick approach] throughout. So it is not like all of a sudden, "Oh, I think now that I have this secure position, I can start dinking around with the ways I use rhetoric and the way I am presenting my information."

Jackie: And that is the point that this person didn't see. In a way it reminded me of something I had just not paid attention to for awhile. It was really very nice to have Pat [Bizzell at the Rhetoric Society of America conference] talk about my work with critical attention. It wasn't necessarily just being laudatory, but by giving it critical attention, after 15 years, just trying to make a space for something. "Ok. Ok. I am here. You can look at this. It has some credibility." That was a very different moment to have that critical attention as compared to the earlier days when I heard people say, "Oh, I didn't know that Black women could read." And then that question reminded me that, there are some people who just don't know. Who don't see the pathway in quite the way I see it.

The way Jackie sees it, that *pathway* is a life force for African American women's history, African American history, and *American* history. Through her re-cutting and re-forging and re-claiming that path, she becomes one of the trailblazers she writes about. In writing about Sarah, one of the children on the *Amistad*, Jackie reclaims her story and the importance of that small,

African girl-child's life, stating Sarah was a person "whose personal history happened to include one of the most dramatic events in African American history" ("Sarah's Story," 1999, p. 47). The small African child, abducted and held captive on a slave ship, became a success story of the abolitionist movement: College educated at Oberlin, she became a dynamic rhetor, teacher, and trailblazer. In conversations with Jackie and in her speeches and scholarship, Jackie often asks, "Where did they get the nerve?" Where did these women of African descent find the strength, tenacity, and nerve to forge ahead in a pathless jungle of the dominant culture so that others could follow? They led lives in constant jeopardy, and where, Jackie asks, did they get the nerve?

SASSY DEFIANCE

This nerve, this self-described "sassiness" as Jackie often says, is a recalcitrant shrug at the white, supremacist patriarchal conventions. The patriarchal conventions of how history is written or how a scholar creates research do not fit Jackie's approach. By piecing together history from sources that are seen as traditionally credible (newspapers, books) and those that leave room for feminist interpretation and gap-filling (photos, personal letters, speculation), the sassy defiance of Jackie's work thumbs its nose at dominant ways of doing things. "Does my sassiness upset you?" Maya Angelou (1986) asks in "Still I Rise." Jackie is not really asking. Rather she, like the narrator of Angelou's poem, is taunting and daring. Whether her sass, intellect, or refusal to cower before the culture that assigns her the traditionally marginalized and disempowered position of black and female upsets is of little concern to her. Sassiness becomes a rhetorical action, like the shamelessness Lynn writes about in "Entitlement": words without shame; words dripping with sass. It reflects a rhetoric of defiance; and still I rise.

Like Angelou and the women Jackie's work reclaims and restores to American history, specifically American rhetorical history, Jackie embodies the same defiance, a feminist spirit of resistance, in her work as scholar, teacher, and administrator. "You can write me down in history, with your bitter, twisted lies/[. . .] But still, like dust, I rise," Angelou narrates in the voice of her sassy woman. Like the dust of the road left unpaved, ignored, but still well traveled, African American women's lives rise up through their own spirit, certainly, but through Jackie's pen and voice as well. By telling the stories others won't, doing her "historical ethnography" that gives stories and identities to those who are lost to history, Jackie not only names others as sassy women, those with nerve to rise and survive despite all odds, but she herself is included in that category.

Jackie knows to include herself with these women she is restoring to American rhetorical history. In her inaugural address as Full Professor to faculty and administrators at OSU, she tells the stories of "Sassy Women"; within her speech, the "they" becomes "we."

> I particularly want to represent how African American women stand solidly in one world, a world that is not particularly accommodating to *them* and by various processes, *they* systematically imagine and create a new vision of a world that is filled with possibility and cast light on various processes that help us transform ourselves so that these imagined worlds become real.
>
> [. . .]
>
> The very inclination to speak, to write, to use literacy is in and of itself an act of resistance, an act of defiance. The very fact of producing language becomes an authorizing event, one that African American women have been able to set *themselves* on pathways to personal empowerment, advocacy, and activism. In focusing on the 19th century, the physical condition of African American women was, whether free or enslaved or later freed, they led lives in constant jeopardy. [. . . .] The hostile context and degrading circumstances, the critical context, gave lots of reasons to lay down and die. *We* didn't. [. . .] [D]espite consistent messages from a world that encourages *us* to think otherwise, African American women are sassy. *We* are irrepressible. Quite consistently *we* simply refuse to have our hearts and minds restrained or our spirits crushed. [italics added]

In her book *Traces of a Stream* (2000), Jackie overtly discusses why she includes herself in the subject group of her research (using *we* instead of *they*). Because she identifies strongly with the women she is researching and writing about, she includes herself among them. "I intend for myself to be viewed as one among those who constitute the subject of this discourse" (p. 13). In her work and in her rhetoric, Jackie rejects the dispassionate, objective stance for one that creates connections that bring power and strength to the work. In fact, this close association with the "Sassy Women" about whom she writes and talks applies feminist ethics to her work. She is not "othering" her research subjects because she includes herself among them. Additionally, by not only recognizing herself as a sassy woman, but positioning herself so publicly, specifically within the context of her inaugural address, Jackie is exercising that tradition of defiance she celebrates in the subjects of her research. At the rhetorical moment of her inaugural address, Jackie is declaiming to her colleagues that she intends to be sassy, defiant, critically conscious, and irrepressible in her leadership role. The rhetoric of sassiness becomes one of public transformation, as if to say, "Regardless of what you thought you were getting, here is who I am." In her speech Jackie is taking her authority, her *ethos* as associate dean, and describing how she will act in that role.

For an African American woman, not only is her public announcement of alliance with the defiant woman of history a radical act, the work of being a university leader in and of itself is a radical location. When I asked Jackie what her most radical feminist act was, she did not hesitate to name her very presence in the academy as such.

> **Jackie:** My most radical feminist act. That depends on your definition of radical. It really does. Because I think it is a radical moment for any African American woman to be in the university context, my very presence is radical. We were talking about defiance before. It is an act of defiance. African American women scholars are by existence a radical scene. There is nothing in the environment that is particularly accommodating to our being there and that some of us have managed to get all the way through the system. That is a radical moment. I do think that is the most radical thing. That and coming here. Being a full professor of English who is an associate dean at a Big Ten university is a radical moment. How many opportunities do you have [to witness that]?
>
> **Kay:** Not many.
>
> **Jackie:** Not many. No. So if your definition of radical includes that, then everyday that I live and breath is a radical day. There are other things that you say I think I put more in the area of defiance. The fact that I have the nerve to study African American women, you know, when I have been told continuously when I first started this, "Now, why are you doing that? What did they do? Are they important?" And the most insidious question I have got is, when I say I am studying the history of literacy of African American women in the 19th century, "Could they read back then?" So for me, that is a radical moment. To have the nerve to do the work. To spend your time in a world that is very hierarchical, very conventional, that does not count lots and lots of things, to choose to do all the things that they say don't count. I don't count as an African American, I don't count as a female, I don't count as someone interested in rhetoric and composition, I don't count as someone interested in African American mentors, I don't count as a person who would say there is an intellectual tradition for African American women. There are lots of

things that don't count about what I do, and I just do them anyway. That's radical.

Although her identity embodies a position that historically "doesn't count," having the power of being associate dean is a tangible way that Jackie's work and voice *do* count. Because they do count, her use of feminist pedagogy and her feminist beliefs that she brings to that work "count" a great deal. As Jackie stated in her keynote speech to the 2001 Race, Gender and Identity Symposium, "It is not when and where I enter, but *how* I enter."[39] The *how* is with a feminist pedagogical style and sensibility. Because of entering her work from a feminist perspective, Jackie defines herself as an academic activist. "I consider myself to be an academic activist, a person who has chosen (even if I have not been chosen) to be a politically conscious watchdog, a sentry for the need for positive change in the world of education" ("Time Alone," 1997, p. 41). One could argue that, by virtue of being selected for leadership positions like that of associate dean, Jackie has been chosen because others are acknowledging and supporting her fiery spirit working for "positive change in the world of education" (she is not just self-selecting the work of academic activism). To codify her position of academic activism, her "Sassy Women" speech publicly claimed that stance.

During the question-and-answer period after the "Sassy Women" speech, someone in the audience asked whether Jackie's use of the word *sassy* to describe the subjects of her research was related to the contemporary stereotype of Black women as hostile. Jackie responded personally (once again shifting the "they" to not just a "we," but an "I"), rather than to the impersonal collective of "hostile Black women." "I got so sick of all the people who asked me why I was so angry. I am not angry. I do operate on a certain level of *passion*," she laughed. "I am passionate. I do resent the dismissive qualities and the way we talk about sassiness. I want to recover the very spirit of sassiness."

That spirit of defiance is not just alive and well in Jackie's scholarship, but an example of feminist pedagogy as it embodies itself in Jackie's leadership. When Jackie demonstrates her commitment to and awareness of dynamics of race, class, ethnicity, and gender, when she wants those she is leading to actively engage in critical consciousness regarding these issues, when she is intensely aware of the voices and silences that surround her and her role in bringing out more of the silenced voices, she enacts feminist pedagogical themes in her leadership. To hear Jackie tell it, however, is to hear a leader describe herself as someone who did not intend this path, did not actively choose it, but knows the imperative deliberateness of her feminist scholarship, teaching, and leadership. As she says of the African American women leaders of the 19th century, "Something in Womanhood made it imperative that they worked for their people. That imperative was so strong that they could not choose *not* to take the opportunity" (Keynote, March 2, 2001). Although Jackie was not talking about herself directly when she made that statement, her feminist leadership dictates a similar consciousness.

A CRITICALLY CONSCIOUS WOMAN IS A DEFIANT WOMAN

The theme of defiance is fundamental to Jackie's own life and work. Defiance is something she also associates with feminism. For Jackie, being a feminist means engaging in defiant acts. Therefore, it would follow that her definition of feminist pedagogy also has this theme running through it. "[Feminist pedagogy] has a willfulness about it. There is a deliberateness about it. A consciousness about it. And then there is a reflexivity in that consciousness." This theme of critical consciousness seems to be a foundational element not only of Jackie's definition of feminism, but Lynn's and Harriet's as well. It reminds me of a conversation a group of graduate students had in a feminist rhetorics and pedagogies class I was in. We were struggling with something, one identifying element, that made feminist pedagogy distinct from other critical or radical pedagogies. At the time, we came to the conclusion that the *one thing* that distinguished feminist pedagogy from other pedagogies was critical self-reflection. The teacher had to use feminist critique and self-reflect on the class, on her own decisions, on the dynamics of her work, the students' work and their interactions together. It was feminist consciousness, feminist critique, applied not only to oneself as the teacher, but the classroom community as a whole and the teacher's role in shaping and leading that community. Because of my work with this project, it is impossible for me to simplify feminist pedagogy in that way, but I do think that the feminist critical consciousness as applied to teaching and the classroom environment is *one of the ways* feminist pedagogy is unique from other radical pedagogies.

In addition to identifying this self-critique as a primary element of feminist pedagogy, Jackie also saw this interrogation as a willful way of engaging with students, a classroom community, and the work of teaching. Echoing back to her definition of *sassy*, Jackie's way of describing feminist pedagogy also reminds me about the way she spoke of her mother: a woman of willful deliberateness; the woman who showed Jackie how a person could be Black and female in the world. "She is very radical [. . .] I grew up with her as the kind of model of how you could do really crazy things and still live, really outspoken things and still live." At one point during my site visit, when I asked Jackie whether other people would define her as feminist, she laughed and said, "They would probably say, 'Oh, she's that crazy woman.'" Crazy, a word that Jackie used to describe not only her mother's actions, but the way others would define Jackie, is evidence of this defiance playing out in the larger cultural context. Traditionally marginalized people who refuse to enact their assigned cultural roles are often described as crazy.⁴⁰

When I taught English in Morocco to Saharan school children who needed to learn English as much as they needed a trip to Disney World (more pressing needs such as hunger and disease kept them squarely in the clutches of poverty), I often integrated poems and songs in the curriculum. Together we would sing and recite verses, committing words of Bob Marley, Langston Hughes, and June Jordan to memory. A staple of this diet of poems and songs of oppression and critical engagement in the world was a Gwendolyn Brooks poem. Entitled "Crazy Woman," it spoke to this same radical willfulness of feminist defiance. "I shall not sing a May song./A May song should be gay./I'll wait until November/and sing a song of gray./I'll wait until November./That is the time for me./I'll go out in the frosty dark/And sing most terribly./And all the little people/Will stare at me and say,/That is the Crazy Woman/Who would not sing in May." Many of the Moroccan students responded passionately to this poem; they identified with the melancholy tone of the woman who did not feel like singing when she was supposed to; they knew the mournful tunes of grey and how often despair can comfort a heart or mind when happiness or physical comfort is not readily available; they understood the idea that "crazy" is an easy label to throw onto someone, instead of looking closely and trying to see the troubled life or unsettled spirit that moves someone to act outside the expectations of cultural norms. The narrator of Brook's poem is engaging in radical acts of defiance. She is, as I am sure Jackie would agree, the essence of a sassy woman.

The insistence on redefinition and renaming also reflects an element inherent to feminism. In the way that Jackie wants to "reclaim sassy," Patrician Hill Collins writes that Black Feminist Thought focuses on renaming/reclaiming the concept of Black Womanhood. In her essay "Outsider Within," Collins defines Black Feminist thought as first self-definition/valuation: challenging *external* definitions of black womanhood and defining themselves not in relation to what is "other," but how they see themselves. Second, it is recognizing the interactive nature of oppression: dualistic thinking (either/or) is the lynchpin in interlocking systems of oppression; binaries imply superiority and inferiority. Black feminist thought also recognizes the importance of African American culture and the material effects and supports of that culture. By virtue of working in the academy, identifying not only as a feminist, but a sassy woman, doing the work she is doing to reclaim and rename the obliterated past of African American women intellectuals and activists, Jackie engages with Collins' idea of Black Feminist Thought. Through her work, Jackie not only displays a model of what it means to be a Black feminist in the world, in the academy, in today's culture, but she also asks us to contemplate and consider the material lives of Black feminists whom history has attempted to erase. "What did it take for these women (of African descent) to believe in their own agency?" Jackie asks. "To act defiantly and dangerously, using speaking and writing?" (Keynote, March 2, 2001).

Even recognizing that these women existed, that they were part of history and deserved to be recognized as such, was an exercise in feminist thought. When describing how she came to do this work of historic ethnographies, Jackie said, "I had seen before, I had known before, but I hadn't noticed before [. . .] my knowing wasn't transformed into knowledge until my head, heart, backbone, and stomach also knew" (Keynote, March 2, 2001). Through this kinetic engagement with the past, through heart, stomach, back, feet, mind, Jackie resuscitates a world and lives that were left for dead. After conference presentations or speeches, Jackie told me it is not uncommon for someone to ask, "Why don't you research black men? Why don't you research white women?" These questions seem cast from the same racist, albeit perhaps naive, lack of critical consciousness that spawns another comment Jackie hears a great deal when she talks about her work: "Could black women read back then?" Do people consistently ask scholars of William Blake why they do not study women? Do scholars of Thomas Jefferson get the regular inquiry as to why they are so focused on White, heterosexual privileged class males? Yet for scholars who are working outside the domain of what the culture has considered worthy of research (feminists, women, traditionally marginalized people), they are often accused of bias and, furthering the critique, weak scholarship.

When Jackie was asked to respond to the question "Is there such a thing as women's rhetoric?" as part of her work in contributing to Andrea Lundsford's collection *Reclaiming Rhetorica*, Jackie responded, "We would never ask if there is such a thing as men's rhetoric." The underlying assumption behind the question was that what is White, what is male, what is privileged class is, obviously, of course, without question, worthy of research. Research outside these boundaries, research that attempts to give voice and life to anyone outside the dominant circle is, well, . . . just craziness.

SHARING THE POWER
AND TRAINING THE TROOPS

Ironically, despite what I believe to be the obviousness of Jackie's trail blazing, Jackie eschews the idea that she is a leader. Jackie told me she does not see herself as a leader; rather more of a facilitator. Jackie measures her success as a leader/facilitator by how well the project thrives in her absence, not in her presence. "I don't see power or ego as useful in a facilitator," she told me as we are walking, *fast*, to an initiation ceremony for the OSU chapter of Phi Kappa Phi (Jackie was a new faculty inductee). "It's more a sharing of power." Her approach to leadership once again speaks to "how" Jackie enters this position of authority. To be a feminist in a position of authority or power (be she administrator, scholar, or teacher) seems to make little difference unless the "how" is different. "It seems just the presence of women in power positions is progress, but how do they *do* things different?" Sattler (1997) asks in her book of feminists in the academy (p. 116).

Jackie is doing lots of things differently, beyond just being a black female person of authority in meetings full of White, privileged class males and females. Perhaps the skills of feminist facilitation and leadership that Jackie employs have been developed over the several years she has spent in leadership and administrative roles. Jackie has worked in administrative positions for 23 of her 25 years working in higher education (writing program administrators and associate deans account for the bulk of those administrative positions). She implies, in telling the chronology of her administrative history, that none of that was intentional. She was tapped as Writing Program Administrator (first at Spelman College and then at OSU) and associate dean (also first at Spelman College and then at OSU). "If I had been a more goal-oriented, long-range planner I wouldn't have done any of these things. But I am deliberate, but not long range. Allowing myself to have possibilities open up for me that I hadn't known were possibilities [landed her] in a field that just feels perfect to me. I love what I do." In other words, the path she has forged was not one she set out to cut; it just happens to be the one she did create, which worked out very well.

> I haven't done a whole lot because it was thought out. I have done it deliberately, but not in a planned way. I can't think of a single thing that I now count as part of critical moment in my professional development that was a real plan. I mean I never planned to come over here. I never planned to be at Ohio State. I never planned to do the work that I do. It was the moment and it seemed interesting at the time. I decided to do it. So it is that kind of deliberation, it is not very kind of goal-oriented type of planning. [. . .] I have done what I do by asking, "What work will I do? Am I enjoying it? How does this play out in the broader cultural context?"

Jackie's need to enjoy the work she chooses reminds me of Harriet's struggles to do the kind of writing she has a passion for and still publish in academic circles. At this juncture, Harriet seems to be having less luck than Jackie in doing the work she "enjoys" while still getting published. The reason for this may be related to something that Jackie wrote in her book, *Traces of a Stream*. In the "Preface and Acknowledgments," Jackie thanks David Bartholomae, a colleague in the field who also works in the capacity of editor for the University of Pittsburgh Press, for telling her to pursue the work she wanted to do, the work for which she had a passion. "I particularly appreciated the encouragement of David Bartholomae, who recognized the possibility of this project and, with his incredible style, said, 'Why don't you think about doing what you really want to do?'" Although one theme of feminist pedagogy is bringing that personal passion to the work, it certainly helps when one has a benefactor with power who is urging one to take the plunge. That is not to suggest that before Bartholomae encouraged Jackie she wasn't doing work that she was passionate about. Rather the distinction between Harriet's experience of doing work that she is passionate about and Jackie's experience seems to be, in Harriet's case, the lack of tangible support and in Jackie's case, the overt and active support of peers and colleagues who are in positions of power. Besides the need to enjoy what she is doing, Jackie is also aware of how it fits into the "broader cultural context." The attention Jackie pays to the larger cultural impact of her work shows a keen eye to critical reflection of what she is doing. Although joy and passion are essential for the work, equally important is the impact her work will have, evidence of what Jackie calls her academic activism. In her administrative role, this activism takes the form of feminist pedagogy as leadership. As I stated in the chapter on Lynn's work (chap. 4), there is little distinction for me between feminist pedagogy and feminist leadership. Feminist pedagogy seems to be the educational twin of feminist leadership as enacted in many grassroots organizations. Because Jackie is primarily an administrator these days, filling her life with facilitating meetings, mentoring young faculty and graduate students, and acting as advisor on issues of professional faculty development to the Dean of Humanities, her feminist pedagogy is daily enacted in a meeting room rather than in a classroom.

I observed several meetings of varying dynamics as part of my site visit with Jackie. Whether she was meeting with a group of faculty members (the Graduate Committee for the college of Humanities), advising a graduate student on his dissertation ideas, having a "working lunch" with an editor to talk about a book project, or reflecting on her approach to leadership in her role as associate dean of research and faculty development, I could see the themes of feminist pedagogy practiced in her leadership.

With each site of leadership, Jackie is aware of her power position in relation to others. She asks graduate students to call her by her first name, she listens first and then offers her opinions when running a meeting or talking with a colleague or student, and she asks more questions than makes statements, all ways of turning her position of power and authority into a more open exchange with people who have less power within a given context. The strategy of listening first connects to Jackie's approach to her research, where she feels she is listening to the traditionally silenced voices of African American women.

> I acknowledge, then, the importance of listening well, of paying careful and close attention to what they [African American women] say on, between, and around the lines; of listening to what they say about the day before, for example, and the day after; and of paying attention to who is in the conversation with them, where it is taking place, and how it interacts with other conversations that may be occurring simultaneously. ("Sarah's Story," 1999, p. 48)

By listening first, Jackie models a form of leadership that empowers rather than dominates.

THE (IN)VISIBLE RACE/GENDER DIVIDE

Her leadership philosophy of listening and then moderating or facilitating was evident in a meeting I observed of the College of Humanities Graduate Committee. The particular meeting I observed embodied not an unusual dynamic for Jackie: She was the only African American woman at a table of White men. Although it did not occur on the day I visited, she said often the men will sit along one side of the table across from her evoking, Jackie said, the mental image of Anita Hill at a Senate hearing. "I kind of chuckled when I realized you were coming on a day of that meeting. [. . .] It is kind of me against the world, in a way, just physically in the way we sit in the room. Now, that wouldn't be so noticeable if there weren't the differences between race and gender, but it makes the line-up just so obvious. Black woman here. White men there." Jackie is quick to point out that, although the physical logistics of the room play out in a way that evokes cultural references of hostility of White men toward Black women, the dynamics of this group are not that way; there is a permeating aura of respect and cordiality. "I come to the meeting with a certain kind of status, if not authority, that makes my participation not to be an onerous one."

> Jackie: The investment I have in the engagement [of conducting the meeting and working with these men] is professional and not personal, in a way in that we are all there in the interest of graduate students. I don't know if that really answers your question.

Kay: Yes. The question was do you find that politeness, that unwillingness to really address the difficult issues, does it play out at much in this job as you see in playing out in 4Cs.

Jackie: And I guess my point in bringing up that example [of her 4Cs address as president of the organization and people's response to the address (see p. 184] is the systemic way it always plays out because the power dynamics are amazingly resilient in this country if not this world. So you can see it if you want to pay attention to it. And then in some ways it is mediated because of position and status that can operate or cannot operate. I think that the men in that room in the meeting you observed are respectful of me.

Kay: Yeah. Very much so. There was definitely a tone of respect, on both sides of the table, so to speak.

Jackie: It's not that way all the time, but it is nice to get that in return. If everybody had been pushing me with attitudes I have experienced before, like "Who do you think you are? Doing this, talking to me, acting like I owe you something?" So I didn't get any of that in there and there isn't much in my day that operates that way. Part of it may be a function of age. Because when I was younger, doing some very similar things, it was a more familiar thing to happen. I was too young to have any authority. I was too Black to have any authority. I was too female to have any authority. So, here when I am the only Black or woman in the room, I can't tell you the number of times I have been in a situation like that.

The race and gender dynamics of these meetings and Jackie's awareness of them re-create the image of authority and leadership to *include* people other than White males. Giddens (1991) names this critical self-reflection of race and gender dynamics the "reflexive self," where, specifically in Giddens' and Jackie's cases, Black women create their "self-perceptions" of their own authority and leadership despite the cultural messages that indicate they should not be these things because of their femaleness, age, or skin color. By re-ordering a self-narrative to include the status of leader, the role of leader is re-created in their own image. Rassool (1995) writes that Black women re-create self-identity and overcome barriers to authority and leadership by (a) networking and finding mentors, (b) choosing a place in the field that has a strategically high number of women, and (c) claiming a rightful place—engaging in a challenge with the male-dominated field just by being there. In Rassool's description, the claiming of ethos seems to be more passive—just by a Black woman's presence, the academy changes. Giddens' theory positions the woman more as an active subject, working to create an ethos, to define her own public version of self to become knowledge and culture producers in the academy. Jackie seems to follow the model Giddens proposes, being actively aware of *how she is entering* this sphere of authority and leadership. By doing so she is actively and consciously changing the ethos of African American women as a group.

By using feminist leadership strategies, Jackie creates an *ethos* that embodies an alternative model of leadership that is more empowering for those who are afforded less institutional power than herself. Although there are distinctions between feminist leadership and feminist teaching (power relationships may be less pronounced because knowledge is more shared than in a classroom situation), there is enough overlap between feminist leadership and feminist teaching to see the themes of feminist pedagogy playing out in administrative tasks facilitated by feminists.

The day I observed Jackie's work world, the Graduate Committee was winding up the semester and adjourning for the summer. Items on the agenda included a discussion of what issues needed to be carried over to the next term's agenda (graduate student funding and relation to attrition, graduate teacher training programs) and a couple of proposals regarding adding a graduate major or simply an emphasis in the areas of film studies and comparative studies. There were four attendees (not counting Jackie or myself), each one from a different Humanities department/program. Although there are two women, besides Jackie, who have been appointed to the committee, Jackie was the only woman present the day I attended. The meeting was held in a room with a long, wide conference table—about three times the size of what was needed for a group of six people. Jackie sat on one side of the table and the committee members (all White men) sat across from her or on the end of the table. The tone of the meeting was friendly and focused, and Jackie moved the group through the morning's agenda with deft organization, all the while making sure everyone had contributed or commented on an agenda item before moving on.

When reviewing transcripts of this meeting, I note that Jackie positions herself as a facilitator rather than a traditional leader, reconstructing hierarchical power. Several ways Jackie worked to share power included giving people choice in the work of the committee and how to approach that work, verbalizing her own biases to the group, and asking members of the committee to draw on their own experience/expertise and share that knowledge with the group. One could argue that Jackie's physical presence of being Black and female in a room of White males complicates this dynamic of leader even more. The group is not unaware of the physical, cultural disruption Jackie's location places on the cultural paradigm of leadership as White and male.

Jackie's commitment to facilitate instead of dominate is evidenced brilliantly by the number of ways she is continually reconstructing power so that it is empowering. The prominence of this theme also plays out in her definition of what she perceives her role as a leader to be: "I have more information and resources, so my job is to present that to others so they can do the work: put it together and stir it up; see what happens." Mixing it up and seeing what happens also offers a way to embrace conflict instead of avoiding it. Instead of controlling and limiting conflict, as is typical not only of traditional leadership but of socialized female/feminine discourse practices, where the goal is smooth sailing rather than rocky currents, Jackie sees the benefit of stirring things up and working through the rough spots.

A CHALLENGE POLITELY IGNORED

Another public example of embracing conflict instead of ignoring it was Jackie's challenge to the members of the College Composition and Communication Conference (4Cs) to e-mail her their responses to her public declamation that members of 4Cs were not confronting issues of race within the organization or the profession of composition and rhetoric effectively, or perhaps at all. In 1995, Jackie was the chair of 4Cs. In that capacity, she opened the annual conference with a speech where she publicly confronted her experience as a Black woman in the organization and what she felt was lack of attention to race issues in scholarship, in classrooms, in presentations, and in professional interactions. At the end of her speech, she invited the audience to talk with her about these issues, to begin a dialogue. She asked her colleagues to "talk back" to her about the speech. Only a handful of people took her up on that offer. I asked Jackie what the nature of the responses were, what she expected when she extended the invitation, and what kind of responses would have been productive.

Jackie: Well, I got a response from one person who wanted to use the talk in their class and engage in a rhetorical analysis (a graduate seminar). I had a response from a woman who was doing her dissertation on deliberative rhetoric who wanted to use it. And I got a couple more general responses like, "Thanks for the opportunity. This is what I am interested in. This is what I am thinking." So, there was less volume than I was expecting. I was taking something of a risk in having my box flooded with response. But then when I thought about it, it is hard for people to respond to issues about race.

Kay: I think it is especially hard for white folks to do that because they feel there is so much baggage with that.

Jackie: So, I think folks were not wanting to take the risk of saying what they thought.

Kay: When you extended that invitation, you just said you were anticipating that you could have had lots of responses, but what were you anticipating as far as what did you think . . .

Jackie: What I hoped for was a dialogue. At the time I thought we were not having such a dialogue in rhetoric and composition and that was a really a little silly for us not to be more actively and directly engaged in these issues since we claim to have the general interest in the field. So, let's see if we can keep our feet to this fire. What I *expected* was no response.

Kay: Really?

Jackie: Really. Because that is what we generally get when we raise issues of race or you get a clap. Or you get a "Yeah. That's right," or "That was so interesting." We get response around the issues instead of to the issues. I remember that day just being hugged to death. I let people cry on my shoulder for about half the day. [. . .] People couldn't say more than, "That was courageous of you." You know, in that kind of breathless way. It was a difficult dialogue to get going and I wanted to get that dialogue going.

Kay: When I was talking to Harriet one of her critiques of the field of comp rhet was that people want to be so nice. They want to be concerned. "I am so concerned about issues of race. I am so concerned about issues of gender and sexual identity." All that kind of thing, but she said that people aren't willing to honestly confront the issues. We have good hearts about it, but . . .

Jackie: Well, a lot have been perceived as doing something about it. But being able to engage in the issues is difficult, being able to look ugliness in the face, be willing to look at our own complicity in certain kinds of things without being distracted by the fact that "This is a bit embarrassing that I am going to admit this," or "I hadn't thought about that. I am kinda guilty of doing this with my students or having this situation ride without my asking a question even though I think of myself as X, Y or Z." So, I agree with her that it is the image of the field that we are the good guys. So, if we are the good guys then we don't have to admit anything. We don't have to do anything. We are just kind of righteous and above ourselves. No, we are not. So it is hard to enable a discussion.

Kay: What would have been the response you would have liked to
           receive? Give me an example of something that would have
           been a meaningful, substantive response.

Jackie: Well, I think for some people an honest response would have
           been to say, "Oh, I think you are full of it. This is not right.
           This is not right. This is not how you should be interpreting
           these things. You are just really being overly sensitive." Show
           me I'm wrong. Or "Let me tell you how I would have inter-
           preted that." So to me that would have permitted conversa-
           tion to happen. To seriously sit down and try to figure out,
           "So why is my perspective this way and your perspective that
           way and what does this difference suggest about the kinds of
           things we are able to do inside this organization when we
           seem like we are on the same page but we are really far apart
           when we try to make sense of our lives?" That would have
           been the kind of conversation I would have ideally wanted to
           have. Or one that would have said, "You know, I am not an
           African American woman, but I often feel that way in these
           types of situations, so how is my situation like yours? How
           is it different? How can I see you in the same light that I have
           experienced my own life in a way that is useful to me? Or
           what do I need to know that would make me see things the
           way you see them?" Any of those kinds of things would have
           been very interesting. Or for somebody to have said, "Oh, I
           really don't think you went far enough with that. There are
           some other issues that you didn't deal with at all from my
           perspective. I wonder what you think about X, because I
           think this." And I don't see that kind of conversation at pre-
           sentations. I think of it as a desire to try to figure out what is
           going on between human beings who are the same in so many
           ways and different in so many ways. Who are trying to do
           certain kinds of things with a certain community of interest,
           but it didn't happen.

Jackie's reflection shows that embracing conflict and actually getting
people to engage with conflict are two different things. Although she was
willing to engage in the difficult discussions of honest dialogues on race with
the predominantly White membership of the 4Cs, the challenge was not
accepted. It was, for the most part, politely ignored. Thinking about this
challenge for critique and conflict that was ignored made me think back to
Harriet's comment on the politeness of the discipline. By way of illustrating
this trope of politeness, Harriet told me about her essay "David and Me"
published in *JAC* and how it was also politely ignored. In the essay, she talks

about her critique of David Bartholomae and how he became, in her dissertation, a theory ("Bartholomae"), not a human being. When she was confronted with the physical reality of the man at a conference, she was taken aback. She wrote the essay as a way of critiquing the theory, but also of attempting to confront the man. She ended the essay with two simple words, "Hello, David," signifying her willingness to engage with *the man* who wrote the theory. I asked her whether David Bartholomae ever responded either publicly or privately to her essay. She said he had not,[41] marking another moment where confrontation and potential conflict were politely ignored.

Then I am reminded of the baldly honest responses Lynn Worsham and Susan Jarratt received on their book proposal for *Feminisms and Composition*. The difference, it seems, is that these critiques were anonymous and therefore did not hold back angry responses to what "they" perceived as a project that was "listing towards feminism." In one context, where a human face must be addressed and the physical reality of another human being must be considered, we become cowards, running from conflict and politely turning away. In another context, where the faces are hidden and our opinions "anonymous," we get to say what we *really* think and feel, with less than productive ends, because it is too easy to dismiss a faceless comment and even more easy to dismiss a faceless comment full of hostile rhetoric, the masked coward on a rampage.

In her leadership, Jackie offers another way: respectful conflict that is honest, meaningful, and thought-provoking. Instead of politely ignoring the issue of race, a subject that makes many liberal-minded White folks hang their heads or wring their hands in concerned abjectness, Jackie names the conflict, the points of contention, and challenges us all to engage instead of run away. However, if we refuse to engage in discussion, to embrace the conflict, the challenge hangs in the air like an empty thought bubble, a gasp void of breath. Instead of claiming and telling the stories that shame us, as Lynn Worsham challenges feminists to do, analyzing and critiquing our own lives from various angles, the 4Cs audience that Jackie addressed chose to politely ignore instead of publicly declaim. Instead of the audience engaging in rigorous self-critique, the response was to use the rhetorical moment as a teaching tool in classes or as an example in a dissertation (demonstrative rhetoric!), or give a clap on the back ("That was so interesting!"), or offer a breathless hug ("You are so courageous!"). Jackie's challenge to tackle the conflict, to name the various rough edges of contact, was politely ignored. The well-meaning, goodhearted people who Harriet typifies as the 4Cs membership shied away from the challenge of conflict, despite the feminist challenge to engage. Jackie's anticipation of no response speaks to her experiences of being black and female, a person who historically, traditionally "doesn't count." Instead of critiquing our shame and working through those deep-running currents of ideological bigotry as they manifest themselves in our lives and work, we pat the head, rub the shoulder, tightly embrace the physical body, but politely decline, in silence, to make similar intimate contact with the issue that has been named. Although in this example the "we" is typically White folks at 4Cs who refused to publicly examine our own racist shame, in the context of feminism the "we" are feminists and the issues encompass much more than race, but class, ability, age, sexual orientation, gender, ethnicity, and religious or spiritual bigotries, among others.

To further integrate Lynn's point that we are all responsible for publicly interrogating our internalized racism, sexism, and homophobia into this example, we must also consider that it is not the African American's duty to point out racism. It is not the lesbian's job to point out homophobia. It is not the woman's job to point out sexism. Instead, we must be self-critical enough in the name of feminism to recognize our own collusion with systems of oppression, in whatever form they take, as well as naming them as they are manifested in the organizations, institutions, and classrooms in which we work. As Harriet expressed weariness of being cast as the spokeslesbian, always called on to give *that* perspective, by virtue of being an African American woman leader, Jackie is called on to be the watchdog of racism. Just as the women Gesa Kirsch interviewed said they were exhausted from serving on several committees as the token female, so are African Americans within the academy called on to serve so the committee/group has the *face* of diversity. The onus of calling attention to issues of "diversity" then falls on the shoulders of these few individuals who are selected (because they are physically marked) to represent the perspectives of an entire group. This dynamic is only compounded by the "watchdog" responsibility of bringing to the table issues of racism/sexism/classism, allowing others to feel blissfully unresponsible to interrogate or publicly name these issues.

The 4Cs address is just one example of how Jackie takes the feminist high road of embracing conflict instead of politely ignoring issues some may feel uncomfortable addressing; another is any given group's expectations that Jackie name or doggedly police racism because she embodies the physical reality of a Black woman. This same dynamic could have been playing out when Emig and Phelps asked Jackie, and others, to comment on the table of contents for their anthology, *Feminine Principles in Composition*. In her response, Jackie leveled a careful, honest critique regarding the absence of African American voices and the acknowledgment of their experience in the history of the field. When talking with me, she said it was a frustrating exercise to be asked to comment on the Table of Contents because she was commenting on someone else's decision. "It was a pointless exercise," she told me. "It was their choice, so why are they asking me?" The answer to this rhetorical question is likely that the editors wanted "The Black

Feminist" perspective. Jackie rose to the unspoken demand and offered that perspective, but again she did so in the feminist spirit of respectfully engaging in conflict rather than politely ignoring it. Reverberating through these examples is Harriet's description of Jackie as embodying the "nexus of smart and warm." The careful and honest critiques Jackie offers, the challenges she extends, and the patience she exudes in the face of tireless demands to speak as The Black Feminist show us the ideals of feminist pedagogy as leadership. Jackie has, in fact, answered the call of Maria Stewart, to "distinguish yourself" (qtd. in Inaugural address, May 22, 2001), furthering the path that Stewart forged along with other sassy women of African descent in our culture's history.

THE BRIDGES BETWEEN FEMINIST NURTURING AND MENTORING

Before one becomes a leader, one looks to others for models of what it means to effectively move a group or community toward common goals. Inherently there is a connection among mentoring, being mentored, and leadership. To learn to lead effectively, one looks to others who embody effective, compassionate, and empowering leadership and, in the best of circumstances, is mentored by a role model. In turn, as a leader one mentors others, both directly and indirectly as novices and plebeians keep keen eyes cued to the *how*. As Jackie articulated, a good leader, as manifested in her own philosophy, "trains the troops" so that the work can be carried on even when the leader is not physically present. In feminist pedagogy, a leader shares the power of authority and trusts those with less power to make decisions, and make mistakes, and do things differently, recognizing the unique needs of each community. This style of mentoring and leadership involves careful listening, turning an ear to voices that are traditionally disempowered and silenced, hearing the stories they tell, their ways of viewing the world. This style of mentoring is also a manifestation of feminist pedagogy.

As a Black woman in the academy, Jackie found mentors hard to come by. Her mentors, instead, were the women who surrounded her as a child and then the women she came to know through her research. As Harriet created relationships with writers whose work she admired, a fictional mentoring to substitute for the physical absence of a mentor, Jackie found mentors in the stories of the women she researched. Through the stories of people like Anna Julia Cooper, Maria Stewart, and Ida B. Wells (among many others), and through her work of historical ethnography, Jackie has not only come to know these women's stories, but to see them as mentors, models of effective leadership, a way to take a defiant feminist stand to integrate voices and perspectives long ignored. "What does it mean to look into the eyes of a woman of African descent and know there are stories that should be told, could be told, *need* to be told?" Jackie asks (Keynote, March 2, 2001). By clearing the way to these stories, she and others find ways of leadership and mentoring that speak to the lives and perspectives of Black women.

"I feel conspiratorial with the women who I have met through texts, like Anna Julia Cooper," Jackie told me during my site visit.

> And the women I have grown up with. And by that I literally mean I feel like I breathe with them. So I have found great comfort in understanding that we share the same air in our spirits. So, in that way, yes. I look to them. But I look to them for the inspiration, not for the "This is what they would do." In fact it has often been the other way around. When I first started looking at 19th Century women who were all doing incredible things, I would often say, "If they could do what they did under those awful circumstances of their lives, I have no excuse. What is not possible?"

The conspiracy Jackie feels with these women is one of sororal, even feminist leadership and access to power. The way women like Anna Julia Cooper used rhetorical skills to gain ethos and a public forum *despite* their racial and gendered locations and the way Black women in Jackie's immediate childhood world seized power through acts of public defiance blazed a trail to follow. Repeatedly in her conversations, speeches, and scholarship, Jackie asks her audience if these women could do what they did at the disempowered location of being black and female in the 19th century through even the latter part of the 20th century, then "what is *not* possible?" Jackie places the responsibility for action not only squarely on her own shoulders, but everyone in the audience: "If not now, when? If not me, who?" Although the site for interrogation is the 19th century, Jackie finds role models and mentors of how to enact feminist leadership in her life and in the academy.

That is not to discount or ignore the contemporary mentors and role models Jackie has learned from. As she articulates it, "I have had a lot of nurturing, but little mentoring." The distinction between nurturing (offering encouragement and support) and mentoring (showing the way and taking someone by the hand to help them through) is an important one to make. For Jackie there was a bridge between feminist principles and where and how Jackie found mentors. Through the strong connections she had with the women who showed her the way, through their support and nurturing, these mentors showed Jackie how to survive, live, work, and proceed as a Black woman doing her work in the academy. Although these women may not use the label of feminist to describe themselves, Jackie said she found feminist principles in the way they chose to work, speak, and live. This

bridge between feminist mentoring and leadership, arching between genera-
tions of Black women, has strong groundings in feminist theory. Without
that theoretical base, the bridge would be more rickety in structure, largely
unable to sustain the history it holds. Through feminism, Jackie found a way
to see these women, to tell their stories, showing the strength and power of
these women's lives and how they paved the way for their daughters of the
future. Because of her work, others will find hope and strength on this path,
as Jackie did. But the power of women was not first revealed to Jackie in the
academy, but as a feminist tool in the home and community in which she
grew up.

Kay: When did you first have an inclination towards feminist theory? Do you remember when that happened?

Jackie: Well, probably on the first day. I don't remember not having a
particular inclination to be, to admire, let's just say women's
power. I grew up around women who did very interesting
things and I watched them all my life, so how can that not
count? I went to a women's college before the words became
vibrant. How can that not count? When I look back over the
various papers that I wrote [as an undergraduate] a lot of those
had an interest in various things of women. And certainly
since I have become a professional in this arena almost everything has been that way. Even having spent 16 years teaching
at a women's college [Spelman]. There are certain kinds of patterns to my life that suggest maybe there was something quite
significant about my context that fed those interests and incli-
nations and what has happened is that they have gained
vibrancy because the times we have lived in have been fed by
the system of what we do. So, you have a field [feminist theo-
ry] that was evolving just as I needed labels for what I was
interested in. And that happens with both rhetorical studies
and feminist studies. I can't think about them alone. I still
define myself as a person who is centered in language studies.
That is what I do. But my interest in that area has really been
informed by my own experience and the fact that these other
things were bubbling around me at just the right time with a
collection of people. I was lucky to have very interesting
friends. Very interesting work. [My mother] loomed large in
my life all the time. She's not famous or anything, but she is
very active. [. . .] A leader in her community, she has always
been very involved. She is what I would call a radical woman;
she is very radical, much more radical than I am. I grew up
with her as the kind of model for how you could do really

crazy things and still live, very outspoken things and still live. She certainly wouldn't have used any of this vocabulary that we used today to talk about this, in the same way that Anna Julia Cooper would not have called herself a Black feminist, but for me that is how she functions. [. . .] I just happened to have the advantage of being born with the people that I knew. And they were very strong. There were really strong men, too, but the women were the real movers and shakers in my life. And in the world, too. They were the movers and shakers. And by the time I was in high school I just knew that if you wanted to do something it wasn't impossible if you really wanted to do it. And I think that is kind of an "ah-ha" moment that most people have to come to and I really didn't have to come to it in that way.

Project Journal: March 19, 2001

When looking over the transcriptions of the site visit with Lynn, I highlighted a particularly captivating quote. She said, "My mother was the only thing that stood between me and doom." Jackie expressed that her mother was the first model that represented the power of being a woman. It seems that for these feminists, and for me, too, because it is also true in my experience, that our first model of womanhood was a prototype for our feminist beliefs. It was through observing our mothers that we came to know not only the oppression of women, but the power to overcome that or the strategies to use to get beyond it. Also, it seems significant that we all have these strong women behind us. They not only showed us a way, but then followed us through. That seems significant. It is all so intensely interesting and complicated because Harriet, on the other hand, had a mother who Harriet describes as being "afraid of everything." Harriet only found the strength and courage of women through Women's Studies courses and community activism. So, I can't make a generalization that we are all following the models our mothers created for us. I wonder, however, if this primary relationship to a prototype of feminist consciousness allows people like Lynn, Jackie, and myself to approach our feminist work with less trepidation or apology (in Jackie's words: more sass)?

Rather than a defining moment when Jackie felt the "click" of feminist consciousness, the self-actualization through female power was more gradual and seamless from the time she was born. She said her mother's light and voice follow her through her days, inhabiting her head and whispering in her mind's ear. "Her way of making the decisions and her outspokenness are the voices I hear in the back of my head. And so they have always constituted affirming instances for me," Jackie told me. But her mother's voice is not the only one that guides her. "When I was at Spelman one quotation particularly from one of [the women who Jackie discovered doing archival research] who said she had 'A righteous disdain for second best.' [. . .] So, it is true there are words that I found inspirational."

> **Kay:** So it sounds like, with your mom or the people you have found in the text, a lot of people you look to kind of as a mentor are either people who are in the immediate surrounding, like family, or people you historically find through your research. Are there people you can identify within the academy?

> **Jackie:** I have had a lot of nurturing by all kinds of people. But I haven't had a lot of mentoring. I haven't had a lot of people within the profession who have mentored me. I have had a lot of people who have supported me, who have been kind in various ways, you know, folks who have written recommendations for me, you reap some benefits from that. But I think of mentors as being people who advise and guide. And I have to say that I just have stumbled along on my own or in the company of people who are stumbling along with me rather than people who are actually leading, advising, counseling who could smooth the wake in a way I try to do for people now. At one point in *Traces* I talk about the mentoring program that we ran for *Sage* when the co-director and I said we wanted to do what we wished someone had done for us when we were at that stage. I often find myself in that spot.

All three of the women in my ethnographic studies talked to me about their difficulty finding mentors. I do no want to cast these women as lonely or isolated in their work. That is not the case. Each of them talks about mentors they did find and others, perhaps not feminist mentors, who greatly helped them along the way. Rather, I want to recognize that there are difficulties being a feminist, even within the privileged location of the Ivory Tower. I also want to point out that 30 years of the Second Wave still makes for a relatively new movement, and so young feminist scholars of 20 years ago, in this project specifically Harriet, Jackie, and Lynn, definitely did feel the absence of established scholars who could take them under a wing and show them the way. For Jackie, the problems of being a traditionally marginalized person within a subculture dominated by the traditional (re: the academy as White, male, heterosexual, and decidedly unfeminist) becomes exponentially more difficult when a person is not only marginalized by gender, but race as well. Mirza (1995), the author of the much celebrated play *To Be Young, Gifted and Black*, wrote the play in response to her Ph.D. advisor who told her she would never complete her work because she was a single, black mother. Mirza reflected, "I did not end up in university because of role models [. . .] my motivation lay in my determination to reveal the myths about black women's under achievement" (p. 145). Safia Mirza, like Jackie, felt an obligation to forge another trail, blazing the way for a new vision of Black womanhood not defined by the dominant culture, but instead defined by the people's whose lived experiences, whose lives, would not be pushed aside or silenced.

Kay: What do you attribute that [lack of mentors] to? Do you think there just weren't people?

Jackie: Who would there have been? And that is not to discount the people who have been supportive. People who have been kind in different ways. But mentoring, it wasn't a big deal when I was in graduate school. People didn't mentor people when I was in graduate school. [I]n the absence of mentoring I got very lucky, rather than in the presence of mentoring I understood what my choices were and I was able to make a good decision. I didn't have that. You know, you guys are very lucky.

Kay: It is true, though. I think it is very true. And I don't even think you have to go back 25 years; 10 years ago the idea was competition, not helping along.

Jackie: And then I look at other things like who like me was here to help me see the kind of work I was doing? Nobody. I am here for people now. Ten years ago I was not here for people like me. A few people were in my place. There were a couple of senior African American women who were doing other things who were, again, kind to me. Often not even realizing the extent of their kindness at the time. That is mentoring, when you don't know you are doing. There is credit I pay to having good people in my life at some very good moments. But the kind of specific relationships and nourishment and attention that you give and you can take more for granted these days, I didn't have. In rhetoric and composition in particular now we are doing very well. [. . .] [But still] there is a lot of pressure, or need, among African American graduate students. And then there is blame. If we don't connect or don't work well together or they don't like what I am telling them, then it is my fault. I am not being a mentor to them. And it is just because we are two very different people. We

don't connect. There is no fault in that. But because I am the
only one, if not me, who?

The incredible responsibility Jackie places on herself to do the work she
is doing, to use her voice to reclaim and declaim the journeys and paths of
the women obliterated by the dominant culture's master narratives, manifests itself as a feminist act of defiance, a most radical act. Through her feminist scholarship and leadership, she holds back the undergrowth so that others can see their way through. Her resilience to the hostile elements, a sassy
woman on an expedition of a lifetime who refuses the trail that has already
been paved and cleared by hegemony for one that leads in a territory not on
the map, allows others the option of making a similar journey. "Who like me
was here to help me see the kind of work I am doing? Nobody. I am here for
people now," she said. Her presence is evidence of a new way. As Audre
Lorde wrote, "We [African American women/girls] were never meant to
survive." Jackie realizes that her act of survival, in the world and specifically
in the academy, is a living, breathing embodiment of sassy defiance. Jackie
herself said, "Everyday that I live and breathe is a radical day."

AFRAFEMINIST, BLACK FEMINIST, WOMANIST

Although Jackie claims the label of feminist easily, she is also quick to add
that for her "it is never without modification." Primarily this modification
entails placing the modifier *Black* before the word *feminist*[42] to emphasize a
consciousness about being a woman of African descent in the world, in this
particular time, at this specific geographical location. In the last chapter of
Traces of a Stream, where Jackie describes her methodology, she substitutes
her own rhetoric, "Afrafeminist," for Collin's (1999) term of Black feminist
or Alice Walker's term of Womanist. She writes that it is this Afrafeminist
ideology that grounds her scholarship, teaching, and administrative work.
Afrafeminist ideology, Jackie writes, defines African American women as
"sentient beings who are capable of proactive engagement in the world. I
deal consciously with the world as a place that is materially defined by
social, economic, and political relationships" (p. 271). This Afrafeminist ideology signals new feminist rhetoric to describe Jackie's own pedagogy, leadership, and research as well as the women she is writing about. The term signals African American women's "action despite hostility." To be pro-active-
ly engaged with the world as an African American woman, despite the systemic hostility imposed by the dominant culture, to do the work in the face
of the barricades, instead of bridges, describes Jackie's life and work.

In addition to this Afrafeminist ideology, feminist theory allows Jackie to look more "critically at systems of power and privileged and authority and those issues that seem very constructive to me. I try to think about them fairly constantly." This critical consciousness, when Jackie challenges herself to constantly keep feminist theory and its ideas at the front her mind, is a deliberate process. "There are occasions when I find myself slipping and not being consciously aware of the implications of location, position, privilege, power in how a situation is operating," Jackie told me. The theme of self-critique and self-monitoring, to make sure one is enacting feminism and living the theory through daily lived practices, is prominently featured here. Jackie said she first and foremost sees feminism as a theory that works well when applied to the areas she is interested in. When I asked her to reflect on how her scholarship was a site of feminist pedagogy, she said,

> I think it is feminist in subject. It is about women. It is feminist by theoretical frame. I am speaking through lenses that are specifically identified as feminist theory. Attention to class, race, culture. Attention to systematic forces. And all things that come through other methodologies as well that still resonate with feminist pedagogy. But the fact that much of my work is ethnographic, one way of looking at a scene or an event is inadequate to generate what is going on there. So this multi-lens approach that I came to through having been taught linguistics by an anthropologist. That gets translated in my work, the multi-lenses. They are central concerns to feminist theory.

NEW ROUTES TO KNOWLEDGE THROUGH FEMINIST EPISTEMOLOGY

Working through a multilensed approach creates a feminist epistemology where experiences, stories, histories, cultures, and identities interact with historical documents of record to create a new way of knowing, seeing, and understanding the people Jackie works to "recover." Jackie told me she is interested in creating knowledge in a new way. The last chapter in her book (*Traces*) is devoted to articulating Jackie's theory about making knowledge in a way that is meaningful to those outside the traditional power structures. "It is a theory I have developed on how one is able to acknowledge, when you are talking about people who have not been privileged by mainstream power structures," she told me during my site visit. In her book she writes that she is "forging ahead in unchartered territory," creating a new space, a new way, a new path or route for others to follow (p. 252). This Afrafeminist scholarship, or perhaps epistemology, "creates bridges from which to speak and interpret" (p. 276) and creates a collective of the heart, mind, body, and soul where intellectual work, critical awareness and analysis, and passionate attachments coalesce into new knowledge-making.

This approach to epistemology is also evident when Jackie presents her research to others. An example of this is the slides Jackie uses when making presentations. The slides are used to introduce her research, jump start the audience, and confront the material reality of existence of her "knowing subjects."

Project Journal. March 28, 2001

> I had lunch with Beth Harrick today. We were talking about the Gender, Race, Orientation Symposium a couple weeks ago. Beth didn't know that Jackie (who gave the keynote) was one of the people I was doing ethnographic research on. She said, "Well, her presentation was itself a site of feminist pedagogical approach." I didn't really understand what she meant. I knew that the methodology that Jackie uses is what I would consider to be feminist (both epistemologically and methodologically), but the presentation itself? Beth said, "Sure! Those slides. In the psych department (Beth is finishing up her dissertation in psychology) we talk about people all the time. All the time. But we would never think of showing them. The material reality of those women in the slides. It changed everything." Beth saw the slides as a big transgression of structure, form, approach. It wasn't a presentation where the "expert" was "reading a paper," in effect banking information to a passive audience. Instead, Jackie was forcing the audience to confront the material reality of these women. To confront the fact that they lived. To look in their eyes. I don't know if that is feminist pedagogy, I'll have to think more about that, But it definitely is feminist rhetoric because it transgresses norms in form and structure to further a feminist message.

During my site visit, I told Jackie about what Beth said. She said that transgression of boundaries was something she was aware of, and did intentionally, to confront her audience with the material lives of these women who had been erased from history. She said it is also an approach she uses in her classes. "I often structure my talks on an experience-based arena. In order for you to understand what I am saying [in my talks], you have to have the experience where you are able to stand and place people here [in your physical reality]. And if you can see it and hear it, it might make more sense than if I just say it." Jackie told me that in her experience, when she talks about her research that extends outside the dominant culture or dominant history, people do not understand what she is talking about. But when she confronts them with the physical evidence, the slides and the faces, it becomes real. She likens it to a bridge that she needs to build before they can move across the chasm between what they know and what they need to know. "You have to walk across the water, but if there is nothing there yet, you aren't going to get there. I have to build it for them."

Jackie also uses this strategy of forcing her audience to confront the physical realities of the people she is writing about in her book on Wells, *Southern Horrors and Other Writings* (1997). At the end of the introduction in that text, Jackie includes a full-page spread that is a facsimile of editorial cartoons that *Harper's Weekly* published on lynching. The graphic images of White men pontificating while two Black men swing from a lynch rope bring the reader face to face with the grizzly reality of lynch laws, the subject of much of Wells' work. These images are followed by photographs of the people who Wells looked to for support and guidance: Frederick Douglass, Victoria Earle Matthews, and Maritcha Jones. The reader, once again, must confront the physical reality of these people, looking into their eyes as they are represented in the photographs, creating a tangible connection between the words on the page, the story recorded there, and the lived realities of human lives. The use of graphics and photographs in Jackie's own rhetorical work moves the audience to a place where they must confront the physical realities of these people's lives. By doing so, Jackie transgresses the academic norm where the audience is comfortably at home in the words, having removed themselves totally from the physical and bodily manifestation of the subject.

Transgressing the boundaries in the way one presents information embodies feminist pedagogy. This approach asks teachers to not only be critically conscious of their strategies to meet the needs of students, but to take risks and model a new way of using authority and leadership. By using these alternate strategies, by building bridges that previously did not exist and leading students and colleagues trip-trapping over that bridge, Jackie creates a road of defiance that furthers a feminist pedagogical approach. Through her feminist leadership, as administrator, teacher, and scholar, Jackie uses these strategies as a way of forging ahead. By doing so she embraces labels of crazy, sassy, and defiant. It is all part of the work, creating new ways of knowing and moving through the world, paving roads so others may join or follow her, leaving more than traces of these lives and minds in her wake.

There Are No Conclusions,
Only New Beginnings

I have an old t-shirt somewhere in my stack of thread-bare, tattered tees. On the front, in big red letters, it proclaims, "Feminism is the radical notion that women are people." The slogan on the shirt has felt outdated for a number of years. I understand feminism as working toward the radical notion that not only are *women* people, but so are Blacks, Hispanics, queers, transsexuals, transgendered people, transvestites, children, the poor, and all the other identities that are rejected, ignored, or marginalized by hegemonic systems of power. In other words, feminism is about everybody getting access to systems of power, especially those traditionally marginalized people who have been held back at the turnstile for so long: "Sorry, but you need to be white, male, heterosexual, privileged class, abled-body before you can go on *this* ride."

Now, when I am asked what a feminist is, I say, "a person who is committed to confronting and dismantling systems of oppression wherever they exist, whether in the form of classism, sexism, racism, homophobia, ageism, etc." That pesky "etc." It leaves so much out, but the list seems not only infinite, but ever-changing. Perhaps it would be easier to say, "a *person* who is committed to confronting and dismantling systems of oppression that exclude traditionally marginalized people from the status of personhood." That is not exactly right, however, on two counts. First, because I really mean "a *woman* who . . . when I say "a person who. . ." Or rather, I do not mean "a man who. . . ." I do not believe men can be feminists because they do not reside in that position of gender disempowerment. Men can only work toward feminism (men can be profeminist, but not feminist) because they inherently embody an identity on which the systemic oppression of those gendered female is built. Second, this definition obscures my belief that men, and not just women, can benefit from feminism. When we dismantle the oppression of socialized gender identities, boys/men win, too. However, because the dominant culture portrays feminism first as "male-bashing" or man-hating, it is often difficult to convince people, both men and women, that males have something to gain from feminism.

Teaching Journal. May 6, 2001

> I finished up the Foundations of Education course yesterday. Turned in grades. So many of the students wrote heartfelt, critically smart reflections about their work and the semester in their portfolios. I was quite surprised by all the "this class changed my perspective" comments. I felt like I was constantly struggling throughout the semester against their unwillingness to take responsibility for and critically engage with the material. And, as always, I had a lot of "this was *so much* work for a three credit general ed course." It's maddening. They carry the unquestioned belief that gen ed or liberal arts requirements should be coast classes.
>
> B. (the persecuted white guy; there is always one) wrote a very hostile reflective letter saying I really didn't know anything and shouldn't be teaching. It was a two-page single spaced mantra of hurled insults. To demonstrate how little I knew about education theories and practices, he cited the fact that Freire was Chilean, not Brazilian, and then he wrote that I needed "to get your facts straight." I copied the back of *Pedagogy of Oppressed* where it outlines Freire's bio (his life in Brazil before he fled for Chile and the U.S.) and slipped it into his portfolio. He also said, in addition to my stupidity, I didn't know what feminism was about. I had, he wrote in his reflective letter, been claiming things for feminism that weren't feminist, like gender equity (feminists really want dominance, not equity) and freedom from gender oppression for males and females. I still haven't figured out how to avoid this kind of hostility from the occasional white male student, or how to most effectively deal with it when I am confronted by it. I photocopied that letter to keep me humble and reflective.

The undercurrents of how to define *feminism* and *feminist pedagogy* churn throughout this project, at moments towing me under and making me writhe with discomfort. "You can't say *that*! Who do you think you are! *You* don't get to decide what feminist pedagogy is, or tell these teachers what they are doing is *feminist* if they don't see it that way!" Certainly there are a multitude of definitions for *feminism*. Each feminist will likely define it for herself. But is there some general agreement? One could argue that gender oppression may be the central issue, but I reject that as an old version of feminism. Confronting gender oppression may be my primary attraction to feminism because I am a white privileged class female living in the United States. Ending racial oppression may be the primary focus of someone else's feminism. Although I identify as queer, I am not often marked or identified by others as queer, so typically I experience the privilege of heterosexuality; queer issues are a part of my feminism, but may not be the primary focus *today*. Tomorrow, it may be. These shifts and changes make my definition more general than specific. I want to believe that feminism can embrace other realities where the primary association is not gender oppression. As Nancy Fraser writes, feminists are more than remiss if they ask people to choose a priority identity (race, class, gender, or sexual orientation). But this is not a new take on feminism; Audre Lorde wrote over two decades ago that there was no hierarchy to oppression, meaning gender oppression does not trump homophobia, classism, racism, or all the other systematic ways groups of people are denied tangible power. Instead, feminism embraces all these multiplicities. When I was talking with Harriet, she attempted to describe how she articulated these complexities, relying on a story she has told before, both in her classrooms and in her book.

Harriet: I actually told this in class recently, too, a story about when my mother came up from the country with her second husband and we were going out for a walk and it was getting chilly and he didn't have a jacket and so I had to offer him one of my sweaters and it sort of gave my mother an anxiety attack. When I was dismissive of that she said, "Oh, Harriet. I know that you say there are no differences between genders." And I said, "Well, yes. There are huge differences between genders, I just don't think there are differences between sweaters." But I went on to say that if she had accused me of a different feminist prejudice, I would have taken a different tack. You know, multiple feminisms, and who knows what they all are.

Kay: But for you personally. What would you say? If someone said, "You're a feminist? What does that mean?" What would you say?

Harriet: It would be really hard to say what it is for me at this point. In a certain way I would say, it's comparable to me being Jewish. It's like my relationship to the Jewish religion. I have a lot of irritation about it. A lot of it is a reaction to my over-exposure and to being forced to be certain things and yet it was meaningless. And yet, Jewishness is a big part of my

identity, and yet, not unlike a lot people I know, I am not celebrating it. I am not into celebrating it. I forgot that it was
Passover this week. It slipped my mind totally. I just don't
care about those types of things. And my sort of gestalt; I
think feminism is the same thing. It is so hard to describe. For
anyone to understand what it means to be Jewish, if you
don't have any relationship to religion. And I feel like feminism would be wholly unintelligible to the world and to
myself. It is part of my physical make up kinda thing. I just
couldn't define it. And if I had to, I would probably have a
lot to do with audience, who asked me.

I agree that audience is important when defining feminism. Jackie indicated
the same when she told me it depends on the context whether she identifies
herself as a Black Feminist or a Womanist. Jackie also sees feminism as a theory that fits well with her scholarly interests, whereas for me it is more of an
identity.

Kay: How do you think feminism affects how you approach lead-
             ership?

Jackie: Feminism for me is never without modification. I don't have
             any problem putting myself in the feminist circle, but when I
             take it on as a personal identity, I usually like to add "Black"
             to be very conscious about being of African descent in the
             world, in this particular time period and geographical loca-
             tion, ideology, and experience that foregrounds things that
             are not necessarily foregrounded in feminism. So that is what
             Black feminism signals for me. What feminism as a scholarly
             area does that I like very much for the things that I want to
             do is that it allows me to look more critically at systems of
             power and privilege and authority and those issues that seem
             very constructive to me. And I try to think about them fair-
             ly constantly. I think it is a deliberate process. I have been
             doing this for the past ten years, there are occasions when I
             find myself slipping and not being consciously aware of the
             implications of location, position, privilege, power in how a
             situation is operating. My guess is that, as a person who is in
             rhetorical studies, I am concerned about processes. What is
             going on? How is it going on? What is the impact of it going
             on? Those kinds of questions are fairly consistent for me. So,
             actually I am going to talk about this next week (in her inau-
             gural address), the alliances that I have formed in scholarly
             arenas have been in those fields that centralized those inter-

ests. So I draw into my circle feminist thought, African dias-
poras, and rhetorical interests. All those studies. It is all very
interdisciplinary. All those contexts are very much part of the
way I have formed my ways of being and doing in the professional area.

Kay: What is the distinction in your mind between a Womanist
and a Black feminist?

Jackie: I don't know what those distinctions are. Labeling is problematic for me at best. I think there are ways in which
Womanist satisfies some of what I like to think of myself as
being and doing. I am using that quotation from Alice
Walker in my talk. But it draws from a popular, a cultural
arena, and in some ways I find that unsatisfying when I think
about ways I want to theorize African American women's
rhetorical history. So the feminism, as studies rather than an
activist orientation, is something that is more vibrant in an
academic way. The way in which Black Feminist and feminist
studies, African diaspora studies, women's studies, they work
for me in my work, in my academic work. What I want to do
more often than not is the combination between theory and
practice. So there is part of me that goes beyond the academic, where all those things are still true, but most of the time it
is in this circle and I want to be able to theorize about life
experiences, achievements, practices in ways that [particular]
vocabulary helps me to do. So I am rather selfish in being
absolutely free to use whichever one of those I personally
like. I am not offended by either one. And I especially understand why some African American women choose Womanist
over Feminist because of the association with white woman's
identity.

Still, I yearn for, and at moments feel desperate for, a definition of feminism
that can act as a signifier for the group of people committed to doing this
work—the work of changing power structures and standards so they are
more open and embracing of alternative and disruptive perspectives, those
of TMP. As a feminist in the Midwest, that solidarity in numbers feels
important. In fact, typically I am so thrilled when another human being simply identifies as a feminist out loud and in public that I could not care much
about what that means to them, although privately I cringe whenever
Camille Paglia is trotted out by the national press as the spokesfeminist
regarding the gender crisis du jour. My Midwest Feminist experience has
proved to be less than pleasurable at times: Women in the Midwest do not
generally like to publicly identify as feminist. It is not unlike openly identi-

fying as queer; most people feel the amount of explaining and overt discrimination they would have to go through to claim the label is not worth it. It is not that they "hide" who they are, but they do not, as I have heard more than one person put it, "advertise it."[43]

As a feminist in the geographic location in which I live and work, I feel I have to publicly proclaim that belief system and carry the banner high and proud to educate others—to make it understood that feminism is not about male-bashing or man-hating. By the same token, I give little attention to academic feminists spending reams of paper trying to define various categories of feminisms (ludic, liberal, radical, Marxist) because these categories seem essentializing and a betrayal of the complexities in the reality. Because every feminist enacts her feminism, and defines her feminism, differently, these static categories irk me and, in my mind, contribute to the ever-widening divide between feminist theory and feminist activism. In Jane Roland Martin's (1999) book, *Coming of Age in Academe*, she attempts to confront the murkiness of feminist theory and its various conflicts; a kindred spirit, Martin also believes that the chasm between activism and academia is ever growing due to the rhetoric of theoretical labeling: "The language of the academy places its speakers at an aerial distance from the world's ills" (p. 28).

Some theorists believe the solution to the problem of language and naming is to abandon the word *feminism* and create a new word. I resist getting rid of the term because I believe it is vitally important that we historically honor and claim the work that has been done on behalf of gender equity and systemic oppression. Rather I want feminists to realize we are all radical, liberal, ludic, Marxist, and various other kinds of feminists depending on the context, day, audience, and situation. No one is ever 100% a radical feminist in every corner of their lives and psyche. Yet within these various contexts and corners, isn't there some idea of what feminism is that will help us identify a solidarity? Instead, it seems at various times those who would like to or do identify as feminists feel paralyzed by the accusation of essentializing. To avoid that scarlet letter "E," we tie ourselves in knots writing theory that seems to go nowhere. These accusations of essentialism (which is always, used in the context of feminist theory, seen as very bad) stifles the work. This "self-policing kills our courage, silences our voices and restricts our vision" (Martin 23).

Personal Journal. March 15, 2001

A full day at 4Cs. I quickly get over-stimulated at these things. Too many people. Not enough alone time. I went to a session this afternoon that made me want to spit. The title of the session was something about critical pedagogies. But only one of the panelists actually talked about teaching. One young woman presented a paper on how the new site of radical feminism is the internet. It was as if liberal feminists never engage online. Or that radical feminism is the "good" kind of feminism and liberal feminism is the "stupid" kind of feminism. The presenter went on to say while "liberal" feminist organizations like NOW were still trying to mobilize in the old fashioned way, radical feminists were using web sites and chat rooms. I had to hold my head onto my shoulders. Lots of feminist organizations (including NOW) use web sites and chat rooms and email list groups to discuss, distribute, and call to action. No one person or organization is a "radical feminist" (a signifier that has come to represent "the right kind of feminism" when actually it means, at least the way I remember theorists originally defining it, as feminists who believe a new system and structure needs to be created to replace the old order that marginalizes women and keeps them from power and self-actualization) all day every day. Depending on the audience and what I am trying to convince them to do, I can be radical, liberal, Marxist, whatever. Sometimes I am not even a feminist, or at least I catch myself not acting or thinking in very feminist ways. There seems to be no awareness of a feminist continuum we all slide across on a minute by minute basis. My frustration is also related to people talking all about categories but never critically reflecting on their own lives to realize there is no way to embody one category fully and completely 100 percent of the time. I wanted to ask the woman doing the presentation, "So what feminist activist work have you done lately and how would you categorize that work? How many NOW meetings have you been to and why do you categorize them as a 'liberal' organization?" My frustration today reminded me of my response to the *JAC* trilogue about feminism in the last issue ("Negotiating the Differend: A Feminist Trilogue"). It was almost like the three theorists were calling for abolition of the "f" word because they just couldn't resolve the messiness of the slippery day to day work that is feminism. They talk a lot about listening and hearing, but not about their own political action. They want to cling to or reject the categories ("I'm a ludic feminist and you're a radical feminist!") but they don't seem able to move beyond those static categories to say, "Well, primarily I have these beliefs and this is how the work I do reflects those beliefs. Here is how I am living these beliefs." I know they would say "rhetorical listening" and hearing can be radical feminist acts, but I want more critical self reflection: what are they doing in the community to further their feminist beliefs? Writing and rewriting the circular argument of "What kind of feminist are you?" isn't enough.

As I struggle with my discontent with how some theorists or scholars are defining or categorizing feminism(s), Harriet originally expressed a similar concern regarding feminist pedagogy. For her, the category was problematic because there was nothing in the way she had heard people describe feminist pedagogy that seemed distinct from other theories of pedagogy. More than once during this project, I have wondered whether I am doing with feminist pedagogy what I adamantly resist about theorists who attempt to parcel out feminisms into various distinct categories. I answer these nagging questions in my own mind by saying feminist pedagogy needs a historical definition to save it from the misrepresentation it now suffers: a weak-minded form of critical pedagogy where the feminine, nurturing mother situates herself in the touchy-feely classwomb where students feel validated and empowered. The field of composition needs to reflect on how feminist pedagogy has contributed to current composition theory and practices. With this project, I want the argument to be clear: Feminist pedagogy has not only contributed but largely defined what we consider to be good teaching practices in the field of composition.

The definitions of feminist pedagogy articulated in the articles I read on the subject, the articles and books from which the 16 themes sprung, varied considerably. None provided as comprehensive a definition. The editors of *The Feminist Teacher Anthology* rely on the basic definition of incorporating issues of race, gender, and class into the classroom. Diana Gustafson compiles a series of definitions offered by other theorists at the beginning of her article "Embodied Learning," but ends this collaborative definition by stating, "Just as there are multiple and sometimes contradictory feminisms or feminist perspectives so too are there multiple feminist pedagogies" (p. 250). I think this is one of the main problems people have with embracing the idea of "feminist pedagogy": too many varying definitions. Instead, what I am arguing in this project is that we need to reflect on the compilation of this historical definition and analyze how these theories have influenced the field of composition without being named as feminist.[44]

When I asked Lynn how she would define feminist pedagogy, she acknowledged that, because of the ambiguity surrounding the idea of feminist pedagogy, the term was used in wildly different ways. The conflation of feminine pedagogy and feminist pedagogy seemed to be at the heart of these ambiguities.

Kay: How do you define feminist pedagogy? In a lot of the articles I read you use the term "radical pedagogy." Is there a distinction? Is feminist pedagogy a type of radical pedagogy?

Lynn: It can be. It can also be terribly conservative. I think that liberal feminism is a very conservative type of feminism. I wouldn't call it radical. Liberal is radical even that it is arguing for equal rights. But, I wouldn't call it a true radical pedagogy. But not splitting hairs, I would say that feminism is a kind of radical pedagogy, in the category of radical pedagogy. I use the term "radical pedagogy" as an umbrella term to gather and group together a lot of these different kinds types of pedagogies.

Kay: OK. So then there is post-modern pedagogy. Is post-modern pedagogy a type of radical pedagogy, or is it a different kind of pedagogy?

Lynn: It's a type of radical pedagogy. And critical pedagogy is a pedagogy with a real leftist, harder, Marxist, approach than a post-modern approach. So critical pedagogy would be a type of radical pedagogy. I think we use this kind of categorizing to make sense of all this stuff. So the question is what is feminist pedagogy?

Kay: Yeah. How would you define feminist pedagogy as a distinct pedagogy? Distinct from other kinds of radical pedagogy.

Lynn: Well, Essentially it is a way of teaching and a subject matter that keeps gender very up front. My sense of feminist pedagogy is not that it must be collaborative, must be nurturing in some sort of feminine way of nurturing. One of the things I have a lot of personal experience with as a female and feminist teacher is the demand that I need to be everybody's momma. And guess what? I am nobody's momma, and I don't want to be [anybody's momma]. (laughs) So, it is very interesting to experience the resentment when you do that. Not because you are an uncaring person, or even an un-nurturing person, it is just that you want to express nurturance in a different way.

Kay: Do you think feminist pedagogy has evolved a little bit over the past ten years to include other issues like class, race, sexual orientation?

Lynn: Absolutely. So when I said it keeps gender at the forefront, it also shows that gender isn't the only category intersected by the institutions of hetero-normativity, of white supremacy, etc. I am directing a dissertation in which the person is arguing that feminism is a bad thing. And this is a Queer Studies person so he's not arguing this from a conservative position, but he is saying that feminism is entirely hetero-normative and trying to show that in composition studies it becomes hetero-normative. I wouldn't argue against him on that point. But he wants to lump feminism together with Women's Studies, and that we're part of the hetero-normative institution. And I don't think he's wrong, but my point is I really want to keep the word feminism. I don't want to have it become gender studies or I don't want Women's Studies to become Gender Studies. I want feminism to remain the term. Not the "F" word, but a term for naming a political classroom, pedagogy, area of study, all those things, and we still have a lot of work to do. So when I said earlier that feminism puts gender up front as an important category of struggle and of knowledge and so forth, it wasn't to the exclusion of anything else. I consider myself a Material Feminist and Material Feminism is trying to be very careful about understanding the complexity of the relationships between gender, race, class, sexual preference, able-bodiedness, ageism, those sorts of things.

I think that the operative term of what I try to teach is critique and all my courses are about learning how to do cultural critique. There is certainly focus on critiquing the patriarchy, but also heterosexism and capitalism—the hardest thing of all to get students, especially undergraduates, to think about and talk about because capitalism has plans. That kind of criticism of everything, including feminist pedagogy, is what my version of feminist pedagogy is. It's not about being the nurturing mother.

Students say about me that I am hard. And I actually published this as a footnote, so I don't mind telling you that, my first semester in Milwaukee as an assistant professor and I got two student evaluations. One of them is not important, but I will tell you it anyway. He wrote, it had to be a guy, one of my evaluations said, "I like to get up behind her and smell her hair." (Laughs) It was years before anyone [again] got anywhere near enough to smell my hair. But the other one said, which I thought was an *amazingly* hostile thing, he said, "She's a good teacher, but she has invisible tits."

Kay: Oh, my god!

Lynn: And to me that is about not being feminine enough. Not being capable of being sexualized enough. And so I had somehow failed, not as a teacher. I was a good teacher, he said; I had failed as a woman. And I am telling this story because I think that is the reality of not just being a female teacher but being a feminist teacher because that was a power play, an aggressive move. It was an act of aggression. He meant, because of course he knows I am going to read it, he meant to get at the part of me that is vulnerable to having my femininity questioned.

Kay: Wow.

Lynn: So, I am a good teacher, you know, but not a good woman.

In feminist rhetorical theory, the descriptor *dangerous moves* is some-times used to distinguish feminist rhetoric from women's rhetoric. Feminist rhetoric breaks the norms enough to be dangerous. For Sojourner Truth to stand up before a group of White people and point to the physical reality of her Black, female body and challenge "Aren't I a Woman?" was a dangerous move. For Margaret Sanger, imprisoned for distributing birth control infor-mation to poor women, refusing to be silenced by threats of prosecution and prison was a dangerous move. For Leslie Feinberg to follow her heart and live as a transgendered person, speaking and writing about her experiences of persecution and hope is a dangerous move. To be *feminist* rather than *feminine* is what makes the assumption of power a dangerous move. To walk into a classroom as a teacher is to assume a position of power. As with the heart-stopping example Lynn offered, being a *feminist* teacher, instead of the expected *feminine* teacher, disrupts the dynamic of the classroom and sends some students reeling. For many students, however, feminist pedagogy pro-vides a liberating, empowering model of knowledge-construction and criti-cal thinking, and this is disruptive because it challenges traditional models of learning and knowing. For educators to be better able to adopt or conscious-ly reject feminist pedagogy, it needs to be more clearly understood. *That* was my goal for this project. Through historical research of the feminist move-ment and Women's Studies, I attempted to synthesize the many ways that feminist pedagogy has been defined into a more comprehensive and histor-ical definition. I wanted to apply this definition specifically to the field of composition and rhetoric to show how feminists and feminist pedagogical principles have changed the way contemporary writing and rhetoric teach-ers teach. Finally, I wanted to show how three feminist teachers enacted their feminist pedagogy. I wanted to hear about their experiences with being feminist teachers and leaders. I wanted to *show* how the theory of feminist pedagogy plays out in day-to-day practices, from class to class, from meet-ing to meeting, in an article, a conference presentation, or a speech.

In the end, I have more questions than answers. Although I believe that a clearer definition of feminist pedagogy is desperately needed, I continue to struggle with the danger of essentializing. What I offer here is the most com-prehensive, historical definition, understanding that tomorrow this defini-tion will change, evolving as feminism always evolves, in answer to specific issues and concerns that previously we had obscured or ignored. What I have come to understand is that feminist pedagogy, like feminist rhetoric, is practiced differently depending on context, audience, and purpose. Teachers make choices about how to practice their feminist pedagogy based on those three things. In the lives and work of Lynn, Harriet, and Jackie, I see the powerful passion that is feminist pedagogy, and feminist ideology, spinning out in dynamic and exciting ways. Being able to see a glimpse of their lives has not only codified my belief that feminist teachers are smart, funny, and amazingly self-critical educators, but that they are the *best* kind of teachers, changing more worlds than they will ever know. For me, it all began in an Intro to Women's Literature course in 1985. A feminist teacher changed my life. Over 20 years later, I am still awed and thrilled by what feminist peda- gogy offers, as a teacher, student, and a scholar. I am sure I will be critiqued for being a romantic, a bleeding heart, a dewy-eyed idealist. There are worse things, I suppose.

It is only through my continued questions and challenges that I will move further in figuring it out. As I said in the introduction, figuring it out always means ending with more questions than what I started with. Hopefully the questions are more sophisticated, more complicated, further along. In the spirit of feminist conversation and helpful critique, I ask you here, now, "What questions do *you* have? How can I help to pull the thread that begins an answer?"

Notes

1. Scholars such as Susan Jarratt are researching historical Black colleges and universities and the voices of women at those sites of learning, but nothing that I have read has investigated the role of women specifically as teachers in such institutions. In the past few years, there have been articles and books focusing on women in administrative positions at historically Black colleges and universities. There has also been research on Native American boarding schools, institutions of education that the federal government established to force native children to assimilate to the dominant culture and that resulted in the coerced betrayal and abandonment of their own cultural heritage. These schools were often run by religious orders, many times by women in the vocation of nuns. However, investigation of the role of women teachers in these systems is outside the scope of my project. Likewise, feminist approaches to teaching that existed in less formal educational sites are not be included in this research. For example, during WWI and post-WWII, the feminist movement integrated with the labor movement where literacy work for immigrant and other under-class women workers was a primary way feminist activists furthered the rights and education of women.
2. Throughout this project, I use *their* as a generic third person in relation to both singular and plural nouns. Although many would see this as a grammatical error, my intention to use *their* as a generic third person is a way of creating nonsexist language. In Standard English, there is no nonsexist third-person plural that does not point specifically to gender.
3. Certainly there were theorists and teachers who identified pedagogical methods as *feminist* prior to 1982. The problem in identifying these scholars is that electronic databases do not contain a comprehensive list of every article published or every presentation given. Through searching databases that compiled citations and records of publications from the fields of education, language and literature, communication, social sciences, and Women's studies, I found the Cully and

Miller citations. These were the earliest references of feminist teaching or feminist pedagogy. That is to say, these were the first articles where certain practices were named as *feminist teaching practices* where the database administrator used those key words (*feminist teaching* or *feminist pedagogy*) as a signifying way of cataloguing the articles. That is not to say there were not theorists who wrote about feminist approaches to teaching before this date. Rather, these were the first instances where feminist teaching as a pedagogical approach was defined explicitly.

4. I created the term *Traditionally Marginalized People* (TMP) because I was wholly unsatisfied with the more common lexicon used to describe people who are outside the perimeters of the dominant culture. I reject the word *minorities* because it continues to reinforce the idea of a White, male majority, which is a fiction of the dominant culture (White males have never been the majority, only traditionally those with power). Likewise, I reject the rhetoric of *People of Color* as inherently racist because the norm is the un-named Whiteness that immediately casts all those who are not white as being colored. Through struggling with how to name those outside the dominant culture, I came to TMP because it encompasses not only those of various races or ethnicities, but all groups that have been systematically denied power in the White supremacist, capitalist patriarchy. Those who have been traditionally marginalized include women, queers, poor people, the aged, the differently abled, and all groups that are not identified as White or Anglo Saxon. I also especially like this term because the acronym TMP implies a temporary position as traditionally marginalized people. As feminists and others do their work to change the cultural norms, the hope is that people who are traditionally marginalized will gain access to power. Therefore, the feminist work is to make sure that, although these groups and individuals have been *traditionally* marginalized, they are only *temporarily* so.

   Some African-American individuals and organizations are working to remove *minorities* and *People of Color* from the popular lexicon, arguing that *minorities* indicates a lesser status. Jordan (1985) prefers the term *the world's majority* instead of *minority* because she finds the latter diminishes not only the realities of all the various groups of people corralled into that one category, but also because her term more accurately reflects reality where, in sheer numbers of people, the only minority when considering the world's population are people of Anglo-Saxon heritage or Whites. The 2000 census reported that one in four Americans identify as either Hispanic or African American. In places such as California, the District of Columbia, Hawaii, and New Mexico, the majority of the population reflects people often defined as *minority* (Harrison, 2005). When I do use the term *minority* I put it in italics to show this is not my term of choice, but how the dominant culture chooses to lump all people who are not of Anglo-Saxon heritage or an arbitrary skin color designation into one category.

5. Even radical feminists who try not to interact with the patriarchy at all must do so on a daily basis if they watch TV, listen to the radio, read texts published by nonfeminist publishers, work with men, buy groceries, or even pay taxes. Even separatist feminists who live on self-sufficient communes with only other women struggle against the indoctrination of patriarchal styles of leadership and systems of thought and knowledge.

6. *Critical thinking* is a term that few people take the time to define. The danger is that my understanding of what critical thinking is may be a radical departure from how someone else envisions that term. There is ambiguity in how various theorists and writers have defined *critical thinking*. Although many theorists I quote in this section use the terminology of critical thinking, few actually define what critical thinking means within the context of their work. Fisher (2001) defines *critical thinking* as skills of argumentation and analysis, as well as ability to critique prevailing (or perhaps dominant) relationships and social structures. This definition would most closely articulate how I define critical thinking.

7. I am not suggesting that boys and men are neither initiators of nor affected by feminist pedagogy. In many ways, male theorists have contributed a great deal to the definition and practices of feminist pedagogy. I single out girls and women here, and in other places, because the roots of feminist pedagogy via Women's Studies began as attention to the education of girls and women and adapting the institutions and ideologies of education to empower and educate girls and women in a culture where females held a disempowered position.

8. I want to make the distinction between feminists in the academy and feminist teachers. Feminists who work in the academy are not necessarily feminist teachers. Feminist teachers are teachers who are committed to feminist pedagogy as a specific way of enacting their feminist beliefs in their lives. Feminist academics do not necessarily identify as feminist teachers or enact feminist pedagogy.

9. Although this quote, taken out of a context of a very long discussion Harriet and I had regarding feminist pedagogy (spanning months), may seem to indicate she does not believe in feminist pedagogy, Harriet was expressing her frustration at earlier descriptions of feminist pedagogy rather than the definition I am using here.

10. That is not to say that this represents a static definition of *feminist pedagogy*. The definition of feminist pedagogy represented here is not the only definition or the end of how feminist pedagogy should and will be defined. Rather, it is a definition that attempts to look back, historically, and outline what feminist theorists have identified as feminist teaching and show how these strategies and practices are part and parcel of how composition is taught. As pedagogical strategies and theories evolve, so will the definition. What the 16 themes represent is a definition that reflects what feminist pedagogy has been defined as from when it was first named until *today*, the definition may change/evolve a year or 5 years from now. The definition should be in constant revision as the theory evolves through practice.

11. When I originally began this project, I had gathered together 15 themes. As I continued working and researching, I added another theme to the category of "Teacher Critical Reflection": *Teaching With the Whole Self*. My hope was that my classroom observations, during site visits, would help me clarify whether this was a distinct theme or rather a manifestation of another theme in that category, *Being Overt With One's Political Location (self-disclosure)*. However, classroom observations did not create a definitive answer regarding whether these two themes were redundant. Currently I am wondering whether the distinction lies between *checking authority* and *being overt/teaching with the whole self*. However, one could argue that checking teacher authority is a way of being overt with students about one's personal location. This offers just one example

of how loosely grouped and named these themes are, and how they often creep into one another in ways that mock the clear lines of categories and themes.

12. I define *radical pedagogies* as those that reject traditional models of pedagogy for approaches that subvert the teacher-focused classroom for one that is student-focused and replace a model of teacher power with one where knowledge is gathered and communicated by all members of the community, where domination in all forms is confronted, and where progressive and innovative theories of teaching are celebrated.

13. The symbol of the 1950s "oppressed housewife in the suburbs" has been called into question by some feminist historians who believe this reality only reflected a small percentage of women's lives, obviously almost exclusively the lives of White, middle- to privileged-class women. In the collection of essays entitled *Not June Cleaver*, the authors debunk the model of middle-class womanhood documented by Betty Freidan (1963) in *Feminine Mystique* as myth. The question for me becomes not whether the reality of the White middle-class housewife existed in the form that Freidan described, but whether cultural propaganda of the 1950s created this image of middle-class womanhood as something to aspire to: the dainty housewife in her sparkling kitchen who waited eagerly for her husband to arrive home from work. Cameron (1995) theorizes that ideology is perpetuated and then re-created in the lives of women through the vehicle of magazine articles and other literature in popular culture. This theory, where the media creates an image that is then internalized and aspired to by the women in the culture, can be applied to the model of womanhood as manifested in the suburban housewife of the 1950s and 1960s. Although the "suburban housewife" identity may have only realized itself in a certain population of women (White, middle to privileged class), the fact that the media and popular culture perpetuated this as the ideal feminine identity would have made it something that most women aspired to. This theory parallels the example Cameron provides in her work on self-help articles in popular women's magazines. Cameron writes that the articles document what a woman is supposed to be concerned with (e.g., passive–aggressive relationships, her weight or thigh size, whether she is orgasmic, how to find her inner spiritual self), and women reading the articles come to believe that these things are part of what a woman needs to be a woman or feminine. In Cameron's theory, the women's magazines create the ideological identity that individual women then aspire to or begin to embody. Women who read the magazines enact these identities, thereby creating a cultural reality that mimics propaganda in the magazine. I am applying this same theory to the image of the 1950s housewife as represented in magazines such as *Life* and *Good Housekeeping*, as well as on TV shows such as *Father Knows Best* and *Leave It to Beaver*. These popular culture media representations of women created a model of womanhood that was then enacted by middle-class women, largely White middle-class women, and aspired to by many others who were not White or middle class. The advertisements of the aproned wife/mother in her kitchen, articles on how to greet your husband when he comes home, and TV shows that portrayed wives/mothers as happy, smiling, and deferential to their family created an image of middle-class womanhood that women who desired to fit into the dominant culture then strived to achieve.

14. I make the distinction here between feminist pedagogy and Women's Studies pedagogy to further clarify that the former is a pedagogy that evolved *from* Women's Studies pedagogy, but also differs from Women's Studies pedagogy.

15. Although *active learning* has been defined in various ways by educational scholars, in the context of this project, I define active learning as learners taking responsibility for their own learning, where the teacher allows space for the students to make their own choices and processes. Ryder and Graves (1998) define active learning as an instructor's acknowledgment of cultural, social, and cognitive diversity, giving attention to the processes of knowledge creation and not just memorizing information. For Ryder and Graves, active learning acknowledges diverse interpretations of information, encouraging students to be aware of their own learning processes and "promot[ing] students ability to monitor and direct their learning" (6-7). In his book, *Experiential Learning in Higher Education*, Cantor reinforces this definition and extends it to critical thinking and ability to solve complex problems.

16. The May 1971 issue of *College English* devoted itself to a focus on feminist literary criticism and how to apply it to the English classroom. It also included articles that discussed the status of women students and how the college classroom was changing because of feminist influences. Hedges (1972), the editor of the issue, wrote that changes resulting from feminist influences are on the horizon and "we are still at the beginning" (p. 5).

17. Between 1973 and 1980, women authored from a third to a half of all articles published in the journal. In *College Composition and Communication*, articles authored by women compared to articles authored by men also reflected this ratio. During the 1980s and 1990s, the split became almost even, with some issues publishing more articles by women than men, although these issues were still the exception and not the rule. Even so, in a field where the majority of teachers and scholars are female, even a 50:50 ratio hints at a male bias.

18. It is in this issue that Tillie Olson's (1972) now famous essay was first published, "Women Who are Writers in Our Century." In this essay, she made the call to teachers that they must teach women writers, but first they must educate themselves since their own training omitted women as writers of literature. "You who teach, read writers that are women" (p. 16). The focus throughout this issue is the study and teaching of women writers (Emily Dickinson, Sylvia Plath, and Anais Nin, to name a few).

19. The connection between themes of feminist pedagogy and theories in composition from the 1970s through 2000 are represented in chapter 2 (this volume).

20. Rose's (1995) description of a democratic classroom focuses on the issue of student "care." Noddings (1988) picks up this rhetoric when calling for an "ethic of care" in the composition classroom. I interpret Noddings description as an attention to the individual student's academic needs and personal location using a careful and critical teacher eye. With her "ethic of care," Noddings challenges teachers not to make assumptions about their students and their realities and to engage in critical self-reflection of their own teaching practices, themes of feminist pedagogy. However, Noddings' rhetoric can also quickly fall into the "maternal teacher/feminine pedagogy" camp, which focuses more on socialized stereotypes of how women approach teaching (nurturing mothers). Elizabeth

Flynn (1988), a scholar of feminine pedagogy, reinforces this connection to feminine contexts by creating the pedagogical binary of the authoritative father (bad pedagogy based on power of the teacher) and the nurturing mother (feminist teaching). Both Flynn's and Noddings' models can quickly become oppressive when considering them in the context of essentialist beliefs, where all females are innately nurturing and maternal, or that a feminine nurturing manifests itself in specific ways.

West (1993) might offer a way to reconsider the essentialist connections between care for students and nurturing mother/teachers. West writes that teachers need "politics of conversation," converting nihilistic cultures to one of love and caring. West uses the example of Malcolm X, Fannie Lou Hamer, and Martin Luther King, Jr. as people who speak in rhetoric that shows they are physically and emotionally upset by the state of Black Americans, but also show deep care and concern for those same Black Americans. Using West's rhetorical analysis of African American revolutionaries, the rhetoric of care moves away from a warm, fuzzy mother figure to one of critical rigor with strategically placed sharp edges, enticing people to action.

21. I define *multiculturalism* as an attempt to integrate voices and perspectives from various cultures outside the dominant culture in both curriculum and class discussions. Recently, there have been critiques of multiculturalism especially in regard to education as a way to further reify the dominance of Whiteness, where all *other* cultures are lumped into one category of multiculturalism. Regardless of this new problematizing of the rhetoric and concept of multiculturalism, the word *multiculturalism* is what these scholars use in their writing and therefore represents my primary reason for using that same rhetoric here. Their use of the word reflects the historical context of when they wrote the article/book, and not necessarily the contemporary view some educators have of what multicultural education or approach to meaning.

22. Although I could find no articles in composition journals that specifically addressed the issue of humor in the writing classroom, when I was observing Lynn Worsham's graduate writing workshop during my site visit to the University of South Florida, one of the students in that class was writing about humor in the classroom. From what I remember of the discussion during the workshop of his project, there was a consensus that teachers integrate humor in individual ways depending on the personality of the teacher and the personality of the class. What works to bring laughter into one class for a particular teacher may not work in another class or for another teacher. Because of the uniquely personal way in which laughter and pleasure are created, it is difficult to construct a knowledge base of "how tos" when it comes to integrating pleasure and joy into the classroom community. Consequently, this may be why there seems to be no scholarship that focuses on this topic . . . *yet.*

23. I believe that leadership is a form of pedagogy. In the ethnographic chapters, this idea of pedagogy as leadership plays out more fully. In the ethnographies, it is clear that Harriet Malinowitz, Jackie Jones Royster, and Lynn Worsham use leadership, with graduate students and colleagues, in the university, and the field of composition and rhetoric, as a site of feminist pedagogy.

24. Throughout this book, I define *ideology* as systems or structures that create a way of being in the world, a way of constructing the world, and a way of creating knowledge about the world. The dominant ideology is one I see as grounded in patriarchy, racism, classism, sexism, homophobia, as well as capitalism and consumerism. These systems of power and knowledge are reflected in institutions of religion, education, marriage/family, and government, among others.

25. I am using *situational knowledge* as defined by Haraway (1998): knowledge produced in and for a specific context. In the ethnography, the researcher produces knowledge, the story she writes, in and for a specific context. In this ethnographic project, the knowledge I am producing resides in the context of the academy, with all the power relationships that exist both within the academy and between me, as a researcher, and the participants. Because I am the younger/student researcher and they are the tenured professors, the power relationship that is part of these ethnographic studies is, in some ways, more complex than the traditional ethnographic research where the researcher (educated academic) is "studying" a person or group of people with less cultural power. In my situation, I have less institutional power (nontenured and younger) than the participants (tenured professors who have a lot of authority and celebrity in the field of composition), but by virtue of being the researcher, I have power. I get to decide what to write about.

26. These feminist principles for composition theorists were not only applicable to pedagogical research, but more traditional rhetorical research. In the latter part of the decade, composition/rhetoric scholars began writing about women's rhetoric or feminist rhetoric, attempting to articulate the differences between women's use of language and men's. Most scholars believed that a woman's position as an outsider to the dominant culture placed her in a rhetorical position where she had to manipulate language to gain ethos in ways that men did not. Extending French feminist theory to the field of composition, Worsham (1991) examined "ecriture feminine" and looked for ways to radicalize the writing of the body. She argued that feminist writing goes beyond "writing the body" to radical mimicry: disrupting the dominant phallocentrism ("laughing at the truth") and creating new visions of language. The dominant culture dismissed any radical language as a fad or fashion, language that was not part of long-standing systems. But, she wrote, feminist composition would move beyond this to teach writing as a mode of learning where radical language choices are celebrated. Scholars such as Biesecker (1993) criticized these attempts as epistemological affirmative action, marginalizing all who did not fit the definition. Instead, Biesecker argued for a language theory that recognizes resistance within power structures, where powers of equal strength push and pull each other.

   Biesecker wrote that there is no difference between the way women use language and the way men use language; instead there exists the need to research and document the rhetorical history of women, long left out of the rhetorical canon. I disagree with the claim that there are no differences between the rhetoric of men and women, as well as the TMP. Because women and others are afforded less power and authority in the culture, they have to work harder at *ethos*-gathering strategies in their rhetoric. Also, the tools of male rhetoric may not challenge the status quo, so purpose changes strategies of rhetoric that some women, especially feminists, use. Because of these reasons, women's rhetorical moves are slightly different than those of men. Men do not have to work as hard to prove *ethos* to their audience; authority and credibility are culturally assigned to men by virtue of being male.

27. In the ethnographic chapters, I refer to these three women by first name only. Some may see my use of the first name as reckless disrespect and disregard for these preeminent comp/rhet scholars who helped me with my research by generously opening their lives to my scrutiny. Even to me it feels a little odd, using a first name instead of just a last name when referring to another person in a scholarly text. From the beginning, in my correspondences with Lynn, Harriet, and Jackie, I used only their first names when addressing them. It seemed the feminist thing to do, a small subversion of hierarchies. Within the dominant culture, and in many subcultures, the use of only a first name when speaking to or about an elder is seen as a sign of disrespect. I thought of this more than once when I (a younger White woman) referred to Jackie (an African American elder) by her first name. Could this be done without evoking the oppression imposed on African Americans for centuries where they were called by first names yet had to address others (Whites) with courtesy titles? What right did I have to call any of these women by their first names, as if they were colleagues or friends? Yet I proceeded this way because I have never called a professor by anything other than a first name. Or at least I cannot recollect a time when I did, although perhaps as an undergraduate student in the early 1980s this was more the status quo. Because that was how I proceeded, addressing these three incredible scholars and teachers by their first names, it felt false to then switch to a last name when writing about my experiences with them, a harkening to some jocular sports jargon: "Way to go, Royster!" Still, as I write this, I wonder if I have a right to subvert this standard of respect in the name of feminism. At moments it feels uncomfortable, but the alternate feels even more so. "Discomfort," I always tell my students, "is often good. It means we are challenging ourselves. And perhaps we will learn something in the process." I am not quite sure, yet, what this discomfort of using familiar first names for people I afford so much respect is teaching me.

28. In traditional (White supremacist patriarchal) philosophy, man is "the knowing subject" and woman (and other traditionally marginalized people) are relegated to the status of "object." In her book *What Can She Know?*, feminist philosopher Code (1991) writes that academic philosophers and researchers often treat "the knower" as "a featureless abstraction" that unquestionably embodies the male gender. A feminist approach to epistemology, therefore, not only positions woman (and other traditionally marginalized people) as knowing subjects, but articulates even further an identity of "the knower," understanding that there is no unbiased standard of knowledge construction. In these ethnographies, I want the reader to position the participants as "the knowing subjects." Rather than "subjects" of my research, they are participants. Rather than "objects" from which I construct knowledge, they are "the knowing subjects" creating knowledge. The knowledge they bring to this project helps us work together to construct something new.

29. *JAC* was formerly an acronym for *Journal of Advanced Composition*. When Tom Kent became editor of the journal in the 1990s, he changed the name of the journal to *JAC*, dropping what he saw as an inaccurate title and replacing it with a descriptive subtitle: "A Journal of Composition Theory." When Lynn took over the editorship, she dropped the subtitle, explaining her decision by writing: "*JAC* has long since stopped functioning as an acronym, properly speaking; those three letters have no fixed referent. Today *JAC*, like the term composition, is a floating signifier. In other words, just as composition has been, and continues to be, articulated to radically different intellectual, educational, and political agendas, and thus continues to be a site for hegemonic struggle, the journal has been devoted during most of its twenty-year history to the struggle over the proper boundaries of composition and over what literacy, broadly conceived, will mean" (*JAC*, 20.1, pp. viii–ix).

30. I know. *Women* is an essentializing category. There is no such thing as a succinct way to define *women* or *women's lives*. However, there are material realities that result in being gendered female in this world, and when I write *women* I am aware that poststructuralist theorists argue against using such categories to define groups of people. But I am also keenly committed to recognizing gendered locations and how they intersect with a wide range of other social orders (race, class, sexual orientation, able-bodiedness, age, etc.). Women are not a unified group, ditto for feminists, but by being gendered female, they take on a location of systematic disempowerment even if that disempowerment also varies with other locations and identities.

31. Quotations that are not attributed to a specific text and page number came from personal interview transcripts.

32. Examples of feminist journals that sprang from the Second Wave feminist activist movement and the discipline of Women's Studies are *Signs*, *Feminist Journal*, and *Frontiers*. Contemporary feminist journals such as *Women's Studies Quarterly* and *The Feminist Teacher* are more squarely rooted in the academic earth, located in the Woman's Studies plot. Whereas the earlier feminist journals attempted to straddle the two worlds of activism and academia and create connections between the two communities, contemporary feminist journals rarely attempt to reach across an ever-increasing divide between grassroots activism and academic feminism, many seeing such work as "unscholarly."

33. As an example, in the first issue Lynn edited (20:1, 2000), the articles focusing on pedagogy include Henry Giroux's "Public Pedagogy and the Responsibility of Intellectuals," G. Douglas Atkins' "On Writing Well," and Bruce Horner's "Politics, Pedagogy, and the Profession of Composition." Of the seven other articles featured in this issue, one focuses on identity issues and activism (Chaput's "Identity, Postmodernity, and an Ethics of Activism"), one critiques the Whiteness of rhetorical history (Ratcliffe's "Eavesdropping as Rhetorical Tactic"), and one applies feminist language theory à la Mary Daly to popular culture (Covino's "Walt Disney Meet Mary Daly").

34. Attributing general theories of shame and guilt to one theorist is difficult, if not sloppy, scholarship. Ruth Benedict (1989) may be one of the first names associated with discussions of shame and guilt. Margaret Mead has also written on the subject. Another theorist who has helped further my understanding of these

distinctions has been Hajime Nakamura (1997). Interestingly, all these researchers wrote about the concepts of shame and guilt in the context of observing other cultures, as if the workings of these social norms were not part of their own cultural experience.

35. Ironically, instead of a jury or judge pronouncing an individual "shamed" for a crime, the judicial system pronounces the person on trial "guilty." In fact, one person cannot pronounce another to be guilty of something because guilt is an internal and individual self-judgment. Instead, the public condemnation of being named as a criminal is an act of shame, not guilt. Equally interesting is the way the dominant culture articulates the distinction between guilt and shame. Guilt is a state of being, an existence, an identity: "He was guilty." Shame more often constitutes a feeling, a temporary emotion: "He felt ashamed." The different rhetoric used when describing the state of guilt or shame reinforces the public/private distinction: internal (feelings) versus external (state of being).

36. Snools are foreground rhetors who govern and legitimate what Daly (1990) refers to as the "bore-ocracy." Only by pushing language from the Background (feminist consciousness and community) into the foreground will feminist ideals ever take root and grow in the dominant culture.

37. The "Unmotherhood" essay was eventually published by Lynn in *JAC*, an example of how Lynn gives space to feminist scholarship that may not get published elsewhere because of feminist approaches or research.

38. Certainly the journal is a feminist publication. Certainly the people who are reviewing [the article] are feminist, or I would assume that they are, or at least that they are defining themselves as feminist. But I would also say the more radical feminist response to Harriet's article would be a closer, more critical self-reflection of the reviewer's own discomfort with the essay: "I am uncomfortable with this, but I am uncomfortable with this probably because I am entrenched in the structure that this article is disrupting. So, in the name of transgressing old structures or creating other models that are more engaging, that are more welcoming, that are more inclusive of different feminist voices and different feminist approaches and perspectives, I want this to be published. And thereby begin a discussion about changing the standards of publication."

39. The reference to "When and Where I Enter" comes from Cooper's (1988) essay, "A Voice from the South by a Black Woman of the South," her only published work. She wrote, "Only the BLACK WOMAN can say 'when and where I enter, in the quiet, undisputed dignity of my womanhood, without violence and without suing or special patronage, then and there the whole *Negro race enters with me*'" (p. 31). Giddings (1984) resurrected the phrase (and Cooper's use of it) in her book, *When and Where I Enter: The Impact of Black Women on Race and Sex in America*. In her book, Giddings describes the physical reality of being Black and female and how that identity shifts the contexts of her rhetorical moments. A Black woman does not assume a rhetorical position, but first must consider when and how she will enter that rhetorical space so that the audience will respond in ways that allow them to hear the message.

40. If the people acting counter to expectations of the dominant culture are reflecting traits of the dominant culture, they are not labeled as *crazy*, but as *eccentric* or *maverick*. The examples of Ted Turner, Hugh Hefner, or William Randolph

Hearst spring to mind. These white, heterosexual males, excrutiatingly wealthy, and controlling an inordinate amount of financial, natural, political resources are not seen "crazy" in their unconventional behavior or quirks but "eccentric." These men are entrenched in the capitalist empire, therefore their behavior, often seen as out of bounds in relation to what is defined as "normal," were/are typically described as eccentric or maverick, but rarely, if ever, as crazy.

41. Bartholomae's nonresponse to Harriet's article about him seems a tad ironic because Jackie attributes her book *Traces of a Stream* to have, in part, resulted from Bartholomae's support and encouragement regarding her work.

42. I asked Jackie about the distinction between Black feminist and Womanist. She responded by saying that the distinction between Black Feminist and Womanist (a term coined by Alice Walker, 1983) seems to lie between a definition that is scholarly (Black Feminist) and one that is cultural (Womanist). "[Womanist] draws from a popular, a cultural arena, and in some ways I find that unsatisfying when I think about ways I want to theorize African American women's rhetorical history. So feminism, as studies rather than an activist orientation, is somewhat more vibrant in an academic way. [...] There is part of me that goes beyond the academic, where all those things are still true, but most of the time it is in this circle and I want to be able to theorize about life experiences, achievements, practices in ways that vocabulary helps me to do. So, I am rather selfish in being absolutely free to use whichever one of those terms I personally choose. I am not offended by either one. I especially understand why some African American women choose Womanist over Feminist because of the association with white woman's identity." In fact, in her inaugural address, Jackie defines and claims the term *Womanist* instead of Black Feminist, showing that the rhetorical situation and context dictate which label she chooses to use.

43. Another t-shirt memory. The Omaha chapter of the National Organization for Women sold t-shirts during the Bush administration (The First Reich) that pictured a close-up of a young, White blonde woman's face in the throws of an anguished scream, harkening back to comic book cels of the 1950s and 1960s. From her caption bubble came the desperate cry, "Oh, my GOD! I'm a Feminist in Nebraska!"

44. In the end, my need for a definition of feminism is not that much unlike my definition of feminist pedagogy, in that the definitions represent broad theories and the *practices* define the individual's unique interpretation or enactment of the theory. How feminist pedagogy is enacted depends, as with feminism, on context, audience, and purpose.

References

"A Student's Right to His Own Language." Committee on CCCC Language Statements. *CCC* 25.3 (1974). Special Issue. Ed. Edward P. J. Corbett.

Allison, Dorothy. *Two or Three Things I Know for Sure*. New York: Plume Books, 1996.

Altbach, Philip. *The Knowledge Context: Composition Perspectives on the Distribution of Knowledge*. Albany: State U of New York P, 1987.

Angelou, Maya. "Still I Rise." *Maya Angelou Poems*. New York: Bantam Books, 1986. 154-55.

Annas, Pamela. "Silences." *Teaching Writing: Pedagogy, Gender and Equity*. Eds. Cynthia Caywood and Gillian Overing. Albany: State U of New York P, 1987. 3-18.

Anzaldua, Gloria. *Borderlands/La Frontera: The New Mestiza*. San Francisco: Aunt Lute, 1987.

Aronowitz, Stanley, and Henry Giroux. *Education Still Under Siege*. 2nd ed. Westport, CT: Bergin and Garvey, 1993.

Ashton-Jones, Evelyn. "Collaborative Learning." *Feminine Principles and Women's Experience in American Composition and Rhetoric*. Eds. Louise Phelps and Janet Emig. Pittsburgh Series in Composition, Literacy, and Culture. Pittsburgh: U of Pittsburgh P, 1995. 5-26

Bartholomae, David. "Inventing the University." *When a Writer Can't Write: Studies in Writer's Block and Other Composing-Process Problems*. Ed. Mike Rose. New York: Guilford, 1985. 134-65.

Bauer, Dale, and Katherine Rhoades. "The Meanings and Metaphors of Student Resistance." *Antifeminism in the Academy*. Eds. Veve Clark, Shirley Nelson Garner, Margaret Higonnet, and Ketu H. Katrak. New York: Routledge, 1996. 95-114.

Bauer, Dale. "The Other 'F' Word: The Feminist in the Classroom." *College English* 52 (1990): 385-96.

Behar, Ruth. *Translated Woman: Cross the Border with Esperanza's Story*. Boston: Beacon P, 1993.

Bell, Sandra, Marina Morrow, and Evangelia Tastsoglou. "Teaching in Environments of Resistance: Towards a Critical, Feminist, and Antiracist Pedagogy." *Meeting the Challenge: Innovative Feminist Pedagogies in Action.* Eds. Maralee Mayberry and Ellen Cronan Rose. New York: Routledge, 1999. 23-48.

Benedict, Ruth. *Chrysanthemum and the Sword: Patterns of Japanese Culture.* Boston: Houghton Mifflin, 1989.

Bensimon, Estela Mara. "Lesbian Existence and the Challenge to Normative Constructions of the Academy." *Feminist Critical Policy Analysis II: A Perspective from Post-secondary Education.* Ed. Catherine Marshall. Washington, DC: Falmer Press, 1992. 141-56.

Berthoff, Ann. "'Reading the World . . . Reading the Word': Paulo Freire's Pedagogy of Knowing." *Only Connect: Uniting Reading and Writing.* Ed. Thomas Newkirk. Portsmouth, NH: Boynton/Cook, 1987.

_____. "Foreword." *Literacy: Reading and the Word and the World.* Eds. Paulo Freire and Donaldo Macedo. Critical Studies in Education Series. New York: Bergin & Garvey, 1987. xi-xxiii.

Biesecker, Barbara. "Coming to Terms with Recent Attempts to Write Women into the History of Rhetoric." *Rethinking the History of Rhetoric: Multidisciplinary Essays on Rhetorical Traditions.* Ed. Takis Poulakos. Boulder: Westview P, 1993. 153-73.

Bishop, Wendy. "Students' Stories and the Variable Gaze of Composition Research." *Writing Ourselves into the Story: Unheard Voices from Composition Studies.* Eds. Sheryl Fontaine and Susan Hunter. Carbondale: Southern Illinois UP, 1993. 197-215

_____. *Ethnographic Writing and Research: Writing It Down, Writing It Up, Reading It.* Portsmouth, NH: Heinemann, 1999.

Bizzell, Patricia. *Academic Discourse and Critical Consciousness.* Pittsburgh: U of Pittsburgh P, 1992.

Bleich, David. "Homophobia and Sexism in Popular Values." *Feminist Teacher* 4.2/3 (1989): 21-28.

Bridwell-Bowles, Lillian. "Discourse and Diversity: Experimental Writing Within the Academy." *Feminine Principles and Women's Experience in American Composition and Rhetoric.* Eds. Louise Phelps and Janet Emig. Pittsburgh Series in Composition, Literacy, and Culture. Pittsburgh: U of Pittsburgh P, 1995. 43-66.

_____. "Freedom, Form, Function: Varieties of Academic Discourse." *Women/Writing/Teaching.* Ed. Jan Zlotnik Schmidt. Albany: State U of New York P, 1998. 177-98.

Brodkey, Linda, and Michelle Fine. "Presence of Mind in the Absence of Body." *Disruptive Voices: The Possibilities of Feminist Research.* Ed. Michelle Fine. Ann Arbor: U of Michigan P, 1992. 77-96.

Brooks, Gwendolyn. "The Crazy Woman." *Norton Anthology of Literature by Women.* Eds. Sandra Gilbert and Susan Gubar. New York: Norton and Company, 1985. 18-56.

Bruffee, Kenneth. "Collaborative Learning and the 'Conversation of Mankind.'" *College English* 7(1984): 635-52.

Cameron, Deborah. *Verbal Hygiene.* New York: Routledge, 1995.

Campbell, Kathryn Kohrs. "Biesecker Cannot Speak for Her Either." *Philosophy and Rhetoric* 26.2 (1993): 153-59.

_____. *Man Cannot Speak For Her*. Vol 1. New York: Praeger, 1989.

_____. *Man Cannot Speak For Her*. Vol 2. New York: Praeger, 1989.

Cantor, Jeffrey. *Experiential Learning in Higher Education: Linking Classrooms and Community*. Washington, DC: George Washington U, 1997.

Caywood, Cynthia, and Gillian Overing, eds. *Teaching Writing: Pedagogy, Gender and Equity*. Albany: NY: State U of New York P, 1987.

Chomsky, Noam. "Introduction." *Journal for Advanced Composition*, 11.1 (1991): 90-94.

_____. *JAC*. 11.1 (1991): 19.

Code, Lorraine. *What Can She Know? Feminist Theory and the Construction of Knowledge*. Ithaca: Cornell UP, 1991.

Cohee, Gail, Elisabeth Daumer, Theresa D. Kemp, Paula M. Krebs, Sue A. Lafky, and Sandra Runzo, eds. *The Feminist Teacher Anthology: Pedagogies and Classroom Strategies*. New York: Teacher's College P, 1998.

_____. "Collectively Speaking." *The Feminist Teacher Anthology: Pedagogies and Classroom Strategies*. Eds. Cohee, Gail, Elisabeth Daumer, Theresa D. Kemp, Paula M. Krebs, Sue A. Lafky, and Sandra Runzo. New York: Teacher's College P, 1998. 1-10.

Collins, Patricia Hill. "Learning from the Outsider Within: The Sociological Significance of Black Feminist Thought." *(En)Gendering Knowledge: Feminists in Academe*. Eds. Joan E. Hartman and Ellen Messer-Davidow. Knoxville: U of Tennessee P, 1991.

Connolly, Colleen. Personal interview. 22 Feb. 2001.

Cooper, Anna Julia. *A Voice From the South by a Black Woman of the South*. (1892). New York: Oxford U P, 1988.

Cooper, Marilyn. "From the Editor." *CCC* 52 (2000): 185-87.

_____. "The Ecology of Writing." *CCC* 48 (1986): 364-75.

Covino, William. "Magic, Literacy, and the National Enquirer." *Contending with Words*. Eds. Patricia Harkin and John Schilb. New York: MLA, 1991. 23-37

Cronan Rose, Ellen. "'This Class Meets in Cyberspace': Women's Studies via Distance Education." *Feminist Teacher* 9.2 (1995): 53-60.

Culley, Margo. "Feminist Pedagogy: Lost Voices of American Women." *Teaching Women's Literature From a Regional Perspective*. New York: MLA, 1982.

Cushman, Ellen. "The Rhetorician as an Agent of Social Change." *CCC* 47 (1996): 7-28.

Daly, Mary. *Gyn/Ecology: The Metaethics of Radical Feminism*. 1978. Boston: Beacon P, 1990.

_____. *Pure Lust: Elemental Feminist Philosophy*. Boston: Beacon P, 1984.

Damarin, Suzanne. "Would You Rather Be a Goddess or a Cyborg?" *Feminist Teacher* 8.2 (1994): 54-60.

Daumer, Elisabeth, and Sandra Runzo. "Transforming the Composition Classroom." *Teaching Writing: Pedagogy, Gender and Equity*. Eds. Cynthia Caywood and Gillian Overing. Albany: NY: State U of New York P, 1987. 45-62.

de Lauretis, Teresa. "Woman Can Never Be Defined." *New French Feminisms: An Anthology*. Eds. Elaine Mark and Esabelle Courtivron. Amherst: U of Mass P, 1980. 137-41.

Deay, Ardeth, and Judith Stitzel. "Reshaping the Introductory Women's Studies Course: Dealing Up Front with Anger, Resistance, and Reality." *Feminist Teacher* 6.1 (1991): 29-33.

Delpit, Lisa. "The Silenced Dialogue: Power and Pedagogy in Educating Other People's Children." *Harvard Educational Review* 58.3 (1988): 280-98.

Diamant, Anita. *The Red Tent*. New York: Picador, 1997.

Ede, Lisa, and Andrea Lunsford. "Response to Part III: Writing Back." *Feminism and Composition Studies: In Other Words*. Eds. Susan C. Jarratt and Lynn Worsham. New York: MLA, 1998. 313-20.

Elbow, Peter. *Writing Without Teachers*. New York: Oxford U P, 1973.

Feinberg, Leslie. *Stone Butch Blues*. Ann Arbor, MI: Firebrand Books, 1993.

Feminist Pedagogy: An Update. Feminist P at the City U of New York, 1993.

Feminist Pedagogy. Feminist P at the City U of New York, 1988.

Fisher, Berenice Malka. *No Angel in the Classroom: Teaching Through Feminist Discourse*. New York: Rowman and Littlefield Publishers, 2001.

Flower, Linda, and John Hayes. "Cognitive Process Theory of Writing." CCC 32 (1981): 365-87.

Flynn, Elizabeth. "Composing as a Woman." *College Composition and Communication* 39.4 (1988): 423-35.

Fraser, Nancy. *Justice Interruptus: Critical Reflections on the "Postsocialist" Condition*. New York: Routledge, 1997.

Freed, Alice. "Language and Gender." *Annual Review of Applied Linguistics* 15 (1995): 3-22.

Freidan, Betty. *The Feminine Mystique*. New York: Norton, 1963.

Freire, Paulo. *Pedagogy of Freedom*. Trans. Patrick Clarke. Lanham, MD: Rowman and Littlefield Publishers, 1998.

_____. *Pedagogy of the Oppressed*. Trans. Myra Bergman Ramos. 1970. New York: Continuum, 1999.

_____. *The Politics of Education: Culture, Power, and Liberation*. Trans. Donaldo Macedo. South Hadley, MA: Bergin and Garvey Publishers, 1985.

_____. *Teachers as Cultural Workers*. Boulder, CO: Westview P, 1998.

Freire, Paulo, and Donaldo Macedo. *Literacy: Reading the Word and the World*. South Hadley, MA: Bergin and Garvey Publishers, 1987.

Fuss, Diane. "Gender, Race, Class: A Quest of the Perfect Writing Theme." *Teaching Writing: Pedagogy, Gender and Equity*. Eds. Cynthia Caywood and Gillian Overing. Albany: State U of New York P, 1987. 107-12.

_____. *Essentially Speaking: Feminism, Nature and Difference*. New York: Routledge, 1989.

_____. "'Essentially Speaking': Luce Iragaray's Language of Essence." *Hypatia* 3.3 (1989): 62-80.

Gawelek, Mary Ann, Maggie Mulqueen, and Jill Matuck Tarule. "Woman to Women: Understanding the Needs of Our Female Students." *Gender and Academe: Feminist Pedagogy and Politics*. Eds. Sarah Munson Deats and Lagretta Tallent Lenker. Lanham, MD: Rowman & Littlefield Publishers, 1994. 179-200.

Gibson, Michelle, Martha Marinara, and Deborah Meem. "Bi, Butch, and Bar Dyke: Pedagogical Performances of Class, Gender, and Sexuality." *College Composition and Communication* 52.1 (2000): 69-95.

Giddens, Angela. *Modernity and Self-Identity: Self and Society in the Late Modern Age*. Cambridge: Polity P, 1991.

Giddings, Paula. *When and Where I Enter: The Impact of Black Women on Race and Sex in America*. New York: William Morrow, 1984.

Golden, Carla. "The Radicalization of a Teacher." *Feminist Teacher* 1.3 (1985): 22-25.

Gore, Jennifer M. *The Struggle for Pedagogies: Critical and Feminist Discourses as Regimes of Truth*. New York: Routledge, 1993.

Goulston, Wendy. "Women Writing." *Teaching Writing: Pedagogy, Gender and Equity*. Eds. Cynthia Caywood and Gillian Overing. Albany: State U of New York P, 1987. 3-18.

Gramsci, Antonio. *An Antonio Gramsci Reader: Selected Writings: 1916-1935*. Ed. David Forgacs. New York: Schoken, 1988.

Haraway, Donna. "Situated Knowledges: The Science Question in Feminism and the Privilege of Partial Perspective." *Feminist Studies* 14.3 (1998).

Harrison, Roderick J. "Numbers Running." *The New Crisis*. May/June (2001): 14-17.

Hatch, Gary, and Margaret Bennett Walters. "Robert Zoellner's Talk-Write Pedagogy." *Writing Ourselves into the Story: Unheard Voices from Composition Studies*. Eds. Sheryl Fontaine and Susan Hunter. Carbondale: Southern Illinois UP, 1993. 335-51.

Hedges, Elaine. "Women in the Colleges: One Year Later." *College English* 34 (1972): 1-5.

Hennessy, Rosemary. *Materialist Feminism and the Politics of Discourse*. New York: Routledge, 1993.

Hoffmann, Frances L., and Jayne E. Stake. "Feminist Pedagogy in Theory and Practice: An Empirical Investigation." *NWSA Journal* 10 (1998): 79-97.

hooks, bell. *Feminist Theory: From Margin to Center*. Boston: South End P, 1984.

_____. *Remembered Rapture*. Boston: Henry Holt and Company, 1999.

_____. *Teaching to Transgress: Education as the Practice of Freedom*. New York: Routledge, 1994.

_____. *Wounds of Passion: A Writing Life*. New York: Henry Holt and Company, 1997.

Hopkins, Annis H. "Women's Studies on Television? It's Time for Distance Learning." *Meeting the Challenge: Innovative Feminist Pedagogies in Action*. Eds. Maralee Mayberry and Ellen Cronan Rose. New York: Routledge, 1999. 123-40.

Hurston, Zora Neale. *Tell My Horse*. Philadelphia: J. B. Lippincott, 1938.

James, Joy. "Gender, Race, and Radicalism: Teaching the Autobiographies of Native and African American Women Activists." *Feminist Teacher* 8.3 (1994): 129-39.

_____. "Reflections on Teaching: 'Gender, Race, and Class.'" *Feminist Teacher* 5.3 (1991): 9-15.

Jarratt, Susan. "Feminism and Composition: The Case for Conflict." *Contending with Words*. Eds. Patricia Harkin and John Schilb. New York: MLA, 1991. 105-23.

_____. "Introduction: As We Were Saying . . ." *Contending with Words*. Eds. Patricia Harkin and John Schilb. New York: MLA, 1991. 1-20.

_____. *Rereading the Sophists: A Classical Rhetoric Refigured*. Carbondale: Southern Illinois U P, 1991.

Jarratt, Susan C., and Lynn Worsham, eds. *Feminism and Composition Studies: In Other Words.* New York: MLA, 1998.

Jessup, Emily, and Marion Lardner. "Teaching Other People's Children." *Feminine Principles and Women's Experience in American Composition and Rhetoric.* Eds. Louise Phelps and Janet Emig. Pittsburgh Series in Composition, Literacy, and Culture. Pittsburgh: U of Pittsburgh P, 1995. 191-210.

Jordan, June. *On Call.* Boston: South End P, 1985.

Kingston, Maxine Hong. *Woman Warrior: Memoirs of a Girlhood Among Ghosts.* New York: Knopf, 1977.

Kirsch, Gesa. *Ethical Dilemmas in Feminist Research.* Albany: State U of New York P, 1999.

_____. *Women Writing in the Academy: Audience, Authority, and Transformation.* Carbondale: Southern Illinois U P, 1993.

Kraemer, Don, Jr. "Gender and the Autobiographical Essay: Critical Extension of the Research." *CCC* 43 (1992): 323-39.

Kramarae, Chris. "Proprietors of Language." *Women and Language in Literature and Society.* Eds. Sally McConnell-Ginet, Ruth Borker, and Nelly Furman. New York: Praeger, 1980. 58-68.

_____. "Power Relationships in the Classroom." *Gender in the Classroom: Power and Pedagogy.* Eds. Susan L. Gabriel and Isaiah Smithson. Urbana: U of Illinois P, 1990. 41-59.

Kramarae, Chris and Paula Treichler. *The Feminist Dictionary.* Boston: Pandora P, 1985.

Ladson-Billings, Gloria, and Annette Henry. "Blurring the Borders: Voices of African Liberatory Pedagogy in the United States and Canada." *Journal of Education* 172 (1990): 72-89.

Lamberg, Walter. "Self-provided and Peer-provided Feedback." *CCC* 31 (1980): 63-69.

Lather, Patti. *Getting Smart: Feminist Research and Pedagogy with/in the Postmodern.* New York: Routledge, 1991.

_____. "Postbook: Working the Ruins of Feminist Ethnography." *Signs* 27.1 (2001): 197-225.

Lather, Patti, and Chris Smithies. *Troubling the Angels: Women Living with HIV/AIDS.* Boulder, CO: Westview P, 1997.

Lorde, Audre. "Eye to Eye: Black Women, Hatred, and Anger." *Sister Outsider: Essays and Speeches by Audre Lorde.* Berkeley: Freedom Crossing P, 1984. 145-75.

_____. *Sister Outsider: Essays and Speeches by Audre Lorde.* Berkeley: Freedom Crossing P,, 1984.

Lunsford, Andrea. "Chair's Address." *Conference on College Composition and Communication* 1989.

Maher, Frances. "My Introduction to 'Introduction to Women's Studies:' The Role of the Teacher's Authority in the Feminist Classroom." *Feminist Teacher* 3.1 (1987): 9-11.

Malinowitz, Harriet. "A Feminist Critique of 'Writing in the Disciplines.'" *Feminisms and Composition Studies: In Other Words.* Eds. Susan Jarratt and Lynn Worsham. New York: MLA, 1998.

_____. "Construing and Constructing Knowledge as a Lesbian or Gay Student Writer." *PRE/TEXT: A Journal of Rhetorical Theory* 13.3-4 (1992): 37-52.

_____. "David and Me." *JAC.* 16.23 (1996): 209-23.

_____. "Extending Our Concept of Multiculturalism: Lesbian and Gay Reality and the Writing Class." *Vital Signs 3: Restructuring the English Classroom.* Ed. James L. Collins. Portsmouth, NH: Heinemann-Boynton/Cook, 1992.

_____. "Textual Trouble in River City: Literacy, Rhetoric, and Consumerism in *The Music Man.*" *College English.* 62.1 (1999): 58-82.

_____. "Unmotherhood." *JAC.* 22.1 (2002): 11-36.

_____. Classroom observation. Women in Culture and Society Course. Long Island University, 2 April 2001.

_____. Classroom observation. Ways of Reading Culture Course. Long Island University, 4 April 2001.

_____. Personal interview. 2 Apr. 2001.

_____. Personal interview. 3 Apr. 2001.

_____. Personal interview. 4 Apr. 2001.

_____. Phone interview. 31 May 2001.

_____. *Textual Orientations: Lesbian and Gay Students and the Making of Discourse Communities.* Portsmouth, NH: Heinemann-Boynton/Cook, 1995.

Marshall, Margaret. "Marking the Unmarked: Reading Student Diversity and Preparing Teachers." *CCC* 48 (1997): 231-48.

Martin, Jane Roland. *Coming of Age in Academe.* New York: Routledge, 1999.

Mayberry, Maralee. "Reproductive and Resistant Pedagogies: The Comparative Roles of Collaborative Learning and Feminist Pedagogy in Science Education." *Meeting the Challenge: Innovative Feminist Pedagogies in Action.* Eds. Maralee Mayberry and Ellen Cronan Rose. New York: Routledge, 1999. 1-22.

Mayberry, Maralee, and Ellen Cronan Rose. "Introduction." *Meeting the Challenge: Innovative Feminist Pedagogies in Action.* Eds. Maralee Mayberry and Ellen Cronan Rose. New York: Routledge, 1999. vii-xix.

_____, eds. *Meeting the Challenge: Innovative Feminist Pedagogies in Action.* New York: Routledge, 1999.

Mayberry, Maralee, and Margaret Rees. "Feminist Pedagogy, Interdisciplinary Praxis, and Science Education." *Meeting the Challenge: Innovative Feminist Pedagogies in Action.* Eds. Maralee Mayberry and Ellen Cronan Rose. New York: Routledge, 1999. 193-214.

Middleton, Sue. *Educating Feminists: Life Histories and Pedagogy.* Urbana: NCTE, 1993.

Miller, Janet. "The Sound of Silence Breaking: Feminist Pedagogy and Curriculum Theory." *Journal of Curriculum Theorizing* 4 (1982): 5-11.

Mirza, Heidi Safia. "Black Women in Higher Education: Defining a Space/Finding a Place." *Feminist Academics: Creative Agents for Change.* Eds. Louise Morely and Val Walsh. London: Taylor & Francis, 1995. 145-55.

Morley, Louise. *Organizing Feminisms: The Micropolitics of the Academy.* St. Martin's P, 1999.

Mullin, Joan. "Feminist Theory, Feminist Pedagogy: The Gap Between What We Say and What We Do." *Composition Studies/Freshman English News* 1 (1994): 14-24.

Murray, Donald. "Teaching Writing as Process Not Product." *The Leaflet* (1972): 11-14.

Nakamura, Hajime. *Ways of Thinking of Eastern Peoples*. 1964. London: Kegan Paul International, 1997.

Noddings, Nel. "An Ethic of Caring and Its Implications for Instructional Arrangements." *American Journal of Education* 96 (1988): 215-30.

Olson, Tillie. "Women Who Are Writers in Our Century." *College English* 34 (1972): 6-17.

Omolade, Barbara. "A Black Feminist Pedagogy." *Women's Studies Quarterly* 21.3-4 (1993): 31-39.

Ortiz-Taylor, Shelia. "Women in a Double-Bind: Hazards of the Argumentative Edge." *CCC* 29 (1978): 385-89.

Perry, Merry. Personal interview. 20 Feb. 2001.

Peterson, Linda. "Gender and the Autobiographical Essay: Research Perspectives, Pedagogical Practices." *CCC* 42 (1991): 70-83.

Phelps, Louise, and Janet Emig, eds. *Feminine Principles and Women's Experience in American Composition and Rhetoric*. Pittsburgh Series in Composition, Literacy, and Culture. Pittsburgh: U of Pittsburgh P, 1995.

_____. "Introduction and Commitment." *Feminine Principles and Women's Experience in American Composition and Rhetoric*. Eds. Louise Phelps and Janet Emig. Pittsburgh: U of Pittsburgh P, 1995.

Rassool, Nan. "Black Women as 'Other' in the Academy." *Feminist Academics: Creative Agents for Change*. Eds. Louise Morely and Val Walsh. London: Taylor & Francis, 1995. 22-41.

Ray, Ruth. *The Practice of Theory: Teacher Research in Composition*. Urbana: NCTE, 1993.

Rich, Adrienne. "When We Dead Awaken: Writing as Revision." *College English* 34 (1972): 18-30.

_____. *On Lies, Secrets and Silence: Selected Prose 1996-1978*. New York: Norton, 1979.

Ritchie, Joy. "Beginning Writers: Diverse Voices and Individual Identity." *CCC* 40 1989: 152-74.

_____. "Confronting the Essential Problem." *JAC* 10 (1990): 249-73.

Ritchie, Joy, and Kathleen Boardman. "Feminism in Composition: Inclusion, Metonymy, and Disruption." *CCC* 50 (1999): 585-606.

Roland Martin, Jane. *Coming of Age in Academe*. New York: Routledge, 1999.

Rose, Mike. "The Language of Exclusion: Writing Instruction at the University." *College English* 47 (1985): 341-59.

_____. *Possible Lives: The Promise of Education in America*. Boston: Houghton-Mifflin, 1995.

_____. "Rigid Rules, Inflexible Plans, and Stifling Language: A Cognitivist Analysis of Writer's Block." *CCC* 31.4 (1980): 389-400.

Roskelly, Hephzibah, and Kate Ronald. *Reason to Believe*. Albany: State U of New York P, 1998.

Rothenberg, Paula. "Integrating the Study of Race, Gender, Class: Some Preliminary Observations." *Feminist Teacher* 3.3 (1988): 37-42.

Royster, Jacqueline Jones. Personal interview. 15 May 2001.

_____. "Foreword." *Composition Theory and the Postmodern Classroom*. Ed. Gary Olson. New York: State U of New York P, 1994. xi-xiii.

_____. "History in the Spaces Left: African American Presence and Narratives of Composition Studies." *College Composition and Communication* 50.4 (1999): 563-84.

_____. "In Search of Ways." *Feminine Principles and Women's Experience in American Composition and Rhetoric.* Eds. Louise Phelps and Janet Emig. Pittsburgh Series in Composition, Literacy, and Culture. Pittsburgh: U of Pittsburgh P, 1995. 385-91.

_____. "Perspectives on the Intellectual Tradition of Black Women Writers." *The Right to Literacy.* Eds. Andrea Lunsford, Helene Moglen, and James Selvin. New York: Modern Language Association, 1990. 103-12.

_____. "Reflections on the SAGE Women as Writer/Scholars Internship Program." *SAGE: Scholarly Journal on Black Women* (student supplement, 1988): 4-6.

_____. "Saga of the Dragons or Perspectives on Teaching Writing at Spelman College." *Bard South: Teaching Writing at Historically Black Colleges and Universities.* Eds. David and Vivian W. Wilson. New Orleans: Xavier Review/Southern Education Foundation, 1988. 235-30.

_____. "Sarah's Story: Making a Place for Historical Ethnography in Rhetorical Studies." *Rhetoric, the Polis, and the Global Village: Proceedings from the 1998 Rhetoric Society of America Conference.* Eds. Jan Swearingen and David Pruett. Mahwah: Lawrence Erlbaum Associates, 1999. 39-51.

_____. "Sassy Women." Associate Dean of Humanities Inaugural Address. Columbus, OH, 22 May 2001.

_____. "Stories Behind the Eyes: Race and Gender in Rhetorical Studies." Keynote Address: Race, Gender, Orientation Symposium. Oxford, OH, 2 Mar. 2001.

_____. "Time Alone, Place Apart: The Role of Spiracy in Using the Power of Solitude." *Women/Writing/Teaching.* Ed. Jan Zlotnick Schmidt. Albany: State U of New York P, 1997. 67-75.

_____. "To Call a Thing by Its True Name." Lunsford 167-84.

_____. "When the First Voice You Hear Is Not Your Own." *College Composition and Communication* 47 (1996): 29-40.

_____. College of Humanities Graduate Committee Meeting observation, Ohio State University, Columbus, OH 15 May 2001.

_____. Keynote Address. Race and Gender Symposium. Oxford, OH, 23 Mar. 2001.

_____. Personal interview. 15 May 2001.

_____. *Southern Horrors and Other Writings: The Anti-Lynching Campaign of Ida B. Wells, 1892-1900.* Boston: Bedford Books, 1997.

_____. *Traces of a Stream: Literacy and Social Change among African American Women.* Pittsburgh: U of Pittsburgh P, 2000.

Ruggerio, Chris. "Teaching Women's Studies: The Repersonalization of Our Politics." *Women's Studies International Forum.* 13:5 (1990): 469-75.

Ryder, Randall J., and Jeffrey Graves. *Reading and Language in the Content Areas.* New York: John Wiley, 1998.

Sadker, David. and Myra Sadker. *Failing at Fairness: How Our Schools Cheat Girls.* New York: Simon and Schuster, 1994.

Sattler, Cheryl. *Talking About a Revolution: The Politics and Practice of Feminist Teaching.* Cresskill, NJ: Hampton P, 1997.

Schmidt, Jan Zlotnik, ed. *Women/Writing/Teaching*. Albany: State U of New York P, 1998.

———. "Story of Women Writing Teachers." *Women/Writing/Teaching*. Ed. Jan Zlotnick Schmidt. Albany: State U of New York Press, 1998. 61-74.

Schweickart, Patrocinio. "Reading Ourselves: Towards a Feminist Theory of Reading." *Gender and Reading: Essays on Readers, Texts, and Contexts*. Eds. Elizabeth Flynn and Patrocinio Schweickart. Baltimore: Johns Hopkins U P, 1986. 31-62.

Secrist, Patrice. *Politics and Scholarship: A Cultural Study of Feminist Academic Journals*. diss. U of Maryland, 1989.

Shaunessey, Mina. *Errors and Expectations: A Guide for the Teacher of Basic Writing*. New York: Oxford U P, 1977.

Shrewsbury, Carolyn. "Feminist Pedagogy: An Updated Bibliography." *Women's Studies Quarterly* 21.3-4 (1993): 148-60.

———. "What is Feminist Pedagogy." *Women's Studies Quarterly* 21 (1993): 3-17.

Shor, Ira. "Anne Sexton's 'For My Lover . . .': Feminism in the Classroom." *College English* 34 (1973): 1082-93.

Slattery, Patrick. "Encouraging Critical Thinking: A Strategy for Commenting on College Papers." *CCC* 41 (1990): 332-35.

Sloane, Sarah. "Invisible Diversity: Gay and Lesbian Students Writing Our Way Into the Academy." *Writing Ourselves into the Story: Unheard Voices from Composition Studies*. Eds. Sheryl Fontaine and Susan Hunter. Carbondale: Southern Illinois UP, 1993. 29-39.

Smitherman, Geneva. *Talkin' and Testifyin'*. Detroit: Wayne U P, 1986.

Sommers, Nancy. "Between the Drafts." *Women/Writing/Teaching*. Ed. Jan Zlotnick Schmidt. Albany: State U of New York Press, 1998. 165-76.

Strotsky, Sandra. "On Planning and Writing Plans: Or Beware of Borrowed Theories!" *CCC* 41 (1990): 37-57.

Tisdell, Elizabeth J. "Poststructural Feminist Pedagogies: The Possibilities and Limitations of Feminist Emancipatory Adult Learning Theory and Practice." *Adult Education Quarterly* 48 (1998): 13956.

Villanueva, Victor. "Considerations for American Freireistas." *The Politics of Writing Instruction: Postsecondary*. Eds. Richard Bullock and John Trimbur. Portsmouth, NH: Boynton/Cook, 1991. 247-62.

———. *Bootstraps: From an American Academic of Color*. Urbana: NCTE, 1993.

Visweswaran, Kamala. *Fictions of Feminist Ethnography*. Minneapolis: U of Minnesota P, 1994.

Walker, Alice. "Womanist." *In Search of Our Mother's Gardens*. New York: Harcourt P, 1983. xi.

Weiler, Kathleen. *Women Teaching for Change: Gender, Class and Power*. South Hadley: Bergin & Garvey, 1988.

West, Cornel. *Race Matters*. Boston: Beacon P, 1993.

Whipp, Les. "Teaching English and Social-Class Relationships." *CCC* 30 (1979): 141-45.

Williams, Patricia. *The Alchemy of Race and Rights*. Cambridge, MA: Harvard UP, 1991.

Woodridge, Linda. "The Centrifugal Classroom." *Gender and Academe: Feminist Pedagogy and Politics*. Eds. Sarah Munson Deats and Lagretta Tallent Lenker. Lanham, MD: Rowman & Littlefield Publishing, 1994. 133-52.

Woolf, Virginia. *Three Guineas*. 1938. New York: Harcourt P, 1966.

Worsham, Lynn. "After Words: A Choice of Words Remains." *Feminism and Composition Studies: In Other Words*. Eds. Susan C. Jarratt and Lynn Worsham. New York: MLA, 1998. 329-56.

_____. "Critical Interference and the Postmodern Turn in Composition Studies." *Composition Forum* 10 (1999): 389-409.

_____. "Eating History, Purging Memory, Killing Rhetoric." *Writing Histories of Rhetoric*. Ed. Victor Vitanza. Carbondale: Southern Illinois U P, 1994. 139-55.

_____. "Emotion and Pedagogic Violence." *Discourse* 15.2 (1993): 113-48.

_____. "Going Postal: Pedagogy Violence and the Schooling of Emotion." *JAC* 18 (1998): 213-45.

_____. "Kenneth Burke's Appendicitis: A Feminist's Case for Complaint." *Pre/Text* 12.1-2 (1991): 67-95.

_____. "On the Discipline *and* Pleasure of Perilous Acts." *JAC* 19 (1999): 707-21.

_____. "Reading Wild, Seriously: Confessions of an Epistemopheliac." *Rhetoric Society Quarterly* 22 (1992): 39-62.

_____. "Romancing the Stones: My Movie Date With Sandra Harding." *JAC* 15 (1995): 565-71.

_____. "Working Titles and Entitlement(s): Feminism, Composition Studies, and the Politics of Publication." *Composition Forum* 8 (1997): 19-29.

_____. "Writing Against Writing: The Predicament of Ecriture Feminine in Composition Studies." *Contending with Words*. Eds. Patricia Harkin and John Schilb. New York: MLA, 1991. 82-104.

_____. Classroom observation. Image of Women in Literature Course. University of South Florida, 21 Feb. 2001.

_____. Classroom observation. Graduate Writing Workshop. University of South Florida, 19 Feb. 2001.

_____. Personal interview. 19 Feb. 2001.

_____. Personal interview. 20 Feb. 2001.

_____. Personal interview. 21 Feb. 2001.

Wright, Janet. "Lesbian Instructor Comes Out: The Personal Is Pedagogy." *Teacher* 7.2 (1993): 26-33.

Author Index

Subject Index

A

abortion, 105, 147, 156
academic discourse, 18, 66, 81, 93, 136, 142
academic feminism, 109, 125
academic feminists, 78, 109, 210
action, 56
active learners 4, 61
active learning, 52, 53, 60, 215
activism, 22, 54, 82, 105, 129, 154, 157, 175, 192
activist, 6, 18, 20, 106, 125, 135, 147
adjunct, 129, 130, 149
administrator, 180
Afrafeminist, 195
African American, 146
African American history, 171
African American women, 22, 103, 146, 152, 165, 166, 168, 171, 172, 174, 177, 181, 186, 200
African American women's rhetoric, 203
African American women's rhetorical history, 203
African diaspora, 203
After Words, 93, 119, 145
ageism, 208
agency, 78

aggression, 208
ambiguity, 207
ambivalence, 83
anthropologists, 115
anti-feminist, 29
argument, 84, 83, 96, 108, 132, 189, 202, 205
assumptions, 39, 41,50, 84
audience, 6
authority, 8, 30, 46-47, 66, 82, 100, 146, 179
autobiographical, 141

B

basic writers, 50, 70
basic writing, 137
bias, 40, 42, 59, 64, 85
Black, 182
Black English, 67
Black Feminist, 46, 178, 188, 200
Black Feminist Thought, 177
Black woman, 175, 181, 182, 190
Black womanhood, 194
Blue Betty, 100, 120
book reviews, 126
boundaries, 116, 197
bridges, 191, 196
Brooklyn, 127

post-modern pedagogy, 31, 207
poststructural theory, 20, 68, 219
power, 38, 41, 47, 64, 79, 105, 136, 179, 200
  in the classroom. *See* teacher authority
praxis, 38
process, 200
process theory, 70, 132, 133, 136
pro-choice, 140, 146
pro-feminist male, 199
pro-life, 147
publish or perish, 78, 82

Q

queer, 132, 150, 199, 201, 207
queer rights, 126

R

race, 22, 44, 53, 59, 175, 181, 184
race issues, 53
racism, 3, 73, 135, 166, 199, 201
radical, 109
radical act, 174
radical pedagogies, 19, 207, 214
rape, 86, 147, 156
reader response theory, 28
reclaim, 169, 172
reproductive choice, 140
reproductive rights, 146
research participants, 79, 89, 90
researcher and participant, 79
resistance, 56, 109
revise, 89, 107, 108, 132, 140, 142, 144, 160
revolution, 120
rhetor, 98
rhetoric, 95, 114, 119, 136, 171
rhetoric for social change, 55
rhetoric of change, 55
Rhetoric Society of America, 171
rhetorical analysis, 89, 141, 184
rhetorical canon, 163
rhetorical situation, 58, 66, 76
rhetorical theory, 94, 95, 103, 209
Rich, Adrienne, 152, 153
risk-taking, 42
roads, 168

rubric, 57, 111

S

scholarship, 92, 107
Second Wave, 15, 193
self-criticism, 49
self-critique, 22, 97, 118, 155, 176, 196
self-disclosure, 45, 93, 138, 141, 154
self-interrogation, 154
self-reported data, 89
September 11, 162
service learning, 49
sex biases, 38, 40
sexism, 3, 17, 73, 135, 189, 199, 201
sexual harassment, 55
sexual identity, 185
sexual orientation, 6, 22, 53, 59, 188
sexuality, 6
sexualized, 208
shame, 101, 104, 113, 115, 188
shamelessness, 117
silence, 16, 27, 39, 61, 63, 68, 175, 181
sisterhood, 75, 121
site visits, 85, 87
situational knowledge, 79, 217
skepticism, 151
skeptics, 71
small group discussions, 65
snools, 119
social action, 54, 57, 73
social activism, 54, 100, 154
social justice, 150
socio-economic class, 56,65, 147
socio-economic class issues, 147, 159
sociolinguists, 115
speaking out, 22, 68, 69
Spelman College, 166, 191
spokeslesbian, 152
standard curriculum, 17, 64, 67
Standard English, 66, 67
standards, 12, 25, 58, 81, 131, 139, 144, 145, 170, 203
status of women, 23
stereotype, 116
stories, 108, 114, 116, 109
storytelling, 97, 98, 141
student concerns, 62
student differences, 63

CPSIA information can be obtained at www.ICGtesting.com
Printed in the USA
LVOW040716130911

245974LV00001B/73/A

9 781572 737129